Labour Market Segmentation in Malaysian Services

T0083574

Labour Market Segmentation in Malaysian Services

Khong How Ling with Jomo K.S.

NUS PRESS
SINGAPORE

© 2010 NUS Press
National University of Singapore
AS3-01-02, 3 Arts Link
Singapore 117569

Fax: (65) 6774-0652
E-mail: nusbooks@nus.edu.sg
Website: http://www.nus.edu.sg/nuspress

ISBN 978-9971-69-487-6 (Paper)

All rights reserved. This book, or parts thereof, may not be reproduced in
any form or by any means, electronic or mechanical, including photocopying,
recording or any information storage and retrieval system now known or to be
invented, without written permission from the Publisher.

National Library Board Singapore Cataloguing in Publication Data

Khong, How Ling.
    Labour market segmentation in Malaysian services / Khong How Ling
with Jomo K.S. – Singapore: NUS Press, c2010.
    p. cm.
    Includes bibliographical references and index.
    ISBN-13: 978-9971-69-487-6 (pbk.)

        1. Service industries workers – Employment – Malaysia. 2. Labor market
– Malaysia. 3. Sexual division of labor – Malaysia. 4. Service industries –
Malaysia. 5. Malaysia – Economic conditions. I. Jomo K. S. (Jomo Kwame
Sundaram) II. Title.

HD8039.S452
331.129133847 -- dc22   OCN427792642

Typeset by: Forum, Kuala Lumpur, Malaysia
Printed by: Vinlin Press Sdn. Bhd.

Contents

List of Tables

List of Figures

Acknowledgements

This book has its origins in Khong How Ling's PhD thesis submitted to Cambridge University in June 1991. It was written to address the dearth of information on and lack of understanding of the labour market in Malaysia, especially in the service sector. Khong sought to develop a framework with which modern sector and traditional sector services could be analyzed within the broader context of Malaysian labour market processes.

While there are a number of private sector studies on modern services, most of these tend to be written to address specific issues or topics within a particular sub-sector (e.g. finance, tourism) and not within the overall context of the Malaysian labour market. Studies on traditional services, in turn, tend to be conducted mostly by sociology students whose aims are often quite different from those of economic enquiries.

In the course of preparing the thesis, various people provided invaluable help and encouragement to her. Khong would like to thank Dr Frank Wilkinson of the Department of Applied Economics, Cambridge, for taking the time to help improve the thesis. Dr Wong Poh Kam and Dr Stacey Birks were helpful in providing some unpublished research materials. This study would not have been possible without the co-operation of trade union representatives, industrial leaders, workers and the many small entrepreneurs who consented to be interviewed. They helped provide the broader context in which official statistics could be realistically interpreted.

Khong would also like to thank the Cambridge Commonwealth Trust (for granting Khong a Tate and Lyle scholarship), the Foreign and Commonwealth Office, the Smuts Memorial in Cambridge, the Luca d'Agliano Centre in Italy, Wolfson College and the University of Malaya; they all contributed in some way or other towards providing the financial resources for Khong's PhD study. Special thanks go to numerous friends and colleagues at Wolfson College and the Faculty of Economics and Politics at Cambridge, and the Faculty of Economics and Administration of the University of Malaya, for their intellectual and moral support. Khong would especially like to thank members of her extended and church families for their patience and support.

This work could not have been updated and revised for publication without the help of Jomo and many others. Chang Yii Tan and Chong Lim contributed much to Chapter 1, while Wee Chong Hui, Vijayakumari Kanapathy, Siti Rohani Yahya, Tan Kock Wah, Clarissa Koh, Kalaiselvi, Brian Ong, Suzette Limchoc and Foo Ah Hiang helped to update much of the data in this study. Clarissa and Brian also helped to edit this book. Most of this work was done while Jomo was at the University of Malaya and later at the Asia Research Institute of the National University of Singapore.

Khong How Ling and Jomo K.S.

Preface

Most studies of labour in developing countries have focused on the agricultural workforce and, more recently, on industrial workers, despite the fact that the services sector has long accounted for more of the labour force than manufacturing. This is as true of Malaysia as it is for most developing countries. Studies of those working in services have tended to focus on those in the public sector and, in recent decades, the informal sector, with the former considered "modern", and the latter "traditional". This study of workers in services also covers those in private enterprises, both modern (e.g. financial services) and traditional (e.g. transportation services), although such categories are themselves moot. After all, money-lending is an activity which has long existed, even in pre-modern times, while most transportation services today are decidedly modern.

The other novel element in this study is the focus on what has been called labour market segmentation, with considerable emphasis on ethnic and gender segmentation besides the other types of segmentation considered by the relevant literature, which emerged in the 1970s and 1980s. This study uses the labour market segmentation approach to develop an overview of labour market processes in the Malaysian service sector (Khong, 1991: Chap. 1). Of particular importance are the impact of structural change in the economy and the interaction between these processes and the labour market on job and pay opportunities.

The study is based on official data as well as an earlier survey and interviews. The bulk of the empirical data is from secondary data culled from censuses, surveys, journals, bulletins, government publications, international research papers, unpublished materials, press reports, seminar papers and other relevant sources of information. These were thoroughly studied and follow-up open-ended interviews were conducted with leading representatives, experts and policy planners involved in the service sector to solicit perspectives, opinions and other information with which the secondary data could be interpreted to build a composite picture of labour processes in the service sector. Due to the heterogeneity of the service sector, interview questions were structured along general lines to determine the job classifications and their recruitment criteria; the determinants of wages and the dynamics of wage and non-wage differentials within the industry/sector, and how they compare with other industries/sectors; mobility patterns and career prospects associated with each sector and major occupational category; and the problems and prospects of the sector, and their effect on labour within that sector.

In the course of collecting data and conducting interviews, the most frustrating problem was the lack of readily available up-to-date information and the reluctance of government officials to provide unpublished research studies undertaken by the Malaysian government and international bodies such as the International Labour Organization. Available statistics were usually a few years out-of-date as official census/survey statistics are usually published after long delays. Several government officials cited the amended Official Secrets Act of 1986 as a constraint, while bureaucratic red-tape in the private sector also limited the openness and readiness of executives to discuss company data although they were willing to provide information on the industry as a whole.

The first chapter reviews the transformation of the Malaysian economy in the last half century since Malaya gained independence in 1957. The second chapter traces the origins and dynamics of ethnic, gender and class segmentation in the Malaysian labour market while recognizing the significant role of the state intervention in the allocation of labour. The third and fourth chapters review the determinants of differential job access and remuneration associated with traditional and modern services respectively, with emphasis on the role of ethnicity, gender and some other socio-economic and political factors shaping career paths and life opportunities. These chapters compare and contrast the diverse factors influencing recruitment, pay and mobility systems in modern and traditional services. The concluding chapter reviews the transformation of Malaysian services, and its interaction with labour market segmentation, before making recommendations for promoting social integration and stability in an ethnically polarized society.

1

Malaysia's Post-Colonial Economic Transformation

(with Chang Yii Tan)

This opening chapter offers an overview of the changing nature of the economy in Malaysia. It begins with a review of trends in economic growth, structural change, and government spending in the post-colonial period to the expansion of services, especially modern services, particularly in the public sector. The relationship between economic performance on the one hand and Malaysian development policy initiatives, as well as other legal, regulatory and institutional reforms will be explored throughout this book.

In the post-Second World War period, Malaysia experienced relatively rapid growth, particularly during the Korean War boom, the oil boom of the seventies and the relocation of East Asian industry into Southeast Asia from the late 1980s. In 2004, the Malaysian economy had a real GDP of RM248,000 million (in constant 1987 prices) and a nominal GDP of RM447,548 million. The economic growth rate was 7.1 per cent, based on private investments of RM25,790 million and public sector investments of RM41,206 million. Total investments, private and public, as a proportion of GDP were estimated at 23 per cent. In comparison, in 1960, GDP in current prices was estimated at RM6 billion (RM12.2 billion in 1978 prices) while per capita GDP was about RM1,500 (in 1978 prices).

Economic Growth

Since Malayan independence in 1957, the Peninsular Malaysian economy has been growing rapidly, with real GDP posting average annual growth rates of

4.0 per cent during 1956–60, rising to 5.2 per cent during 1961–70. With the oil and commodity price upward movements of the mid-1980s, growth rose dramatically to average almost eight per cent during 1971–80, before declining to 5.3 per cent during the global recession of 1981–85, and then surging again to average over eight per cent during 1987–97 before the catastrophic contraction by 6.1 per cent of 1998, followed by the more modest growth since then. Malaysia's economy has grown rapidly by international standards, with GDP growth averaging about 7 per cent over 1971–2000 (Tables 1.1 and 1.2, Figure 1.1).

Trends in private and public investment can be seen in Figure 1.2. Investments have been primarily financed by domestic, rather than foreign sources, though changes in gross domestic capital formation have been reflected by the changing contributions of foreign capital inflows. Annual foreign direct investment (FDI) ranged from RM90–300 million in the 1960s, rising to RM0.3–1.4 billion in the 1970s, and RM2–3 billion in the early 1980s. By the first half of the 1990s, annual FDI was between RM6–9 billion (Bank Negara Malaysia, *Annual Report, 1994*: 112), before declining with the 1997–98 crisis and recovering more modestly thereafter. The contribution of FDI to total

Table 1.1 Malaysia: Long-term Economic Indicators, 1970–2005

	1971–80	*1981–90*	*1991–97*	*1998–2005*
GDP growth (% p.a.)	7.5	6.0	9.2	5.3
CPI inflation (% p.a.)	5.9	3.8	3.6	1.9

	1970	*1980*	*1990*	*1997*	*2005*
Per capita GNP (RM)	1,071	3,734	6,513	11,429	18,040
Per capita GNP (USD)*	348	1,683	2,414	2,939	4,772
Unemployment rate (%)	2.4	5.6	6.0	2.4	3.5
Inflation (%)	1.9	6.7	3.1	2.7	3.0
RM/USD	3.078	2.218	2.698	3.8883	3.7800

Notes: * Calculated by dividing per capita GNP (RM) by the exchange rate (RM/USD). *The Economic Report, 2000/2001* gives Malaysia's per capita GNP in 1997 as US$4,376.

Sources: Ministry of Finance, Malaysia; *Economic Report*, various issues.

Table 1.2 Malaysia: Growth by Sector, 1965–2005 (% p. a.)

	1965–70*	1971–75	1976–80	1981–85	1986–90	1991–95	1996	1997	1998	1999	2000	2001–05
Agriculture, forestry & fishing	6.3	4.8	3.9	3.4	4.6	2.0	4.5	0.7	–2.8	0.4	0.6	3.0
Mining & quarrying	1.1	0.4	8.9	6.0	5.2	2.9	2.9	1.9	0.4	–2.6	3.1	2.6
Manufacturing	9.9	11.6	13.5	4.6	13.7	13.3	18.2	10.1	–13.4	13.5	21.0	4.1
Construction	4.1	6.6	12.6	8.1	0.4	13.3	16.2	10.6	24.0	–4.4	1.0	0.5
Electricity, gas & utility	8.1	9.8	10.2	9.1	9.8	13.1	9.6	–5.8	11.1	8.7	7.5	5.6
Transport, storage & communications	3.0	13.0	9.6	8.4	8.6	9.9	7.4	11.8	–0.3	5.7	7.3	6.6
Wholesale & retail trade, hotels & restaurants	3.2	6.3	8.2	7.0	4.7	10.6	7.9	8.0	–3.4	2.6	5.8	4.3
Finance, insurance, real estate & business services	5.4	7.2	8.0	7.2	8.4	10.7	17.0	18.9	–1.9	5.6	5.1	8.1
Government services	5.2	10.1	9.0	9.8	4.0	6.7	1.7	8.6	1.1	7.7	1.4	6.7
Other services	4.7	9.3	6.6	5.1	4.9	7.7	7.9	7.0	1.9	2.6	1.5	4.8
GDP at purchasers' price	5.5	7.1	8.6	5.8	6.7	8.7	10.0	7.5	–7.5	8.5	8.5	4.5

Notes: GDP in 1965 prices for 1965–70; GDP in 1970 prices for 1971–80, in 1987 prices for 1981–95 and current prices for 1996–2000.
  * For Peninsular Malaysia only and GDP is at factor cost.

Sources: 2MP, Table 2-5; 4MP, Table 2-5; 5MP, Table 2-1; 6MP, Table 1-2; 7MP, Table 2-5; 9MP, Table 2-2; BNM, *Monthly Statistical Bulletin*, various issues.

Figure 1.1 Malaysia: Real GDP and Investment Growth, 1960–2003

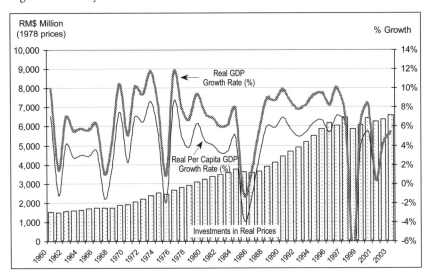

Figure 1.2 Malaysia: Private and Public Investment, 1960–2000
(RM billion and as share of GDP)

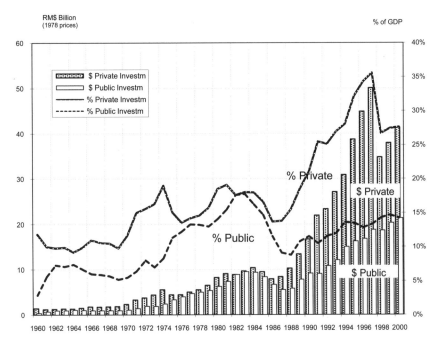

gross domestic capital formation rose from the 1960s to the 1970s, declined in the early 1980s, rose again from the late 1980s, and has been lower since the late 1990s.

Meanwhile, Malaysia's population has grown from 14.8 million in 1980 and 17.8 million in 1991 to 25.6 million in 2004. By 1995, there were an estimated two to four million migrant workers in Malaysia, of whom only about one million were documented. Immigrant labour, mainly involved in the plantation, construction, services and manufacturing sectors, mostly comes from neighbouring countries such as Indonesia, Philippines, Myanmar, Bangladesh and other South Asian countries.

Structural Change

After Malayan independence in 1957, and especially during the 1960s, the Malaysian economy diversified from the twin pillars of the colonial economy, i.e. rubber and tin. Nevertheless, primary commodity production continued to dominate the economy in the early years after independence as Malaysia extended its colonial pre-eminence in rubber, tin and pepper to oil palm, pepper and tropical hardwoods. Agriculture and forestry's share of GDP fell from 29.6 per cent in 1970 to 6 per cent in 2005, while manufacturing's share rose from 14.6 per cent in 1970 to 34.9 per cent in 2005. The manufacturing sector led growth, with the manufacturing growth rate rising in the late 1980s, before declining after the mid-1990s. Services have grown since independence to become the largest sector in the economy, rising from 36.9 per cent of GDP in 1970 to 52.2 per cent in 2005. Agriculture and forestry's share of employment fell from 53.5 per cent in 1970 to 12.0 per cent in 2005, while manufacturing's share rose from 8.7 per cent in 1970 to 29.5 per cent in 2005. Services have long been the largest sector in the economy, rising from 32.5 per cent in 1970 to 50.0 per cent of employment in 2005.

Rapid growth has been accompanied by rapid structural transformation (Tables 1.2 to 1.4). When it gained independence in 1957, Malaya (later Peninsular Malaysia) inherited a dualistic economic structure characterized by a large, relatively low-productivity peasant agriculture sector, and a capitalistic plantation (mainly rubber) and tin mining sector. Extractive industries were the mainstay of the economy, in terms of generating national income, export earnings and employment. The service sector then consisted mostly of petty commerce and the export-import trade of agency houses associated with the plantation and mining sectors, the public sector, and the transport and communications sectors.[1]

Table 1.3 Malaysia: Gross Domestic Product and Employment by Industry, 1970–2005

Industry	Gross domestic product (%)					Employment (%)				
	1970	1980	1990	2000	2005	1970	1980	1990	2000	2005
Agriculture & forestry	29.6	23.5	18.5	7.8	6.0	53.5	39.6	26	20	12
Mining & quarrying	14.4	10.6	9.6	5.4	4.5	2.6	1.7	0.5	0.5	0.4
Manufacturing	14.6	20.1	26.7	32.5	34.9	8.7	15.7	19.9	23.9	29.5
Construction	4.5	5.2	3.4	2.4	2.4	2.7	5.6	6.3	7.4	8.1
Services	36.9	40.6	41.8	51.9	52.2	32.5	37.4	47.3	48.2	50
Total	100.0	100.0	100.0	100.0	100.0	100.0	100.0	100.0	100.0	100.0

Note: GDP in 1978 prices except for 2005, which is in 1987 prices.
Sources: 5MP, Table 3-5; OPP2, Tables 2-3 and 3-2; OPP3, Table 2-5; 8MP Table 2-6 and 4-2.

Table 1.4 Malaysia: Employment Creation, 1970–2005 (% increase)

	1970–75	1976–80	1980–85	1985–90	1990–95	1996	1997	1998	1999	2000	1996–2000	2000–05
Agriculture & forestry	7.4	0.2	2.2	4.4	-17.8	-0.1	-1.6	-2.5	-0.2	-0.8	-5.7	-1.2
Mining & quarrying	1.4	-9.5	-24.5	-11.9	10.0	1.2	-1.6	0.7	-0.7	-1.2	1.7	2.4
Manufacturing	107.0	21.2	9.7	50.8	53.9	10.0	6.0	-6.0	6.7	9.2	26.2	22.1
Construction	126.4	31.2	40.2	-0.6	55.5	11.0	10.1	-12.6	-2.2	0.8	5.3	1.0
Services	42.9	16.1	-19.9	-16.2	-15.6	6.5	5.4	1.3	3.9	5.1	-17.5	-19.1
Total	31.0	10.1	13.5	17.7	18.4	5.3	4.6	-2.9	3.5	4.6	15.9	17.5

Sources: Calculated with data from 5MP, Table 3-5; 6MP, Table 1-11; 7MP, Table 4-2; 8MP, Table 2-4; 9MP, Table 11-2; *Economic Report*, various issues.

Table 1.5 reflects the changing structure of the Malaysian economy in terms of output, employment and location. While the decline in the primary sector has been substantial, inter-sectoral growth rates have not followed the industrial market economies' well-defined patterns of structural shifts from extractive activities to industry to services.[2] During this period, industry consistently increased its share of GDP from 17.7 per cent in 1970 to 24.2 per cent in 1980, 30.5 per cent in 1990, 36.7 per cent in 2000 and 39.0 per cent in 2005.[3] There has been a hint of de-industrialization since the 1997–98 financial crisis, with industry's share of GDP, but not total employment, declining to 34.8 per cent. The service sector was already substantial in the early period of post-colonial growth. Its subsequent growth to 36.2 per cent of GDP in 1970, 40.1 per cent in 1980, 41.9 per cent in 1990, 52.4 per cent in 2000 and 53.1 per cent in 2005 was at the expense of agriculture, not industry.

Table 1.5 Malaysia: Shifts in Percentage Shares of Output and Employment, 1957–2005

Output/employment by sector	*1970–1990*	*1990–2005*	*1970–2005*
Primary output	15.9	17.6	33.5
Primary employment	−29.6	−14.1	−43.7
Secondary output	−11.0	−7.2	−18.2
Secondary employment	14.8	11.4	26.2
Services output	−4.9	−10.4	−15.3
Services employment	14.8	2.7	17.5

Source: Calculated from Table 1.3.

Malaysia shared the experience of industrial market economies in terms of sectoral shifts in employment that far exceeded sectoral shifts in output. In general, between 1957 and 2005, shifts in employment exceeded shifts in output, especially after 1970, with the greatest relative shift recorded by the service sector. There have also been important changes in services employment with a significant shift from traditional to modern services (Table 1.6). However, it is unclear if the significant increase in service employment is demand-determined or due to changes in supply factors, owing to the significant expansion of educational achievements (Table 1.7) as well as the role of state-induced employment restructuring, as suggested by the spectacular growth of government services employment from 1970.

Demand factors — including increases in per capita income, urbanization (Table 1.8) and industrialization — have been important sources of growth in the service sector.[4] A newly-industrializing country must necessarily invest

Table 1.6 Malaysia: Distribution of Services Employment, 1970–2005 (%)

Service activity	1970	1990	2005
Transport, storage and communications	3.6	4.5	5.8
Wholesale and retail, restaurants and hotels	n.a.	18.2	17.7
Finance, insurance, real estate and business services	10.0	3.9	6.7
Other services	18.0	20.6	20.8
Total	100.0	100.0	100.0

Notes: n.a. – not available.
1970 employment figures are for Peninsular Malaysia only. The total figures are different from those provided by official Malaysian plan documents.
Sources: Department of Statistics, National Accounts Statistics, various years; Economic Report, various years; Department of Statistics, Population Census, 1970; Labour Force Survey, various years.

Table 1.7 Malaysia: Educational Profile of Labour Force, 1990–2005 (%)

Highest level achieved	1990	2000	2005*
Primary	33.8	27.2	26.9
Lower & middle secondary	57.4	58.8	54.8
Tertiary	8.8	14.0	18.2
Total	100.0	100.0	100.0

Note: * For employed only.
Source: OPP3, Table 6-2; Yearbook of Statistics, Malaysia, 2005, Table 9.5.

Table 1.8 Malaysia: Urban Shares of Total Population, 1970–2005 (%)

Year	1970	1980	1990	2000	2005
Urban share	28.8	37.5	54.7	61.9	63.0

Sources: Department of Statistics, Population Census, 1957, 1970; Malaysia Plan documents, various years; Malaysia, Yearbook of Statistics, 2005.

in infrastructure projects, including transportation and utilities, as this leads to rapid public sector growth. Associated with rapid economic growth is rapid urbanization owing to the transformation of the economy from a rural agricultural base and, since the 1970s, the active encouragement of industrialization and public sector growth with bureaucracies concentrated in urban areas. Except for government services, the fastest growth in output during the 1970s and for a decade from the late 1980s was recorded by the manufacturing sector, resulting in demand-induced growth of the service sector through linkages.[5]

With the exception of social and personal services,[6] producer and distributive services posted high growth rates. While all sectors experienced deteriorating growth rates during the mid-1980s' recession, the services sector experienced the highest growth rate of 3.9 per cent in output, suggesting that the sector was generally more insulated from the vicissitudes affecting tradeables. This was sustained by the government's early 1980s' counter-cyclical policy of expanding public services before growing budget deficits led to an austerity drive from mid-1982, freezing public sector employment. With public sector services employment largely frozen since then, the subsequent growth of services employment has largely involved the private sector, including the privatization of previously public sector services. And despite some recent trends involving casualization, it is unlikely that much of this service sector growth is accounted for by the informal sector. However, as Tables 1.9 and 1.10 show, much of the significantly increased demand for services has been met from abroad, resulting in a significant rise in the deficit in the invisibles or services component of the trade balance, especially since the late 1970s.

With the exception of social and personal services between 1970 and 1980, service employment grew at a slower pace compared to service output. The highest employment growth rates were posted by finance and business services, wholesale/retail and hotels and restaurants, and government services, casting doubt on the argument that lower productivity is the source of employment growth. As will be discussed in Chapter 4, employment growth in modern services such as public sector services and modern producer services are due to a combination of demand factors discussed earlier and the human resource policies of an interventionist state.

As mentioned above, Western literature on the growth of the service sector has attributed the relatively faster growth of service employment *vis-à-vis* manufacturing to the lower labour productivity in service industries. Bearing in mind the complexities and limitations in conventional measurement of productivity of the service sector, available evidence (Khong, 1991: Chap. 1) suggests that the growth rate of labour productivity in all services (except

Table 1.9 Malaysia: Balance of Payments, 1965–2005 (RM million)

	1965	1970	1975	1980	1985	1990	1995	2000	2005
Merchandise account	521	1,067	724	5,238	8,883	7,093	97	79,144	125,562
Exports		5,020	9,057	28,013	37,576	77,458	179,491	374,033	536,955
Imports		3,953	8,333	22,775	28,693	70,365	179,394	294,889	411,393
Services account	-86	-507	-983	-3,993	-4,957	-4,651	-8,891	-10,670	-9,011
Freight & insurance	-162	-325	-621	-1,781	-1,852	-3,837	-9,028	-11,736	-16,433
Other transportation	-16	—	—	-56	64	-25	737	—	—
Travel[a]	-80	-105	-105	-885	-1,332	632	4,143	11,158	19,448
Government transactions	225	-77	-257	-7	-31	-3	-23	-62	-350
Other services	-53	—	—	-1,264	-1,806	-1,418	-4,720	-10,030	-11,676
Investment income	-255	-355	-727	-1,820	-5,434	-5,072	-10,338	-27,934	-23,426
Transfers[b]	-58	-180	-79	-45	-14	147	-2,515	-8,288	-17,445
Current account	122	25	-1,065	-620	-1,522	-2,483	-21,647	32,252	75,681
(% of GNP)	(1.4)	(0.2)	(-4.9)	(-1.2)	(-2.1)	(-2.2)	(-8.9)	(10.3)	(16.1)
Financial account	324	303	1,565	3,115	5,099	4,829	19,140	-23,848	-37,018
Official capital	174	20	869	180	2,504	-2,836	6,147	3,936	-3,150
Corporate investment	150	283	696	2,935	2,595	7,665	12,993	-27,784	-33,869
Errors and omission	-235	-260	-329	-1,493	-368	3,019	-1,896	-16,581	-25,020
Overall balance	211	68	171	1,002	3,209	5,365	-4,403	-8,177	13,644
(% of GNP)	(2.4)	(0.6)	(0.8)	(1.9)	(4.5)	(4.7)	(-1.8)	(-2.6)	(2.9)

Notes: Data are re-organized in consideration of changes in the format used by BNM.
  [a] Includes education for 1985–95.
  [b] Includes employees' compensation for 2000 and 2005.

Sources: Bank Negara Malaysia, *Monthly Statistical Bulletin*, various issues; Ministry of Finance, Malaysia, *Economic Report*, various issues.

Table 1.10 Malaysia: Net Services Trade Balance, 1965–2005 (RM million)

	1965	1970	1975	1980	1985	1990	1995	2000	2005
Freight & insurance	–162	–304	–621	–1934	–1,852	–3,837	–9,028	–11,736	–16,433
Other transportation	–16	–21	98	–11	64	–25	737		
Travel	–80	–105	–105	–521	–1,332	632	4,143	11,158	19,448
Investment income	–255	–355	–727	–1,954	–5,434	–5,072	–10,338	–27,934	–23,426
Govt. transactions	225	68	47	36	–31	–3	–23	–62	–350
Other services	–53	–145	–402	–792	–1,806	–1,418	–4,720	–10,030	–11,676
Services balance	–341	–862	–1,710	–5,176	–10,391	–9,723	–19,227	–38,604	–32,437
% of GNP	n.a.	–7.1	–7.9	–10.1	–14.4	–8.5	–7.9	12.3	6.7

Sources: Bank Negara Malaysia, *Quarterly Economic Bulletin*, various issues.

commerce, finance and other personal services) has consistently exceeded that of manufacturing.[7] In terms of inter-sectoral productivity levels, as measured by the GDP per head and relative product,[8] the service sector has, on average, lower productivity levels than manufacturing, but higher productivity levels than the extractive sector. This is due to the low productivity levels of traditional services such as petty commerce and social and personal services, and government services. Government services are generally deemed the least productive of all modern sector services, probably because government employment is usually not governed by profitability or productivity considerations.[9]

The modern, capital-intensive financial services and utilities enjoyed significantly higher productivity per head, particularly the financial service sector whose productivity level was significantly higher than the service sector's average. The less productive sub-sectors in the service industries resulted in overall services' average productivity level being lower than that of manufacturing.[10] The highest growth rates in productivity between 1970 and 1985 were registered by government services followed by transport and utilities.[11] The commerce and personal service sectors remain services with low productivity levels and productivity growth rates, a significant phenomenon given their higher than average growth rate in employment. Hence, Malaysian data do not provide unequivocal support for the hypothesis that service sector employment expanded rapidly due to relatively lower productivity levels or productivity growth.

However, Malaysian data support the argument that service sector employment is, in general, more insulated from business cycles than the tradeables sector, especially the manufacturing and primary commodities sectors. Khong (1991: Table 2.5) found that the shares of redundancies in services were much lower than their share of overall employment in the 1980s.[12] Within the service sector, the highest redundancies are found in commerce, comprising wholesale/retail trade and hotels and restaurants, which are vulnerable to business cycles. In addition, these services are without effective workers' organizations, and utilize a greater proportion of secondary and marginal workers who incur low labour-turnover costs to employers.

Modern institutionalized services, such as finance and government services, provide greater security of employment. The higher degree of unionization in these services and collective agreements between employers and workers generally result in negotiations for wage freezes or recruitment freezes, rather than lay-offs, to avoid high labour-turnover costs associated with these services' utilization of a large proportion of elite-primary and secondary-primary workers. Case studies will show that the service sector's role as an unemployment sponge during economic downturns generally only applies to the non-enumerated informal sector, which are not reflected in the official statistics, and the self-employed.

Despite rapid economic growth, Malaysia did not achieve "full employment" (i.e. an unemployment rate of less than 4 per cent) until the 1990s, with a decade of very rapid economic growth from 1988 until 1997. Table 1.11 suggests generally higher unemployment before the 1980s among ethnic Indians, who have been also relatively more dependent on wage employment compared to the more urban ethnic Chinese and the more rural ethnic Malays, for whom self-employment was far more important. With the massive urban migration of all ethnic communities, especially the Malays, since the 1970s, the unemployment rate among Malays has exceeded that of Indians since the 1980s, after the huge expansion of the public sector employment in the 1970s came to an end from 1982.

Table 1.11 Unemployment Rates by Ethnicity, 1967–2005

Year	Malay	Chinese	Indian	Others	Total
1967/68	5.7	5.1	8.4	4.9	5.8
1970	8.1	7.0	11.0	3.1	8.0
1975	6.1	6.3	10.5	9.2	6.7
1980	6.5	3.9	6.3	3.6	5.6
1983	7.0	4.0	6.4	3.8	5.8
1985	8.7	5.5	8.4	5.0	7.6
1990	5.8	4.5	4.9	1.7	5.1
1993	3.3	2.5	2.7	2.3	3.0
1995	4.6	1.5	2.6	0.4	3.1
2000	4.6	1.6	2.7	2.1	3.4
2003	4.9	1.9	3.0	2.4	3.8
2005					3.5

Notes: 1985–2003 figures are for Malaysia; the earlier ones are for Peninsular Malaysia only.
Sources: *Fifth Malaysia Plan, 1986–1990*: Table 3.5; *Seventh Malaysia Plan, 1996–2000*: Table 3.2; *Eighth Malaysia Plan, 2001–2005*: Table 3.7; *Mid-Term Review of the Eighth Malaysia Plan, 2001–2005*: Table 3.7.

Government Spending

Tables 1.12 to 1.14 show trends in government expenditure generally, as well as its components (by sector as well as operating or current versus development or capital expenditure). Government expenditure increased greatly during the

1970s and early 1980s reflecting changing policy priorities (Tables 1.12 and 1.13). The public sector's share of total investments after independence rose from about 20 per cent in 1960 to 38 per cent in 1967 (Lo, 1972: 6–8). The contribution of government investments continued to grow during the 1970s (with the redistributive New Economic Policy to reduce poverty and reduce inter-ethnic economic disparities), and during the early 1980s (to finance new heavy industries). The public sector's share of GDP rose from 29.2 per cent in 1970 to a peak of 58.4 per cent in 1981, before falling to 25.3 per cent in 1993 and then rising again in response to the 1997–98 financial crisis to 38.5 per cent in 2004. Table 1.14 indicates the sectoral allocations of public expenditure in official plans as well as annual budgets, focussing on social services (especially education and health), general administration and defence.

Table 1.12 Malaysia: Government Expenditure as Share of GDP, 1966–2005

Years	Total expenditure	Operating expenditure	Development expenditure
1966–70	23.1	17.2	5.9
1971–75	21.9	19.8	8.1
1976–80	28.5	19.3	9.2
1981–85	38.2	23.6	24.6
1986–90	29.7	23.3	6.4
1991–95	24.2	18.7	5.5
1996	22.3	17.3	5.0
1997	21.0	15.9	5.1
1998	21.8	15.7	6.0
1999	22.7	15.5	7.1
2000	23.8	16.5	7.3
2001	29.3	19.1	10.2
2002	28.7	19.0	9.7
2003	28.7	19.0	9.7
2004	26.4	20.4	6.1
2005	25.2	19.7	5.5

Sources: Malaysia plan documents; Bank Negara Malaysia, *Monthly Statistical Bulletin*, various issues.

Table 1.13 Malaysia: Federal Government Finance, 1963–2005 (RM million)

Period	Revenue	Operating expenditure	Current balance	Development expenditure	Overall balance
1963–65	4,188	3,959	229	1,527	−1,298
1966–70	9,897	9,309	588	3,187	−2,599
1971–75	18,645	18,026	619	7,371	−6,752
1976–80	47,189	38,199	8,990	20,659	−11,669
1981–85	93,025	82,004	11,021	46,571	−35,550
1986–90	114,422	109,480	4,942	28,738	−23,796
1991–95	215,394	164,225	51,169	48,429	2,740
1996–2000	301,265	236,360	64,903	90,668	−25,764
2001–2005*	461,391	397,222	64,669	162,415	−97,746

Note: * estimate.
Source: Ministry of Finance, Malaysia, *Economic Report*, various issues.

Table 1.14 Malaysia: Federal Government Expenditure by
Functional Classification, 1963–2005 (%)

Total expenditure	Social services	Economic projects	Defence & security	Adminis-tration	Others (transfers, debt servicing)
1963–65	27	26	21	9	18
1966–70	28	22	22	9	19
1971–75	30	24	22	8	16
1976–80	28	26	20	8	18
1981–85	27	27	18	6	22
1986–90	27	22	14	9	29
1991–95	30	20	17	10	24
1996–2000	33	21	13	11	22
2001–2005	37	17	13	11	22

Source: Ministry of Finance, Malaysia, *Economic Report*, various issues.

As Figure 1.3 shows, public spending clearly increased in response to the downturns of the mid-1970s as well as in 1998 in countercyclical fashion, but fiscal contraction exacerbated the mid-1980s' downturn. Public investment cuts and privatization during this period reversed earlier trends until the late 1990s, when public investments rose again with some re-nationalization as well as government refinancing and restructuring of distressed banks and large corporations, including previously privatized ones. Public sector expenditure grew to RM167 billion in 2004, up from RM35 billion in 1985 and RM78 billion in 1995. As a proportion of GDP, public sector expenditure dropped from 45 per cent in 1985 to 38 per cent in 1995, before climbing to 77 per cent in 2004.[13] Table 1.12 traces social expenditures before and in response to the last three major Malaysian economic downturns of 1974–75, 1985–86 and 1997–98 respectively as well as the initial (but later reversed) fiscal contraction following long-serving (since mid-1981) Prime Minister Mahathir's retirement in late 2003.

It seems very likely that the rapid growth and structural transformation experienced by the Malaysian economy has had varied consequences for the labour force and their dependents. Malaysian public policy discourse is generally pre-occupied by the inter-ethnic distribution of income. Tables 1.16 and 1.17 suggest that real incomes have grown significantly and that inter-

Figure 1.3 Malaysia: Government Services as Share of GDP in 1987 Prices and Annual Change in Total Government Expenditure, 1973–2005

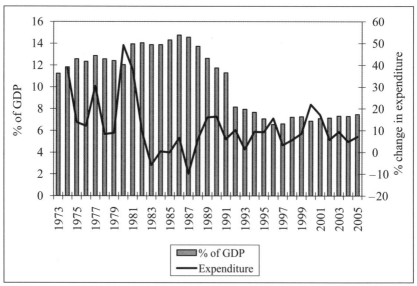

Source: Calculated with data from Bank Negara Malaysia, *Monthly Statistical Bulletin*, various issues.

Table 1.15 Malaysia: Changes in Total Government Expenditure and Expenditure on Social Services, 1973–77, 1985–89, 1996–2005 (% of nominal value per annum)

	1973	1974	1975	1976	1977	1985	1986	1987	1988	1989	1996	1997	1998	1999	2000	2001	2002	2003	2004*	2005*
Expenditure																				
Operating	9	29	14	19	26	1	0	1	8	14	23.3	1.8	1.8	-0.1	21.1	12.8	7.8	9.5	21.4	7.6
Social:	3	27	16	8	38	9	8	3	5	10	22.1	1.5	1.5	10.3	13.1	32.0	15.8	16.7	12.8	4.3
Education	1	31	10	9	39	n.a.	8	3	14	0	22	-0.4	1.6	8.8	12.8	11.6	17.8	12.1	13.1	7.4
Health	10	22	15	7	38	8	8	-3	6	9	27	9	2	8.9	13.9	13.3	10.1	22.2	11.3	4.2
Housing	n.a.	n.a.	n.a.	n.a.	n.a.	n.a.	59	-44	46	16	n.a.	8.7	-97.3	-1.1	5.7	331.5	-65.7	30.2	404.5	-70.8
Development	-9	67	15	11	35	-15	6	-37	10	47	4.1	7.7	14.9	24.9	23.6	26.1	2.1	9.4	-26.7	5.7
Social:	17	40	17	-4	43	-6	21	-59	13	67	13.4	23.5	23.5	19.9	59.7	38.9	17.3	-1.9	-42.1	-17.9
Education	27	32	13	7	21	-14	22	-24	7	44	2.3	20.6	15.6	32.6	83.7	46.0	20.0	-18.0	-57.7	-20.7
Health	26	24	36	-18	-6	-10	5	-55	30	216	30.2	-11.1	59.9	16.8	52.2	23.4	-4.3	78.4	-12.2	-48.8
Housing	n.a.	175	-6	-7	321	7	8	-93	-27	214	24.3	46.7	40.1	5.0	10.5	6.3	42.5	6.6	-17.4	8.5
Total	4	39	14	16	29	-4	2	-10	9	20	17.9	3.3	3.3	6.9	21.9	17.2	5.7	9.5	4.9	7.2
Social:	5	29	17	6	39	4	12	-17	6	19	20.1	6.2	6.2	13.0	26.8	34.6	16.3	8.8	-8.1	-1.1
Education	4	31	11	9	36	4	10.6	-3	13	7	17.8	3.1	4.4	14.0	30.7	23.8	18.7	-0.7	-11.6	2.7
Health	12	22	18	4	33	6	9	-7	7	21	27.0	5.9	8.6	10.3	21.1	15.7	6.5	34.9	4.3	-9.0
Housing	n.a.	n.a.	n.a.	n.a.	n.a.	n.a.	11	-90	-3	116	n.a.	14.1	72.1	4.5	10.1	29.5	16.7	8.3	18.1	-20.0

Note: * Estimate.
Source: Ministry of Finance, Malaysia, *Economic Report*, various issues.

Table 1.16 Peninsular Malaysia: Mean Monthly Household Incomes by Ethnicity and Location, 1970–2004

	1970	1973	1976	1979	1984	1987	1990	1995	1999	2004
All	423	502	566	669	792	760	1,167	2,020	2,472	3,022
Bumiputera (B)	276	335	380	475	616	614	940	1,604	1,984	2,522
Chinese (C)	632	739	866	906	1,086	1,012	1,631	2,890	3,456	4,127
Indian (I)	478	565	592	730	791	771	1,209	2,140	2,702	3,215
Others	1,304	1,798	1,395	1,816	1,775	2,043	955	1,284	1,371	2,150
Urban (U)	687	789	913	942	1,114	1,039	1,617	2,589	3,103	3,680
Rural (R)	321	374	431	531	596	604	951	1,326	1,718	1,744
Disparity ratio (C/B)	2.30	2.21	2.28	1.91	1.76	1.65	1.74	1.80	1.74	1.64
Disparity ratio (I/B)	1.73	1.69	1.56	1.54	1.28	1.26	1.29	1.33	1.36	1.27
Disparity ratio (U/R)	2.14	2.11	2.12	1.77	1.87	1.72	1.70	1.95	1.81	2.11

Notes: Figures for 1970–87 in constant 1978 prices; figures for 1990–95 are constant 1990 prices; 1999, 2004 in 1999 constant prices.
Sources: *Fourth Malaysia Plan, 1981–85, Mid-Term Review of the Fifth Malaysia Plan, 1986–1990, Seventh Malaysia Plan, 1996–2000, Eighth Malaysia Plan, 2001–2005; Ninth Malaysia Plan, 2006–2010.*

Table 1.17 Peninsular Malaysia: Household Incomes by Ethnicity and Location, 1970–2004 (RM/month)

Ethnic Group	1970	1973	1976	1979	1984	1987	1999	2002	2004
Bumiputera									
mean income	172	209	237	296	384	679	1,984	2,376	2,711
median income	120	141	160	197	262	479			
Chinese									
mean income	394	461	540	565	678	1,119	3,456	4,279	4,437
median income	268	298	329	373	462	799			
Indian									
mean income	304	352	369	455	494	852	2,702	3,044	3,456
median income	194	239	247	314	347	625			
All									
mean income	264	313	353	417	494	841	2,472	3,011	3,249
median income	166	196	215	263	326	578	1,704	2,049	
Urban									
mean income	428	492	569	587	695	1148	3,103	3,652	3,956
median income	265	297	340	361	463	785			
Rural									
mean income	200	233	269	331	372	667	1,718	1,729	1,875
median income	139	159	180	222	269	492			

Notes: Constant 1970 prices up to 1984; 1980 RM prices for 1987 and current prices thereafter.
Sources: 1970–76 figures from *Fourth Malaysia Plan, 1981–85*: Table 3.9; 1979 and 1984 figures from *Fifth Malaysia Plan, 1986–1990*: Table 3.4; 1999 and 2002 figures from *Mid-Term Review of the Eighth Malaysia Plan, 2001–2005*: Tables 3.3 and 3.4; Shireen Hashim (1998); *Ninth Malaysia Plan, 2006–2010*.

ethnic disparities declined significantly after 1970. The Bumiputera average income ratio to both Chinese and Indians rose significantly until the late 1980s, though the record since then has been more ambiguous. There has been a corresponding improvement in the rural-urban income ratio for the same time period as well. However, the trend since then seems more ambiguous with income disparities growing again except around the 1997–98 crisis when public expenditures also rose sharply as the debacle probably also had a greater negative wealth effect on higher incomes.

2

Labour Market
Segmentation in Malaysia

Labour market segmentation in Malaysian services cannot be understood without studying labour market structure in the overall Malaysian economy. Segmentation in Malaysian labour markets is rooted in the country's economic, social and political history. Attempts to redress inter-ethnic imbalances in wealth and income distribution through the New Economic Policy (NEP) have changed labour force profiles since 1970. The NEP also changed the boundaries and significance of labour market segments, owing to the effects of educational policies and other forms of pro-Bumiputera state intervention, including an expanded public sector. Parallel with significant changes in labour supply, labour demand has also been transformed. The decline in agriculture and the expansion of industry and services have changed the environment within which the labour market operates. New types of labour market entrants, such as women, immigrants and different ethnic proportions with different education and training, have substantially affected labour market adjustment processes as the economy experiences increasing global interdependence and vulnerability related to openness.

A labour market segmentation analysis is used to guide examination of the structure and dynamics of the Malaysian labour market in general, and services labour in particular (Khong, 1991). Specifically, the labour force is "horizontally" distinguished by educational levels, and vertically segmented by ethnicity and gender. Horizontal and vertical segmentation are not solely economic in nature. They are also shaped by socio-economic and political relations and structures, which influence job access as well as, pay and promotion prospects in the Malaysian service sector.

The Evolution of the Malaysian Labour Market

When Malaya became independent from Britain in 1957, labour was ethnically segmented along employment status, industrial and occupational lines. Although structural change and state policies since independence, and especially from 1970, have mitigated some of these features, Malaysia still has strong social divisions along ethnic, cultural, religious and linguistic lines. The population is usually said to be composed of three main ethnic groups, the Malays and other *Bumiputera*[1] or indigenes, Chinese (about a quarter) and Indians (about eight per cent), who, in turn, comprise smaller sub-ethnic communities. These ethnic groups are unequally distributed geographically, with a higher concentration of Malays in rural areas and a greater Chinese presence in urban areas.

The roots of such ethnic, regional, social and economic stratification can be traced back to British colonial transformation.[2] Free wage labour did not exist in pre-colonial Malaya.[3] Instead, Malaya was a predominantly peasant agricultural economy, with native Malays involved in rice farming and fishing. Lying on the maritime crossroads of Asia, Malaya was a good trading centre for merchants from India, China and the Arab world, some of whom settled down. Contact with European colonialism began with the Portuguese conquest of the port of Malacca in the early sixteenth century, but this did not have any major impact on the economic organization of the rest of the country. British colonialism began in 1786 with the annexation of Penang Island. Initially, British interests were centred in the Straits Settlements of Singapore, Penang and Malacca. Through a series of treaties with the Malay sultans and Siam (which controlled the northern Malayan states of Perlis, Kelantan, Kedah and Terengganu) in the late nineteenth century and early twentieth century, Britain consolidated its hold over Malaya.[4] After the annexation of the Straits Settlements, Britain began to intervene in the Malay hinterland when British economic interests were supposedly threatened by inter-factional fighting over mining rights between Chinese secret societies allied with rival Malay territorial chiefs.

Tin Mining and Chinese Labour

Unlike the early Straits Chinese who came as free men, becoming part of the bourgeois trading network and accumulating sufficient capital to start tin mining in the Federated Malay States, labourers in tin mines were either indentured coolies imported by Chinese mining capital or "voluntary" Chinese emigrant labour escaping famine and war in Southern China.[5] Straits Chinese-owned mines utilized primitive labour-intensive methods. Minimization of the wage bill was a key to profitability and viability, and indentured immigrants provided the necessary cheap labour. Until the end of the nineteenth century, there was no official policy protecting the rights of these Chinese workers in terms of wages or working conditions. Consequently, labour mortality was high because of malnutrition, addiction and overwork.[6] With the help of various British government policies, denomination of the tin mining industry passed over to British dredging companies in the early 1910s. With this, the structure of employment changed, because of the much more capital-intensive methods used by British-owned mining dredges. Small-scale operations became marginalized, and the control Chinese capital over labour was broken through official abolition of indentured labour, secret societies as well as other British measures to "protect" Chinese labour.

Even after the official abolition of indentured labour in 1914, workers continued to be recruited by foremen and supervisors who were sent back to China for that specific purpose. Various remuneration practices let to the debt-bondage of labourers to their employers. Such recruitment led to the use of kinship and village ties to control workers. Chinese labour was organized in craft guilds, clans, associations and dialect groups, while Chinese vernacular schooling, usually funded by wealthy Chinese, trained a labour force almost exclusively for Chinese employers (Jomo, 1986: 169). As the proportion of British-owned mines increased, so too did the use of non-Chinese labour, especially Indian[7] workers, as part of a "divide and rule" strategy. This strategy included different pay and treatment of workers by ethnicity, with Chinese labourers paid more than Indian workers, but provided with fewer other non-monetary forms of remuneration, partly because the Chinese workers, although considered more skilful and productive, ostensibly worked better on an arms-length, daily contractual basis.

Only the richer Chinese could afford to buy land. Those with skills resorted to self-employment, becoming small-scale producers, artisans, craftsmen or petty traders. These small Chinese enterprises were often linked by kinship and dialect group ties, reinforced by business collaboration. Other Chinese settlers became middlemen or retailers in Malay villages, usually financed by larger Chinese or European capital. Chinese capitalists continued to flourish without much intervention from the colonial government. For various reasons, Chinese employers usually resorted to Chinese labour. As a result, significant trade and occupational specialization was consolidated along ethnic, dialect and clan lines.[8]

Plantation Capital and Indian Labour

Large-scale immigration of Indian labourers did not begin until the early twentieth century, with the rubber from 1906. Before that, Indians in Malaya were primarily employed as labourers, domestic servants and clerks for the colonial administration since English was also the official language in colonial India.[9] Before the rubber boom, British sugar-cane and coffee plantations mainly employed Indian labourers, rather than Chinese labourers who were more independent, expensive and prone to strike. With the rubber boom, large tracts of land were granted at low cost to British planters, encouraging the growth of rubber plantations.[10] Labour was scarce, as Chinese workers preferred to work for Chinese mines, while Malay peasants had their own land and were not keen to work for wages. Therefore, India, a British colony with a large labour surplus, was an obvious source.

Similar to the recruitment of Chinese labour, Indian labour recruitment also went through several stages of indentured labour before the 1890s, before being replaced by the *kangany* system and assisted immigration.[11] Most recruitment relied on kinship village and other informal ties. The colonial state served as the largest employer of Indian labour for building and maintaining railroads, roads and ports. Although Indian labourers could work for other sectors of the economy, most were confined to plantations (their first employer/ sponsor) because of barriers to entry in to Chinese and European-controlled private enterprises and peasant agriculture. Additionally, the indenture system prevented them from working for another employer during the period of bondage. Similarly, the *kangany* system indirectly controlled the mobility of workers through debt-bondage.

Indian labour in Malaya was segmented along occupational and caste lines. South Indian Tamils and Telegus were plantation labourers; Malayalees were skilled estate workers, white-collar workers or even professionals; Sikhs were policemen, watchmen or security-guards; Chettiars were moneylenders from Madras; Gujeratis and Sindhis were involved in the textile trade; and Ceylonese Tamils were in the lower administrative positions in the Civil Service or were professionals (see Ampalavanar, 1981: 1–5; Stenson, 1980: 6–8).

Chances of upward mobility for Indians in remote areas were mainly accessible through education. However, only the most basic of primary schooling, in Tamil was available to the children of Indian labourers. Urban Indians, on the other hand, could achieve some degree of inter-generational mobility with access to the English medium schools, which enabled access to white-collar employment, including professional occupations.[12] On the whole, Indians most tied to the colonial economy as wage earners in the public as well as private sector, especially the plantation sector. After independence, their share of public sector employment would collapse, especially following NEP style affirmative action policies. Plantation wages and working conditions would be squeezed by commodity prices and new immigrant labour, while

Tamil and even minimal Malay medium schooling denied much room for upward mobility.

Malay Peasantry and Aristocracy

In various agreements with the Malay rulers, the British promised protection and special privileges for the Malays *vis-à-vis* other ethnic groups, in return for albeit indirect *de facto* rules through "residents" and "advisors". The British idea of protection and preservation of Muslim Malay culture and identity involved preservation of a yeoman peasantry through minimal Malay medium schooling and protected rights to land for the Malays, who were encouraged to remain self-employed as rice farmers and fishermen. Although many were lured by the attractive returns to rubber cultivation, Malay smallholdings (using family labour) were actively discouraged by various discriminatory colonial practices from planting rubber.[13] British educational policy only provided basic vernacular schooling in the Malay language to village Malays.[14] This tended to reinforce the isolation of the Malay community, and limited their access to modern sector employment often requiring knowledge of English (Loh, 1975).

Class differences between the Malay "aristocracy" and commoners were reinvented through education and other policies. An elite Malay college was established in Kuala Kangsar, Perak, in 1905 to provide English medium education to the sons of the Malay royalty and aristocracy, to be absorbed into the lower and middle rungs of the colonial administration. Recruitment of middle-level white collar government employees favoured Malays to placate the Malay elite facing competition from English-educated Straits Chinese and middle class Indians, though they lacked any real substance and power in their administrative role despite the myth of power-sharing with the British.

Early Labour Organization

Despite the appalling labour conditions in British Malaya, early labour organization was insignificant and largely illegal until just before the Japanese invasion. The few labour organizations that existed then were limited in their coverage, and ethnically segmented. While the Chinese triad societies were active among labourers, neither they nor the "clannish and closed" Chinese guilds which organized craft-workers and non-mining labour could be regarded as labour unions since both employers and employees were members. The guilds dealt with all aspects of the trades, including wage disputes, working hours and working conditions.[15] Rules were based on custom and tradition, with employers usually having the upper hand. Through these societies and guilds, employers exercised control over Chinese labour. Nonetheless, these early societies and guilds served some of the purposes of labour unions, for instance, in settling labour disputes.

The seclusion of Indian workers on rubber estates eventually encouraged labour organization among them.[16] However, formal labour unions were only allowed in 1940 under the Trade Union Ordinance, designed to contain the influence of more militant union leaders. The post-war Indian identification[17] with the trade union movement can be traced to changing colonial labour policies with greater state provisions for the welfare of Indian labourers, e.g. a Labour Department was set up in 1911, largely preoccupied with Indian labour issues.[18] While Chinese labour matters were handled by the colonial Protector of Chinese. However, the union movement was weak because of general illiteracy, lack of leadership, absence of a union tradition, and most importantly, the colonial state's strong stance against unions and the political leftwing associated with organized labour.

Recent Labour Market Conditions[19]

The population of Malaysia grew at an annual average of 2.6 per cent per annum between 1991 and 2005 to reach 26.8 million in 2005. This relatively high population growth is due to the substantial increase of non-citizens, averaging 8.1 per cent yearly during this period, reflecting the massive inflow of foreign workers into the country. If non-citizens (immigrants) are excluded, the domestic population grew at only 2.3 per cent annually. Due to the relatively young age structure of the Malaysian population, the working age-group (15–64 years) expanded at 3.1 per cent per annum between 1991 and 2005.

Sustained high economic growth has also brought about considerable changes in the structure of employment (see Table 2.1). Out of the 2.4 million jobs created between 1985 and 1995, over 50 per cent was in manufacturing, thereby increasing its employment share from 19 to 26 per cent during this period. Meanwhile, agriculture's employment share declined to 18 per cent, while government employment, which had expanded rapidly in the 1970s and early 1980s, declined as well due to downsizing and rationalization of the public sector from the 1980s. Non-government services now employ about 36 per cent of the total employed compared to about 27 per cent in 1985.

The Malaysian economy suffered a severe setback in its growth pattern following the financial turmoil that struck parts of Asia in mid-1997. The Malaysian ringgit depreciated by more than a third from RM2.5 in June 1997 to RM3.8 from September 1998, while the economy contracted by 7.4 per cent in 1998. Despite a speedy recovery, sustaining high growth since then has not been easy. The ringgit pegging, selective capital controls, debt restructuring and recapitalization of the banking system brought some degree of resilience into the economy, though it continues to face several challenges. The inflow of foreign direct investment (FDI) has slowed down, and is unlikely to reach pre-crisis levels following the emergence of new growth centres, including China and India. FDI is now concentrated in selected services and existing manufacturing operations that are retooling to higher value added activities. The economy is undergoing a transition with services becoming more important and dynamic. Non-government services accounted for about 60 per cent of the new jobs created between 2000 and 2005, increasing its employment share to 41 per cent, while manufacturing contributed 35 per cent and sustained its share at around 28 per cent.

Unemployment

Sustained high growth has transformed the situation of higher unemployment in the mid-1980s to one of full employment by the early 1990s. Though the labour force expanded at 2.9 per cent per annum between 1990 and 1995, it was not able to keep pace with the rate of job creation at 3.2 per cent during this period. Thus, the unemployment rate dropped from 4.3 per cent in 1990 to 2.8 per cent by 1995. This dramatic turnaround in the labour market has raised several key issues and challenges for the economy:

*   Labour and skill shortages
*   Rising wages
*   Increasing reliance on foreign workers
*   Relatively low skill intensity
*   Weaknesses in the education and skills delivery mechanisms

The tight labour market and rising wages led to large-scale importation of foreign labour. A policy decision was made in 1991 to liberalize the intake of foreign workers. Subsequently, the number of foreigners with valid work permits peaked from 290,000 in 1990 to 1.5 million in 1997, amounting to 4.3 per cent and 17.0 per cent of the total employed respectively. The unofficial estimate of irregular migrants was about one million in 1997 (Ministry of Finance, *Economic Report, 1997/98*: 25). In other words, the estimated migrant worker population in 1997 was 2.5 million, or 28.0 per cent of those employed.

Malaysia's growing reliance on foreign labour was interrupted by the 1997–98 financial crisis. The sudden and steep contraction of economic activities in 1998 reversed the steady growth in job creation, but the full impact

Table 2.1 Malaysia: Recent Employment Indicators

	Unit	Period	
Population	mil.	2005	26.75
Labour force	'000	2005	11,290.5
Labour Force Participation Rate			
Total	%	2004	64.4
Male	%	2004	80.9
Female	%	2004	47.3
Unemployment	%	2005	3.5
Persons employed in:			
Agriculture[1]	%	2005	13.3
Industry[2]	%	2005	35.7
Services	%	2005	51.0
Labour productivity growth (manufacturing)	%	1991–2003	1.9
Nominal wage growth (manufacturing)	%	1991–2003	2.3
Employers and Self-employed			
Male	%	2004	76.0
Female	%	2004	24.0
Share of employment	%	2004	20.5
Employees			
Male	%	2004	63.0
Female	%	2004	37.0
Share of employment	%	2004	74.4
Family Workers (unpaid)			
Male	%	2004	30.9
Female	%	2004	69.1
Share of employment	%	2004	5.1
Part-time Employment (manufacturing)			
Male	%	2003	45.4
Female	%	2003	54.6
Share of employment	%	2003	0.7

Notes: [1] Includes mining and quarrying.
       [2] Includes construction.
Sources: Department of Statistics, *Labour Force Survey*, various years.
          Department of Statistics (2005). *Annual Survey of Manufacturing Industries, 2004.*
          Malaysia (2006).

on the domestic labour market was muted due to the cushioning effects of the variable presence of migrant labour. Unemployment rose to a mere 3.2 per cent as labour supply fell by 1.7 per cent, largely due to the repatriation of contract migrant workers. The number of work permits issued to foreign workers dropped from 1.2 million in 1997 to 0.78 million in 1998 (Bank Negara Malaysia, *Annual Report, 1998*: 77).

With economic recovery, the number of migrant workers with work permits has once again risen steadily to 1.9 million by December 2005. The steady increase in the number of documented foreign workers is largely explained by the tough laws and actions introduced in August 2002 to stem undocumented migration. With stiffer penalties for those hiring or harbouring illegal migrants, employers are now more inclined to hire migrant workers though proper channels, at least in the Peninsula. Authorities have also stepped up border surveillance and enforcement of laws governing illegal migration.

Nonetheless, severe sectoral labour market imbalances, particularly in Sabah, continue to attract undocumented migrant labour for the 3-D (dirty, dangerous and difficult) jobs. There were about 147,000 registered workers in Sabah in 2001, and an estimated 100,000 undocumented migrant workers. Given its rural agrarian economy, Sabah has a higher incidence of migrant labour. Almost half of the workforce in Sabah consists of foreigners, and unofficial estimates suggest that for every registered migrant worker, there are two unregistered workers. Sarawak employs about 107,000 registered foreign workers and the incidence of irregular migration is reported to be insignificant.

The official figures are widely believed to grossly underestimate the total number of foreign workers in the country. The proportion of illegal workers in Peninsular Malaysia has been somewhat reduced by the registration and hence, legalization of illegal workers, as well as increased surveillance and enforcement from 1991. However, Sabah is believed to continue to harbour an estimated 200,000 illegal workers, with another 300,000 with valid work permits. The number of foreign workers in Sarawak is relatively insignificant, ranging between 20,000 and 40,000. Thus, the total number of foreign workers in Malaysia has been estimated to be at least 1.2 million, or about 15 per cent of those in employment.

The intake of foreign workers is officially an interim solution to overcome the labour supply deficit. In 2005, the majority of foreign workers were from Indonesia (68.9 per cent), followed by Nepal (9.9 per cent), India (6.9 per cent) and Myanmar (4.6 per cent). The remaining ten per cent came almost entirely from countries in Southeast and South Asia. The longer-term strategy is to upgrade the economic structure towards less labour-absorbing activities and to increase the domestic supply of labour through enhanced participation rates. Currently, the overall labour force participation rate (LFPR) is 64 per cent. While the male LFPR has probably peaked at about 81 per cent, the female LFPR is only around 47 per cent. The latter ratio is relatively low compared to those prevailing in developed OECD countries where it is around 62 per cent. Thus, legislative and non-legislative measures have been implemented to enhance female participation in the workforce.

Despite slower growth, unemployment has remained low since 1997, hovering at around 3.5 per cent. Nonetheless, structural unemployment is an emerging problem with moderating growth and the non-expansion of the public sector since the mid-1980s. The economy faces an acute shortage of low-skilled labour which is met by large-scale import of contract migrant workers. There is also a shortage of very highly-skilled labour that is being addressed through short-term measures such as reverse migration schemes for highly-skilled overseas Malaysians and longer-term skills training programmes. Nonetheless, graduate unemployment has been on the rise. The poor quality of unemployed graduates, mostly from local public institutions of high learning, as well as inappropriate choices of courses are blamed for their failure to gain employment. State support for these graduates include free or subsidized retraining, job search and temporary job creation.

Labour Costs and Earnings

Labour market tightness during the high growth period is reflected in wage trends. The nominal average monthly weighted (by employment) wage in manufacturing, construction, mining and rubber rose from RM574 in 1985 to RM790 in 1992. On average, nominal wages grew by 4.1 per cent per annum between 1985 and 1992, as wage pressures increased with economic recovery and sustained rapid growth. With full employment since the early 1990s wage pressures have risen sharply. The construction sector has recorded the highest wage rise. This is hardly surprising as the construction industry, a labour-absorbing industry, grew rapidly at an average of 12 per cent during this period. Rapid economic growth has pushed up wages across all skill categories, but wages for the very skilled and the unskilled have risen more rapidly, implying greater shortages for these occupational categories.

Rising wages have also narrowed the gap between labour productivity and wages, thus exerting upward pressure on unit labour costs. Labour productivity, measured as value added per worker, rose by 5.2 per cent per annum, whereas wages grew by 4.1 per cent. Thus, unit labour costs rose by about one per cent annually during this period. Overall, wage and labour productivity growth have moved in tandem, but in recent years, wages have outpaced productivity increases. Slower growth and the large-scale import of low-skilled foreign labour have helped to moderate wage increases, but wages continue to outpace productivity growth. Labour productivity in manufacturing grew at 1.9 per cent per annum between 1999 and 2003, whereas wages increased at 2.3 per cent during this period.

The rising wages amidst increasing unemployment during the mid-1980s' recession sparked off debates on wage rigidity and demands by employers for wage reforms. Wages in the unionized sector are determined through three yearly collective agreements which are legally binding. These collective agreements are based on several practices that are not very conducive to wage flexibility in the short to medium term, e.g. predetermined annual increments with no explicit link to performance. Secondly, disputes are settled by the Industrial Court, which recommends that salary adjustments should not exceed two-thirds of the growth rate of the CPI over the previous three years. Thirdly, the collective agreement provides for the payment of annual bonuses equivalent to one or two months of the basic salary. The bonus is also contractual, and therefore, firms are legally bound to pay it regardless of their financial position.

It has been argued that though only one-tenth of wage employees are unionized, their fate tends to influence wage trends in the non-unionized sector. However, the World Bank (1995) suggests that present wage practices in Malaysia incorporate beneficial elements of the flexi-wage system. Malaysian employers use bonuses, overtime payments and other non-wage incentives to retain flexibility in wages and employment, and to lower labour turnover. While bonuses have a component that is collectively bargained, more than half of the bonuses paid in manufacturing in 1992 were incentive bonuses, while the ratio in services was even higher (World Bank, 1995).

The male-female wage gap is fairly large in Malaysia. On average, men's wages are nearly twice as high as women's wages. The gap increases at higher occupational categories, and the trend has worsened in recent years (World Bank, 1995). The main reason for the large gender wage inequality is the predominance of female workers in low-wage activities.

Regional Differences

The rate of employment creation, and hence of unemployment, has not been uniform across regions or states. Where agriculture is still the mainstay of the economy, the unemployment rate has remained relatively higher. Due to locational factors and less attractive infrastructure and other facilities,

Table 2.2 Malaysia: Unemployment by State, 1990, 2008

State	1990	2008
Johore	3.3	2.3
Kedah	4.4	3.8
Kelantan	5.9	3.3
Malacca	4.0	1.1
Negeri Sembilan	3.7	3.1
Pahang	4.0	2.6
Perak	4.5	3.8
Perlis	4.7	3.0
Pulau Pinang	3.4	2.0
Sabah	9.1	4.9
Sarawak	8.9	5.3
Selangor	2.9	3.1
Terengganu	7.4	3.4
Kuala Lumpur	3.9	2.7
Malaysia	5.1	3.3

Source: Malaysia (1996: 145); Malaysia, *Labour Force Survey Report, 2008*.

these states have not been able to attract many industries. In the more industrialized regions, such as Penang, Malacca, Kuala Lumpur and Selangor, the unemployment rate is generally lower (see Table 2.2).

There is much evidence of labour market segmentation in Malaysia, with differences in wages and working conditions by gender, ethnicity, language ability and credentials, though with considerable variation in different sectors of the economy. While there is little formal discrimination against women, subtle and informal discrimination is quite widespread, especially in certain occupations and in matters of promotion. The public sector discriminates in favour of Malays and other Bumiputera (indigenous) communities, at the expense of the commercially ubiquitous ethnic Chinese and the smaller Indian minority, who were once disproportionately over-represented in the public sector, especially during the colonial period and soon thereafter. Globalization and cultural liberalization have enhanced the premium attached to English language ability, and facility in certain other commercially important languages such as Chinese and Japanese. Perhaps more than in most places, educational credentials are an important determinant of employment prospects and occupational mobility in Malaysia. The ethnically segregated and streamed nature of schooling in the country serves to reinforce and formalize ethnic and linguistic differences in job access.

Locational differences in growth and industrialization as well as costs and standards of living have also affected remuneration expectations and practices as well as working conditions. There are significant differences in conditions in the three industrial growth poles of Penang (and Province Wellesley), the Kelang Valley and Southern Johor, and especially with the rest of the country, particularly Sabah and Sarawak, where different labour laws — e.g. for workmen's compensation — were enforced until the late 1980s. Smallholder agriculture is still far more significant in the northern and eastern parts of Peninsular Malaysia as well as in Sabah and Sarawak, where some shifting cultivation persists. With the increasing use of immigrant labour, wage and working conditions in plantation agriculture are now even worse than in most other waged employment. Similarly, such conditions are generally better in larger compared to smaller enterprises in the same industry. Foreign employers are generally considered better than private sector Malaysians, though there is perceived to be considerable variation among the foreigners.

Making Malaysia's Segmented Labour Market

The discussion above traced the colonial origins of Malaya's ethnically segmented labour force, with differential job access for various ethnic and social groups, mostly based on non-economic factors. Informal organizations, such as trade guilds and triad societies, and practices like debt-bondage, besides linguistic and other cultural divisions, continue to perpetuate ethnic segmentation. Hence, well after the elimination of indenture, corvee and other forms of unfree labour, the labour market remains far from being free and perfect. The interests of capital, the state and arguably privileged labour segments have conspired to perpetuate old and even promote new patterns of labour market segmentation. Meanwhile, trade union organization has been constrained due to its limited coverage and legal rights as well as the state and employer incentives for opportunism by union leaders (Jomo and Todd, 1994).

The colonial measures to create a proletariat with immigrant workers resulted in an unevenly distributed ethnically-segmented society.[20] The Chinese and Indian populations were concentrated on the West Coast (in the Straits Settlements and the Federated Malay States), where most of the jobs in mines, estates and commerce were to be found. Moreover, the proclamation of Emergency rule in 1948 against communist insurgents (largely perceived to be Chinese) led to the coerced herding of rural Chinese into concentration camp-like "new villages", closely monitored for communist infiltration. Thus,

Table 2.3 Peninsular Malaysia: Percentage Distribution of the Employed Labour Force by Economic Activity and Ethnicity, 1957, 1970, 1986, 2003

Economic activity	1957				1970				1986				2003			
	Malay	Chinese	Indian	Total	Malay	Chinese	Indian	Total	Malay	Chinese	Indian	Total	Malay	Chinese	Indian	Total
Extractive	75.6 (58.3)	46.2 (26.9)	59.0 (13.9)	61.3 (100.0)	65.2 (67.6)	33.5 (23.0)	47.6 (9.4)	51.6 (100.0)	35.1 (68.6)	14.7 (18.8)	30.1 (11.7)	27.4 (100.0)	10.8 (72.7)	5.1 (18.9)	7.8 (8.4)	11.9 (100.0)
Agriculture	74.6 (60.3)	40.9 (24.9)	56.8 (14.0)	58.5 (100.0)	64.3 (69.3)	29.7 (21.2)	46.0 (9.5)	49.6 (100.0)	34.4 (69.1)	14.0 (18.4)	29.1 (11.6)	26.7 (100.0)	10.5 (73.0)	4.9 (18.8)	7.4 (8.2)	11.6 (100.0)
Mining & quarrying	1.0 (16.9)	5.3 (67.5)	2.2 (11.4)	2.8 (100.0)	0.9 (24.1)	3.8 (67.2)	1.6 (8.2)	2.0 (100.0)	0.7 (48.9)	0.7 (34.6)	1.0 (14.7)	0.7 (100.0)	0.3 (63.3)	0.2 (23.2)	0.4 (13.5)	0.3 (100.0)
Industry	4.8 (23.6)	17.1 (63.6)	7.3 (11.0)	9.6 (100.0)	6.0 (28.2)	21.0 (65.2)	5.9 (5.3)	11.4 (100.0)	18.5 (42.5)	30.9 (46.3)	23.4 (10.6)	23.4 (100.0)	30.5 (56.2)	32.6 (33.0)	36.8 (10.8)	30.4 (100.0)
Manufacturing	2.6 (19.2)	12.8 (71.3)	3.3 (7.5)	6.4 (100.0)	5.1 (29.7)	16.6 (63.8)	4.6 (5.1)	9.2 (100.0)	13.9 (44.1)	20.9 (43.4)	19.1 (12.0)	16.9 (100.0)	22.8 (58.7)	20.2 (28.6)	30.9 (12.7)	21.3 (100.0)
Construction	2.2 (32.5)	4.3 (47.9)	4.0 (18.1)	3.2 (100.0)	0.9 (21.9)	4.4 (70.8)	1.3 (6.0)	2.2 (100.0)	4.6 (38.2)	10.0 (53.8)	4.3 (7.0)	6.5 (100.0)	7.7 (49.8)	12.4 (44.1)	5.9 (6.1)	9.1 (100.0)
Services	19.0 (31.7)	35.4 (44.6)	33.0 (16.9)	28.3 (100.0)	23.7 (40.1)	40.0 (44.8)	40.9 (13.2)	31.6 (100.0)	46.4 (50.6)	54.4 (38.7)	46.6 (10.0)	49.2 (100.0)	58.7 (57.6)	62.3 (33.7)	55.4 (8.7)	57.7 (100.0)
Utilities	0.4 (37.8)	0.4 (28.5)	1.4 (40.5)	0.5 (100.0)	0.7 (53.5)	0.4 (20.2)	2.2 (32.1)	0.7 (100.0)	0.7 (71.4)	0.1 (8.8)	1.0 (19.6)	0.9 (100.0)	0.2 (81.4)	0.6 (10.0)	0.6 (8.7)	0.8 (100.0)

Table 2.3 (continued)

Economic activity	1957				1970				1986				2003			
	Malay	Chinese	Indian	Total	Malay	Chinese	Indian	Total	Malay	Chinese	Indian	Total	Malay	Chinese	Indian	Total
Transport, storage & communications	2.7 (36.5)	3.8 (38.7)	5.2 (21.5)	3.5 (100.0)	2.9 (43.1)	3.9 (38.4)	5.3 (15.0)	3.6 (100.0)	4.0 (49.7)	4.2 (34.1)	6.5 (15.8)	4.3 (100.0)	5.6 (60.0)	4.3 (25.3)	8.6 (14.7)	5.3 (100.0)
Wholesale & retail; hotels & restaurants[1]									12.7 (36.0)	30.0 (55.3)	14.4 (8.1)	19.0 (100.0)	19.0 (44.5)	37.5 (48.3)	19.4 (7.2)	23.8 (100.0)
Finance, insurance, real estate & business[1]	3.2 (16.4)	16.7 (64.7)	10.7 (16.8)	9.2 (100.0)	4.5 (24.1)	18.2 (64.4)	10.2 (10.4)	10.0 (100.0)	3.6 (42.6)	5.9 (46.0)	4.5 (10.6)	4.5 (100.0)	6.3 (49.9)	9.1 (39.6)	8.3 (10.5)	6.9 (100.0)
Community, social & personal services	12.7 (40.0)	14.5 (34.5)	15.7 (15.1)	15.0 (100.0)	15.6 (48.2)	17.5 (47.5)	23.2 (13.7)	17.3 (100.0)	25.4 (65.3)	14.2 (23.8)	20.2 (10.3)	20.9 (100.0)	26.9 (74.7)	11.2 (17.1)	18.5 (8.2)	21.1 (100.0)
All Sectors	100.0 (47.3)	100.0 (35.7)	100.0 (14.5)	100.0 (100.0)	100.0 (53.5)	100.0 (35.4)	100.0 (10.2)	100.0 (100.0)	100.0 (53.6)	100.0 (35.0)	100.0 (10.6)	100.0 (100.0)	100.0 (58.5)	100.0 (32.2)	100.0 (9.3)	100.0 (100.0)

Notes: [1] For 1957 and 1970, these were collectively categorized as the "commerce" sector. The labour force figures in thousands for 1957 were: Total = 2,126.2; Malay = 1,004.3; Chinese = 759.0; Indians = 307.2. 1970: Total = 2,736.4; Malay = 1,435.0; Chinese = 990.0; Indians = 286.1. 1986: Total = 4,726.0; Malay = 2,535.3; Chinese = 1,655.7; Indians = 501.2.

Sources: Department of Statistics, *Population Census*, 1957 and 1970; *Labour Force Survey, 1986*; *Labour Force Survey Report 2003*: Table A 3.10; *Mid-Term Review of the Eighth Malaysia Plan, 2001–2005*: Table 3.7.

at the time of independence in 1957, the population was divided spatially and culturally. While only 19.0 per cent of the Malayan population was urban, 63.0 per cent of urban residents were Chinese. Rural residents accounted for 81.0 per cent of the total population, but almost 69.8 per cent of the rural population were Malays, 17.4 per cent were Chinese and 12.4 per cent were Indian.

Economic development in the Malayan economy was uneven. Non-wage employment — such as self-employment and unpaid family workers[21] — was significant in 1957, accounting for 43.3 per cent of the total labour force, with wage employment constituting the remaining 56.7 per cent. However, as the majority of workers with limited access to land and capital sought wage employment soared with industrialization and urbanization. Since 1957, wage employment has increased greatly among Malays, although it has declined slightly for Chinese and Indians, more of whom have become self-employed.

Self-employed Chinese included many employers, whereas Malay self-employment generally meant own account work with unpaid family members but rarely employing others. While the Chinese accounted for 35.0 per cent of all in employment, 66.9 per cent of all employers in 1986 were Chinese.[22] Besides Malay peasant farms, Chinese employers have run most small-scale enterprises using a high, albeit gradually declining proportion of unpaid family workers. Such Chinese hiring practices in small-scale enterprises helps account for the relatively lower unemployment rates among Chinese.[23] The Indians have remained predominantly working class in character, with the greatest proportion of wage employees (over four fifths) among those employed.

Ethnic Segmentation

The colonial creation of three ethnically segregated[24] labour markets distributed unevenly across economic activities and geographical regions, was moderately, but unevenly eroded by both *laissez-faire* as well as affirmative action labour market policies of the post-colonial government. Table 2.3 indicates that in 1957, 74.6 per cent of the Malay labour force were in agriculture, especially peasant agriculture; 56.8 per cent of the Indian workforce were in plantation agriculture and 33.0 per cent in services. Of the Chinese workforce in 1957, 46.2 per cent were in extractive activities, mostly non-peasant agriculture and mining, while 17.1 per cent were in industry, and 35.4 per cent were in services, especially commerce. Ethnic segmentation of labour in economic activities was and, to a lesser extent, still is reflected in ethnic segmentation by residence, occupations (see Tables 2.4 and 2.5) and economic inequalities among regions as well as ethnic groups (owing to the concentration of poorly-remunerated extractive activities in rural areas, and the concentration of modern industry and services in urban areas).[25]

Table 2.4 Peninsular Malaysia: Percentage Distribution of Employed Labour Force by Occupation and Ethnic Group, 1957, 1970, 1986, 2000

Occupation	1957				1970				1986				2000			
	Malay	Chinese	Indian	Total	Malay	Chinese	Indian	Total	Malay	Chinese	Indian	Total	Malay	Chinese	Indian	Total
Professional & technical	2.7 (41.0)	3.3 (38.3)	2.3 (11.0)	3.1 (100.0)	4.3 (47.1)	5.2 (39.5)	4.9 (10.8)	4.8 (100.0)	8.9 (58.8)	6.9 (30.0)	7.0 (9.9)	8.1 (100.0)	13.6 (63.9)	9.6 (25.8)	10.1 (7.6)	11.0 (100.0)
Administrative & managerial	0.4 (17.6)	2.0 (62.4)	1.0 (12.2)	1.2 (100.0)	0.5 (24.1)	1.9 (62.9)	0.8 (7.8)	1.1 (100.0)	1.8 (35.8)	4.2 (56.0)	2.0 (5.6)	2.7 (100.0)	3.0 (37.0)	7.4 (52.3)	2.8 (5.5)	4.2 (100.0)
Clerical & related	1.7 (27.1)	3.7 (46.2)	4.0 (19.9)	2.9 (100.0)	3.4 (35.4)	6.3 (45.9)	8.1 (17.2)	5.0 (100.0)	10.1 (54.3)	10.4 (36.4)	8.2 (8.6)	10.0 (100.0)	12.2 (56.8)	12.3 (32.9)	11.5 (8.6)	11.1 (100.0)
Sales & related	2.9 (15.9)	15.9 (66.1)	10.0 (16.8)	8.6 (100.0)	4.7 (26.7)	15.3 (61.7)	9.5 (11.1)	9.1 (100.0)	7.1 (32.5)	19.7 (59.2)	10.3 (7.7)	11.6 (100.0)	8.0 (37.3)	18.4 (49.8)	9.0 (6.8)	11.0 (100.0)
Service & related	7.3 (39.7)	8.0 (33.3)	7.6 (12.8)	8.6 (100.0)	6.8 (44.3)	8.6 (39.6)	10.9 (14.6)	7.9 (100.0)	13.9 (59.4)	10.2 (28.6)	13.6 (11.4)	12.6 (100.0)	13.2 (57.7)	8.6 (21.8)	12.1 (8.5)	11.8 (100.0)
Agricultural & related	74.2 (62.1)	38.3 (24.3)	50.2 (12.8)	56.4 (100.0)	62.3 (72.0)	21.2 (17.3)	41.0 (9.7)	44.8 (100.0)	34.7 (69.8)	13.6 (17.9)	28.7 (11.4)	26.7 (100.0)	21.5 (61.2)	6.3 (10.3)	15.1 (6.9)	18.1 (100.0)
Production, transport & related labourers	10.6 (26.5)	28.3 (53.5)	24.6 (18.9)	18.9 (100.0)	18.0 (34.2)	41.6 (55.9)	24.7 (9.6)	27.3 (100.0)	23.5 (44.5)	34.9 (43.1)	32.2 (12.0)	28.4 (100.0)	28.5 (44.7)	37.4 (33.8)	39.4 (10.0)	32.8 (100.0)
TOTAL	100.0 (47.2)	100.0 (35.7)	100.0 (14.4)	100.0 (100.0)	100.0 (51.8)	100.0 (36.6)	100.0 (10.6)	100.0 (100.0)	100.0 (53.5)	100.0 (34.9)	100.0 (10.6)	100.0 (100.0)	100.0 (51.5)	100.0 (29.7)	100.0 (8.3)	100.0 (100.0)
N = '000				2,126.2				2,850.3				4,726.7				9,271.2

Note: Value in brackets denotes the percentage share of each ethnic group for that occupational category.
Sources: Khong (1985: 36); Department of Statistics; *Mid-Term Review of the Eighth Malaysia Plan, 2001–2005*: Table 3.8.

Table 2.5 Malaysia: Percentage Distribution of Full-time Workers by
Occupation and Economic Activity, 2003

Economic activity	Total	Total	Professional & management	Technical & supervisory	Clerical & related	General	Production, directly employed
Manufacturing	100.0	6.3	12.4	6.9	4.2	62.0	8.1
Transport, storage & communication	100.0	21.1	25.4	35.1	0.0	0.0	0.0

Sources: *Annual Survey of Manufacturing Industries, 2004; Census of Transport & Communication Services, 2004; Information & Communication Technology Services Statistics, 2005.*

Associated with ethnic-sectoral segmentation is ethnic-occupational segmentation. Table 2.6 indicates that in 1957, white-collar workers such as professional/technical, administrative/managerial and clerical workers were mostly non-Malays. Malays were then heavily concentrated in peasant agriculture, while Chinese were well represented in commerce or sales-related jobs. The concentration of non-Malays in the urban areas, where educational facilities were better, and their ability to afford higher educational expenses were reflected in their over-representation in white-collar professions.

Hirschman (1975: 48) suggests that the considerable degree of occupational inheritance may be due to the effects of social origins on educational opportunities and employment prospects for the next generation. Firstly, as school qualifications are a major determinant of employment in white-collar jobs, much of the ethnic differential in white-collar jobs reflects unequal educational opportunities. Secondly, educational qualifications are necessary (but not sufficient) conditions in modern wage employment.[26]

Between 1970 and 2000, the Bumiputera share of clerical workers rose from 35.4 per cent to 56.8 per cent, of sales workers from 26.7 per cent to 37.3 per cent, and of other service workers from 44.3 per cent to 57.7 per cent; meanwhile, the ratio of these Bumiputera workers to its rising share of the population rose from 0.67 to 0.86, from 0.51 to 0.56 and from 0.84 to 0.87 ratio (Tables 2.7a and 2.7b). Table 2.7b shows the continuation of these broad trends to 2003 after also including non-Malaysian workers for the first time.

Education and Segmentation

Constraints on inter-sectoral and inter-occupational mobility were due to internalized customary rules effecting on labour demand and supply. While educational expansion facilitated upward mobility, the education system itself tended

Table 2.6 Peninsular Malaysia: Distribution of Working Population by
Ethnicity, Employment Status and Gender, 1957, 1980, 2003

Employment status

1957	Malays	Chinese	Indians	Others	Total	Males	Females
Employer and own account worker	18.9 (66.1)	28.3 (28.8)	9.8 (4.1)	14.5 (1.1)	35 (100.0)	38.4 (82.7)	24.6 (17.3)
Unpaid family worker	14.1 (80.0)	4.2 (17.8)	0.5 (0.9)	4.1 (1.3)	8.3 (100.0)	4.8 (43.7)	18.7 (56.3)
Employee	37.8 (30.8)	67.6 (42.5)	89.6 (22.9)	81.4 (3.7)	56.7 (100.0)	56.8 (75.5)	56.7 (24.5)
In employment	100.0 (47.3)	100.0 (35.7)	100.0 (14.5)	100.0 (2.6)	100.0 (100.0)	100.0 (75.4)	100.0 (24.6)

1980	Malays	Chinese	Indians	Others	Total	Males	Females
Employer	2.6 (35.5)	5.8 (51.5)	4.6 (12.3)	4.1 (0.7)	4.0 (100.0)	4.4 (75.5)	3.0 (24.5)
Own account worker	32.9 (64.5)	24.7 (31.5)	8.3 (3.2)	32.1 (0.8)	27.4 (100.0)	28.9 (71.2)	24.4 (28.8)
Unpaid family worker	9.2 (67.9)	5.4 (26.2)	3.3 (4.9)	10.1 (1.0)	7.3 (100.0)	4.9 (45.8)	12.1 (54.2)
Employee	55.2 (48.3)	64.1 (36.5)	83.8 (14.6)	53.8 (0.6)	61.4 (100.0)	61.8 (68.1)	60.5 (31.9)
In employment	100.0 (53.6)	100.0 (35.0)	100.0 (10.7)	100.0 (0.7)	100.0 (100.0)	100.0 (67.6)	100.0 (32.4)

2003	Malays	Chinese	Indians	Others	Total	Males	Females
Employer	2.4 (25.9)	7.2 (42.7)	3.3 (5.7)	1.4 (25.8)	3.4 (100.0)	4.6 (87.4)	1.2 (12.6)
Own account worker	16.7 (27.4)	15.5 (14.0)	8.3 (2.2)	20.1 (56.4)	15.6 (100.0)	17.7 (72.9)	11.7 (27.1)
Unpaid family worker	4.0 (18.3)	4.3 (10.8)	2.0 (1.5)	8.9 (69.5)	4.8 (100.0)	2.2 (28.7)	9.6 (71.3)
Employee	76.9 (30.8)	73.0 (16.1)	86.4 (5.5)	69.6 (47.6)	76.2 (100.0)	75.5 (63.5)	77.5 (36.5)
In employment	100.0 (29.2)	100.0 (16.1)	100.0 (4.7)	100.0 (50.0)	100.0 (100.0)	100.0 (64.1)	100.0 (35.9)

Note: The second row for each employment status category (value in brackets) represents
the percentage distribution according to ethnicity and gender for each employment
status.

Sources: Data for 1957 and 1980 are from Khong (1985), while those for 2003 are from
Labour Force Survey Report 2003: Table A3.19.

Table 2.7a Malaysia: Employment by Occupation and Race, 1970 (%)

Occupation	Bumiputera	Chinese	Indian	Others
Professional and technical	47.0	39.5	10.8	2.7
Administrative and managerial	24.1	62.9	7.8	5.2
Clerical and related workers	35.4	45.9	17.2	1.5
Sales and related workers	26.7	61.7	11.1	0.4
Service workers	44.3	39.6	14.6	1.5
Agricultural workers	72.0	17.3	9.7	1.0
Production, transport and other workers	34.2	55.9	9.6	0.3
Total	51.8	36.6	10.6	1.0
Ethnic proportions	52.7	35.8	10.7	0.8

Proportional Equality Index of Employment by Occupation

Occupation	Bumiputera	Chinese	Indian	Others
Professional and technical	0.89	1.10	1.01	3.38
Administrative and managerial	0.46	1.76	0.73	6.50
Clerical and related workers	0.67	1.28	1.61	1.88
Sales and related workers	0.51	1.72	1.04	0.50
Service workers	0.84	1.11	1.36	1.88
Agricultural workers	1.37	0.48	0.91	1.25
Production, transport and other workers	0.65	1.56	0.90	0.38
Total	0.98	1.02	0.99	1.25

Note: The proportional equality index is derived by dividing the percentage of employment of each ethnic group in each sector/occupation by the percentage share in population.

Source: Malaysia, *Fourth Malaysia Plan, 1981–85*.

Table 2.7b Malaysia: Employment by Occupation and Race, 2003 (%)

Occupation	Bumiputera	Chinese	Indian	Others	Non-Malaysian
Professional and technical	64.4	26.4	7.8	0.3	0.9
Administrative and managerial	49.6	42.4	4.5	1.2	2.3
Clerical and related workers	53.2	38.7	6.6	0.5	0.6
Sales and service workers	54.7	33.7	4.5	1.2	6.0
Agricultural workers	73.4	7.7	4.9	2.2	12.1
Production, transport and other workers	53.1	13.9	11.0	1.4	21.6
Total	57.4	25.0	7.5	1.0	9.1
Ethnic proportions	61.6	24.2	7.1	1.3	5.9

Proportional Equity Index of Employment by Occupation

Occupation	Bumiputera	Chinese	Indian	Others	Non-Malaysian
Professional and technical	1.05	1.09	1.10	0.23	0.15
Administrative and managerial	0.81	1.75	0.63	0.92	0.39
Clerical and related workers	0.86	1.60	0.93	0.38	0.10
Sales and service workers	0.89	1.39	0.63	0.92	1.02
Agricultural workers	1.19	0.32	0.69	1.69	2.05
Production, transport and other workers	0.86	0.57	1.55	1.08	3.66
Total	0.93	1.03	1.05	0.82	1.54

Sources: Calculated with data from *Labour Force Survey, 2003* and *Vital Statistics, 2003*.

to perpetuate the socio-economic inequalities inherited from the colonial era. Access to modern wage employment in Malaysia depends largely on educational credentials, used as a proxy for skills and other employer desired attributes, such as acceptance discipline and hierarchies, and to legitimize the differentiation of functional roles and positions of authority within the hierarchy.[27]

The stratification of access to wage employment by educational attainment may be best understood with reference to the employment and remuneration policies of the colonial government. During the colonial era, a strictly hierarchical system of wage stratification was instituted, with colonial administrators occupying the top positions with highly-paid salaries to maintain and reinforce their privileged status and power over employees recruited from the local population. Among local employees, strict rules of access to the occupational and wage structure by educational qualifications were imposed, with members of the Malay aristocracy privileged as intermediaries for the system of indirect rule.[28] Over time, the meritocratic idea that those with higher educational qualifications should occupy positions of greater authority and income became entrenched.

Malays, who were overwhelmingly rural, were clearly at a historical disadvantage since virtually all English medium schools were concentrated in large towns until the 1960s. Hence, English-medium education, offering greater upward mobility, was more readily available to the more urbanized non-Malays and to privileged Malays, including the royalty, the aristocracy, and the children of the urban Malay salariat. The high degree of occupational inheritance meant that most common Malays ended up in peasant agriculture work or other poorly-paid jobs because they lacked other skills or educational credentials.

The meritocratic belief has grown in the post-colonial era that one's station in life is determined by ability alone, proxied by educational achievement. Those lacking family privilege may supposedly secure upward mobility by obtaining the best possible education and then employment. But in reality, educational attainment is heavily influenced by parental socio-economic status, culture and means. Despite the introduction of free schooling since 1970, the costs of schooling are still high especially for the poor, because of out-of-pocket expenditure for school transport, books, school uniforms, and stationery. Moreover, the opportunity cost of schooling was high, particularly where employment opportunities for children abound, although this has declined over time. Even if a poor child manages to continue in school, the home environment tends to undermine mar the child's academic performance.[29] As income and occupation depend on educational attainment, in turn influenced by parental socio-economic status, the education system tends to reproduce inequality over generations.[30]

Despite rapid economic growth, Malaysia did not achieve "full employment" (i.e. an unemployment rate of less than four per cent) until the 1990s, with a decade of very rapid economic growth from 1988 until 1997. Table 2.8 suggests generally higher unemployment before the 1980s among ethnic Indians, who are also relatively more dependent on wage employment compared to the more urban ethnic Chinese and the more rural ethnic Malays, for whom self-employment was far more important. With the massive urban migration of all ethnic communities, especially the Malays, since the 1970s, the unemployment rate among Malays has exceeded that of Indians since the 1980s, after the huge expansion of the public sector employment in the 1970s came to an end from 1982.

After independence, the limited interventionism of economic development policy exacerbated initial income inequalities and perpetuated the identification of economic function with ethnicity.[31] The tension among the

Table 2.8 Unemployment Rates by Ethnicity, 1967–2005

Year	Malay	Chinese	Indian	Others	Total
1967/68	5.7	5.1	8.4	4.9	5.8
1970	8.1	7.0	11.0	3.1	8.0
1975	6.1	6.3	10.5	9.2	6.7
1980	6.5	3.9	6.3	3.6	5.6
1983	7.0	4.0	6.4	3.8	5.8
1985	8.7	5.5	8.4	5.0	7.6
1990	5.8	4.5	4.9	1.7	5.1
1993	3.3	2.5	2.7	2.3	3.0
1995	4.6	1.5	2.6	0.4	3.1
2000	4.6	1.6	2.7	2.1	3.4*
2003	4.9	1.9	3.0	2.4	3.8
2005	5.3	2.4	3.1	4.1	4.2^

Notes: * *Economic Report, 2004–05* gives the unemployment rate for 2000 as 3.1%.

^ *Economic Report, 2006–07* gives the unemployment rate for 2005 as 3.5%.

1985–2005 figures are for Malaysia; the earlier ones are for Peninsular Malaysia only.

Sources: *Fifth Malaysia Plan, 1986–1990*: Table 2.5; *Seventh Malaysia Plan, 1996–2000*: Table 2.2; *Eighth Malaysia Plan, 2001–05*: Table 2.7; *Mid-Term Review of the Eighth Malaysia Plan, 2001–2005*: Table 2.7; *Ninth Malaysia Plan, 2006–2010*: Table 16-4.

major ethnic-based political parties in the ruling Alliance coalition and the perception of economic power being in the hands of the Chinese community brought about considerable ethnic unrest,[32] culminating in racial riots following the general elections of May 1969. In 1970, the New Economic Policy (NEP) was promulgated with the twin aims of eradicating poverty regardless of ethnicity and "restructuring society" to eliminate the identification of economic function with ethnicity.[33]

As part of the Malaysian government's development policies, education was vastly expanded, especially in rural areas, and Malay replaced English as the medium of instruction from 1970. In the 1970s, English, Chinese and Tamil essentially became second languages, with Malay as the official *lingua franca*. Communal hiring practices continued, especially among the smaller businesses, legitimized by Chinese and Indians as legitimate responses to the NEP's pro-Malay affirmative action. Numerous government scholarships were granted to Malay students to pursue higher studies locally and abroad, with the aim of creating a Malay middle-class.[34] Education enrolment, particularly at the secondary level, expanded rapidly, improving the educational level of the workforce (see Khong, 1991: Statistical Annex 3).

While 43.1 per cent of the labour force had no formal schooling in 1962, only 18.2 per cent were in this category by 1975, falling to 4.2 per cent in 2003 (Tables 2.9 and 2.10). Meanwhile, the proportion of workers with lower secondary school education went up from just 11.6 per cent in 1962 to 27.4

Table 2.9 Peninsular Malaysia: Distribution of Employed Workforce by Ethnicity, Gender and Educational Level, 1986

Educational level	Malay	Chinese	Indian	Total	Male	Female
Total	100.0	100.0	100.0	100.0	100.0	100.0
	(53.6)	(35.0)	(10.6)	(100.0)	(65.2)	(34.8)
No formal education	11.9	6.9	9.2	9.9	5.6	18.0
	(64.4)	(24.2)	(9.8)	(100.0)	(37.0)	(63.0)
Basic and lower secondary school	56.2	65.7	68.5	60.7	65.7	51.2
	(49.7)	(37.9)	(12.0)	(100.0)	(70.7)	(29.3)
Upper secondary school	22.9	20.1	15.7	21.1	20.5	22.3
	(58.3)	(33.3)	(7.9)	(100.0)	(63.3)	(36.7)
Pre-university	2.7	2.4	2.4	2.6	2.4	2.8
	(55.8)	(33.5)	(9.8)	(100.0)	(61.7)	(38.3)
College/University	5.9	5.0	4.3	5.5	5.6	5.5
	(57.4)	(31.6)	(8.3)	(100.0)	(65.6)	(34.4)

Table 2.10 Peninsular Malaysia: Distribution of Employed Workforce by
Ethnicity, Gender and Educational Level, 2003

Educational level	Malay	Chinese	Indian	Total	Male	Female
Total	100.0	100.0	100.0	100.0	100.0	100.0
	(58.0)	(32.6)	(9.4)	(100.0)	(64.0)	(36.0)
No formal education	2.9	2.2	3.3	4.2	3.6	7.0
	(40.1)	(17.1)	(7.3)	(100.0)	(48.1)	(51.9)
Primary	17.5	20.1	20.1	19.8	24.0	20.5
	(51.3)	(33.1)	(9.4)	(100.0)	(67.6)	(32.4)
Secondary	59.8	56.9	60.2	57.6	57.0	51.4
	(60.3)	(32.2)	(9.7)	(100.0)	(66.4)	(33.6)
Tertiary	19.8	20.9	16.4	18.4	15.4	21.2
	(62.5)	(37.0)	(8.3)	(100.0)	(56.4)	(43.6)

Notes: Workers without any certificate may either not have a formal education or
may not have successfully completed a particular phase in their educational
career.

See Khong (1991: Appendix 1) for an explanation of the Malaysian educational
system. Values in brackets show the percentage distribution of educational level
according to ethnicity, gender and employment status.

No strictly comparable data are available for recent years.

Source: Computed with published data from Department of Statistics.

per cent in 1975 and 45.0 per cent in 1986, while the share with secondary
education rose to 57.6 per cent in 2003. The proportion with tertiary education
also increased from 1.0 per cent in 1962 to 5.5 per cent in 1986 and 18.4 per
cent in 2003.

However, rapid expansion of secondary education resulted in an excess
of secondary-school graduates compared to the number of lower white-collar
occupations created.[35] This process shifted unemployment from those with
basic education to those with secondary education, and even those with higher
education.[36] Consequently, after 1970, the levels and growth rates of real
earnings in lower white-collar occupations — such as clerical and technical/
supervisory occupations — declined relative to skilled and unskilled manual
jobs (see Khong, 1991: Statistical Annex 4). Workers with higher levels of
education displaced workers with less education from lower-level occupations,
even for jobs where formal qualifications beyond a certain level were not
associated with improved labour productivity.[37] With the rapid expansion of
university/college education, the advantage of having a basic university degree

has gradually eroded, as witnessed by the upsurge in graduate unemployment and the decline in real wages for new university graduates.

The rise in educational enrolment was expected to lead to an inter-generational improvement in higher educational qualifications of lower socio-economic groups. However, this assumes that the appropriate jobs are growing commensurately with the emergence of a better-educated workforce. Otherwise, an excessive supply of better-educated human resources merely leads to a credential explosion, which reduces the social and private return, of education in terms of better employment opportunities. In this scenario, the cost of education, particularly to the poor, was less than fully compensated as the credential requirements for good jobs were raised, and an increasing amount of investment in education was required for access to these better jobs.[38] Compounding the problem of increasing educational levels amidst slow growth in corresponding labour demand are the increasing expectations of labour market entrants in terms of pay, status and other non-pecuniary benefits. In addition, the widespread wage and status bias against blue-collar work has resulted in an under-supply of basic technical skills among school-leavers, exacerbated by the official neglect of vocational education.[39]

Table 2.3 shows that the proportion of the labour force in a primary sector declined from 58.5 per cent in 1957 to 49.6 per cent in 1970, 26.7 per cent in 1986 and 11.9 per cent in 2003, while the proportion in industry increased from 9.6 per cent to 11.4 per cent, 23.4 per cent and 30.4 per cent, while those in services rose from 28.3 per cent to 31.6 per cent, 49.2 per cent and 57.7 per cent respectively. Although the NEP achieved some employment "restructuring", its actual influence on the overall structural transformation of the economy and the sharp decline of primary sector activities is unclear. Meanwhile, the proportion of Malays in the primary sector declined from 75.6 per cent in 1957 to 65.2 per cent in 1970, 35.1 per cent in 1986 and 10.8 per cent in 2003, while the proportion in industry increased from 4.80 per cent to 6.0 per cent, 18.5 per cent and 30.5 per cent, and those in services rose from 19.7 per cent to 23.7 per cent, 46.4 per cent and 58.7 per cent respectively.

Although the ethnic shares in services correspond to the overall ethnic shares in the labour force in 2005, closer examination suggests that Malays are now over-represented in public services, but still under-represented in some private services. The proportion of Chinese in the labour force declined from 37.7 per cent in 1957 to 32.2 per cent in 2003, due to lower fertility rates and higher emigration rates despite higher labour force participation rates. The share in the primary sector fell from 46.2 per cent to 5.1 per cent, while the share in industry rose from 17.1 per cent to 32.5 per cent and those in services rose from 35.4 per cent to 62.3 per cent. Chinese remained over-represented in industry, petty commerce, finance and business services. Over the same period (1957–2005), the proportion of Indians in rural primary sector activities decreased from 59.0 per cent to 7.8 per cent, while the share in industry rose from 7.3 per cent to 36.8 per cent, and the proportion in services increased from 33.0 per cent to 55.4 per cent. Indians were still over-represented in services such as transport, but no longer in utilities, probably due to their sharp decline in public services.

With rapid growth and industrialization as well as NEP implementation, the geographical relocation of the population accelerated. Rural-urban migration due to growth of the public sector in urban areas (which now mainly employs Malays, rather than Indians, as in the past), the reduction of the mostly Malay peasants on agricultural land and of the mostly Indian plantation workforce has increased and changed the urban population and labour force profile. The urban share of the Peninsular Malaysia population rose from 19.0 per cent in 1957 to 28.8 per cent in 1970 to 37.5 per cent in 1980 and 61.9 per cent in 2000 (Table 1.8), with a significant increase in the Malay share of the urban population from 27.4 per cent in 1970 to 41.3 per cent in 1985 as the Chinese proportion of the urban population fell from 58.7 per cent to 47.2 per cent during the first interventionist 15 years of the NEP.

Structural and demographic change has been reflected by changing inter-ethnic and intra-ethnic occupational matrices. Table 2.4 indicates that between 1970 and 2000, the shares of professional, administrative, clerical, sales and service jobs increased tremendously, while the proportion of agricultural jobs declined substantially. Although the Chinese were still over-represented in the professional/technical, administrative/managerial, clerical, and sales occupations, their shares declined significantly between 1970 and 2000. While Indian shares in the different occupational categories remained consistent during the period, Malay shares in non-agricultural jobs, particularly in professional, administrative and clerical categories, increased significantly.

Barriers to entry unrelated to qualifications have structured labour supply in terms of training or educational choices. For instance, Malay students tend to choose liberal arts or social science courses (in anticipation of public sector administrative jobs), while non-Malays prefer professional or scientific courses. Between 1970 and 2005, the Bumiputera share of registered professionals rose from 4.9 per cent to 38.8 per cent, while the Chinese share declined from 61.0 per cent to 48.7 per cent and the Indian share fell from 23.3 per cent to 10.6 per cent (Table 2.11). Although there has been a substantial increase in Malay shares in all the professions since 1970, Malays are still under-represented in the medical, legal, engineering, accountancy and technical professions. In contrast, Indians are significantly over-represented in the legal and medical professions, while Chinese are over-represented in all but the veterinary profession.

Table 2.11 Malaysia: Registered Professionals[1] by Ethnic Group, 1970–2005

	Bumiputera		Chinese		Indians		Others		Total	
1970[2]	225	(4.9%)	2,793	(61.0%)	1,066	(23.3%)	492	(10.8%)	4,576	(100%)
1975[3]	537	(6.7%)	5,131	(64.1%)	1,764	(22.1%)	572	(7.1%)	8,004	(100%)
1979	1,237	(11.0%)	7,154	(63.5%)	2,375	(21.1%)	496	(4.4%)	11,262	(100%)
1980	2,534	(14.9%)	10,812	(63.5%)	2,963	(17.4%)	708	(4.2%)	17,017	(100%)
1983	4,496	(18.9%)	14,933	(62.9%)	3,638	(15.3%)	699	(2.9%)	23,766	(100%)
1984	5,473	(21.0%)	16,154	(61.9%)	3,779	(14.5%)	675	(2.6%)	26,081	(100%)
1985	6,318	(22.2%)	17,407	(61.2%)	3,946	(13.9%)	773	(2.7%)	28,444	(100%)
1988	8,571	(25.1%)	19,985	(58.4%)	4,878	(14.3%)	762	(2.2%)	34,196	(100%)
1990	11,753	(29.0%)	22,641	(55.9%)	5,363	(13.2%)	750	(1.9%)	40,507	(100%)
1995	19,344	(33.1%)	30,636	(52.4%)	7,542	(12.9%)	939	(1.6%)	58,461	(100%)
1997[4]	22,866	(32.0%)	37,278	(52.1%)	9,389	(13.1%)	1,950	(2.7%)	71,843	(100%)
1997[4]	10,659	(27.3%)	21,298	(54.4%)	6,653	(17.0%)	515	(1.3%)	39,125	(100%)
1999	15,321	(28.9%)	28,565	(53.9%)	8,183	(15.5%)	884	(1.7%)	52,953	(100%)
2000	29,376	(35.5%)	42,243	(51.1%)	9,739	(11.8%)	1,286	(1.6%)	82,644	(100%)
2002	35,046	(37.2%)	47,270	(50.1%)	10,593	(11.2%)	1,411	(1.5%)	94,320	(100%)
2005	42,414	(38.8%)	53,297	(48.7%)	11,556	(10.6%)	2,085	(1.9%)	109,352	(100%)

Notes: [1] Architects, accountants, engineers, dentists, doctors, veterinary surgeons, surveyors, lawyers.
[2] Excluding surveyors and lawyers.
[3] Excluding surveyors.
[4] There appears to have been a significant change in the counting of professionals between 1999 (*Mid-Term Review of the Seventh Malaysia Plan, 1996–2000*) and 2001 (*Eighth Malaysia Plan, 2001–2005*), with the total number of professionals and the Bumiputera share dropping drastically for the year 1997 in the two estimates.

Source: Malaysian plan documents.

State intervention in the education and labour market system has shaped some of the inter- or intra-ethnic occupational and industrial shifts. Recognizing that restructuring labour supply alone is insufficient to expand the Malay middle-class because of rigidities in employers' hiring preferences, the state has achieved its aims of more equitable Malay representation in the higher and middle-level occupations through a combination of affirmative action policies in the public and private sectors. Clearly, vast differences in occupational income remain a major concern,[40] especially the earnings differential between the top (professional and managerial) and bottom (unskilled factory production workers) categories of the occupational hierarchy in the private sector.[41] Insofar as occupation remains the main determinant of income and social status in the working-class, occupational stratification along ethnic lines has important implications. To the extent that employers resist affirmative action or "restructuring" requirements, imposed upon them, ethnic and gender industrial-occupational segmentation may emerge in new forms, as employers and workers respond to such policies.

Gender Segmentation

Malaysian political culture has tended to focus on inter-ethnic disparities while neglecting other inequalities, including class and gender differences. Gender segmentation has been largely neglected in employment policies, despite the rapid increase in the female labour force participation rate from 30.8 per cent in 1957 to 45.1 per cent in 1986, owing to increased education opportunities and household needs for additional income. Various tables, including Tables 2.12 and 2.13, show that the proportion of women in the labour force has substantially increased since 1957, with the female share of the working population rising from 24.6 per cent in 1957 to 34.8 per cent in 1986 and 35.9 per cent in 2005. Historically, women have been significantly over-represented in unpaid family work and under-represented as employers (Table 2.3). While comprising 35.9 per cent of the total workforce in 2003, women accounted for 71.3 per cent of unpaid family workers, but only 12.6 per cent of employers.

Tables 2.12 and 2.13 suggest that the pattern of female employment in Malaysia is different from that in most industrialized market economies where women are concentrated in services (see also Khong, 1991: Statistical Annex 6). Although women were traditionally concentrated in the agricultural sector (see Khong, 1985: Chapters 3 and 7), women have since been increasingly found in wage employment in selected manufacturing industries (such as electronics and textiles),[42] retail trade (especially supermarkets), and community and personal services. Within these services, they were crowded into particular occupations

Table 2.12 Peninsular Malaysia: Percentage Distribution of Employed Labour Force by Occupation and Gender, 1957, 1975, 2004

Occupation	1957 Male	1957 Female	1957 Total	1975 Male	1975 Female	1975 Total	2004 Male	2004 Female	2004 Total
Professional or technical	2.9 (71.8)	3.5 (28.2)	3.0 (100.0)	5.5 (65.1)	5.6 (34.9)	5.5 (100.0)	16.5 (59.7)	19.7 (40.0)	17.7 (100.0)
Administrative or managerial	1.5 (98.0)	0.1 (2.0)	1.1 (100.0)	1.9 (96.3)	0.1 (3.7)	1.3 (100.0)	10.1 (75.2)	5.9 (24.7)	8.6 (100.0)
Clerical and related	3.5 (92.1)	0.9 (7.9)	2.8 (100.0)	6.9 (64.0)	7.4 (36.0)	7.1 (100.0)	4.7 (32.4)	17.5 (67.6)	9.3 (100.0)
Sales and related	10.0 (90.1)	3.4 (9.9)	8.4 (100.0)	11.6 (73.3)	8.0 (26.7)	10.4 (100.0)	12.8 (55.4)	18.4 (44.7)	14.8 (100.0)
Services and related	12.9 (84.3)	7.4 (15.7)	11.6 (100.0)	6.8 (54.8)	10.7 (45.2)	8.2 (100.0)	15.0 (72.8)	10.0 (27.2)	13.2 (100.0)
Agricultural and related	49.1 (66.9)	54.9 (74.9)	55.4 (100.0)	37.6 (58.8)	50.0 (41.2)	41.9 (100.0)	41.0 (72.0)	28.6 (28.2)	36.5 (100.0)
Production and related	17.8 (87.0)	8.2 (13.0)	15.4 (100.0)	29.6 (75.6)	18.1 (24.4)	25.7 (100.0)	100.0 (64.1)	100.0 (35.9)	100.0 (100.0)
TOTAL	100.0 (75.5)	100.0 (24.5)	100.0 (100.0)	100.0 (65.5)	100.0 (34.5)	100.0 (100.0)	16.5 (59.7)	19.7 (40.0)	17.7 (100.0)
N = '000			2,126.2			3,567.2			9,986.6

Note: Values in brackets are for the shares of each gender and ethnic group for the occupational category. No strictly comparable data are available for recent years. Data on sales and related workers are estimated from the likely categories in *Labour Force Survey Report, 2004.*

Sources: Khong (1985: 36); *Labour Force Survey Report 2003*: Tables 3.4, A.3.24.

and sub-sectors. By 1986, women were over-represented as maids, cooks, housekeepers (95.0 per cent), in the beauty/cosmetic services (75.3 per cent), laundry and cleaning services (63.7 per cent), in medical and dental services as nurses and medical assistants (64.1 per cent); and in educational services, they comprised 47.4 per cent. They were also commonly found in un-enumerated informal employment as street vendors, petty traders or other related gender occupations, e.g. as maids, child-minders or seamstresses.

Women have accounted for a substantial proportion of professional/ technical, clerical and service-related occupations (Table 2.12). Compared with their 24.5 per cent share of the employed population in 1957, women had only two per cent of administrative/managerial positions and 7.9 per cent of clerical positions; by 2004, these female shares were 35.9 per cent, 23.3 per cent and 66.5 per cent respectively. Although women's share of higher-level occupations — such as doctors, lawyers, engineers and middle and senior management — has been gradually increasing, these trends obscure the tendency for women to occupy secondary and subordinate positions within the same industry, occupation or profession. Often, as jobs become feminized, their prestige, skill grading and remuneration decline.[43]

One reason why women have been traditionally confined to bad jobs is their poorer access to education. For some families in Malaysia, parents are more reluctant to invest their limited incomes in their daughters' education because: (i) they may still earn less because of job and wage discrimination, (ii) it is presumed that the gains from education will accrue to their son-in-law's family once the daughter marries, (iii) daughters are needed to help with housework, (iv) other beliefs and ideologies favour boy children of their sisters. As a result, rural illiteracy is considerably higher for women than for men; women formed 63.0 per cent of the 1986 workforce without any formal education, but their share has since fallen to 51.9 per cent in 2003.[44]

Although female access to secondary and higher education has improved tremendously over time, sexual stereotyping in the education system persists. From school to vocational training courses, the system encourages gender specialization of females and males in subjects for jobs stereotyped as feminine or masculine, contributing to segmentation along gender lines (see Shamsul-bahriah, 1988). Schooling and training thus reinforce the sexual division of labour; subsequently, segmentation takes over through job discrimination and wage discrimination.

Despite the Equal Pay for Equal Work Act of 1969, substantial female/ male wage differentials persist, with wider differentials higher in the occupational pyramid, where employment opportunities are fewer for women than for men of equal qualification, and where there is greater likelihood of wage discrimination

Table 2.13 Peninsular Malaysia: Percentage Distribution of Employed Workforce by Industry and Gender, 1957, 1975, 1986, 2005

Economic activity	1957			1975			1986			2005		
	Total	Male	Female	Total	Male	Female	Total	Male	Female	Total	Male	Female
Extractive	61.3 (100.0)	55.7 (68.5)	78.5 (31.5)	43.3 (100.0)	39.6 (59.8)	50.7 (40.2)	27.4 (100.0)	27.2 (64.7)	27.8 (35.3)	15.1 (100.0)	17.6 (74.6)	10.7 (25.4)
Agriculture	58.5 (100.0)	52.7 (67.8)	76.7 (32.2)	42.3 (100.0)	38.2 (59.1)	50.3 (40.9)	26.7 (100.0)	26.2 (64.1)	27.5 (35.9)	14.8 (100.0)	17.1 (74.1)	10.6 (25.9)
Mining and quarrying	2.8 (100.0)	3.1 (83.8)	1.8 (16.2)	1.0 (100.0)	1.4 (87.7)	0.4 (12.3)	0.7 (100.0)	1.0 (84.6)	0.3 (15.4)	0.3 (100.0)	0.5 (93.4)	0.1 (6.6)
Industry	9.6 (100.0)	10.9 (86.3)	5.3 (13.7)	19.6 (100.0)	20.5 (68.5)	17.9 (31.5)	23.4 (100.0)	23.3 (65.1)	23.5 (34.9)	20.3 (100.0)	31.7 (59.6)	24.6 (40.4)
Manufacturing	6.4 (100.0)	7.0 (83.4)	4.3 (16.6)	15.0 (100.0)	13.9 (60.7)	17.0 (39.3)	16.9 (100.0)	13.9 (53.7)	22.5 (46.3)	20.3 (100.0)	18.9 (59.6)	22.8 (40.4)
Construction	3.2 (100.0)	3.9 (92.1)	1.0 (7.9)	4.6 (100.0)	6.6 (93.6)	0.9 (0.9)	6.5 (6.5)	9.4 (9.4)	1.0 (1.0)	8.9 (100.0)	12.9 (92.6)	1.8 (7.4)
Services	28.3 (100.0)	32.4 (86.5)	15.6 (13.5)	36.9 (100.0)	39.9 (70.7)	31.4 (29.3)	49.2 (100.0)	49.4 (65.6)	48.8 (34.4)	55.7 (100.0)	50.6 (58.3)	64.7 (41.7)
Utilities	0.5 (100.0)	0.7 (96.6)	0.1 (3.4)	1.0 (100.0)	1.5 (96.8)	0.1 (3.2)	0.5 (100.0)	0.8 (97.1)	0.0 (2.9)	0.6 (100.0)	0.8 (87.6)	0.2 (12.4)
Transport, storage and communications	3.5 (100.0)	4.6 (98.8)	0.3 (2.0)	4.1 (100.0)	5.9 (93.7)	0.7 (6.3)	4.3 (100.0)	6 (90.7)	1.2 (9.3)	5.3 (100.0)	7.0 (85.0)	2.2 (15.0)

Table 2.13 (continued)

Economic activity	1957			1975			1986			2005		
	Total	Male	Female	Total	Male	Female	Total	Male	Female	Total	Male	Female
Wholesale and retail; Restaurants and hotel							19.0 (100.0)	18.4 (63.3)	20.1 (36.7)	23.1 (100.0)	22.0 (61.1)	25.0 (38.9)
Finance, insurance, real estate and business services	9.2 (100.0)	11.0 (90.4)	3.6 (9.6)	13.8 (100.0)	15.4 (73.1)	10.8 (26.9)	4.5 (100.0)	4.4 (64.5)	4.6 (35.5)	6.9 (100.0)	6.2 (57.5)	8.1 (42.5)
Community, social and personal services	15.0 (100.0)	16.1 (79.2)	11.7 (20.8)	18.0 (100.0)	17.1 (62.1)	19.8 (37.9)	20.9 (100.0)	19.9 (62.0)	22.9 (38.0)	19.8 (100.0)	14.6 (47.3)	29.1 (52.7)
Total	100.0 (100.0)	100.0 (75.4)	100.0 (24.6)	100.0 (100.0)	100.0 (65.5)	100.0 (34.5)	100.0 (100.0)	100.0 (65.2)	100.0 (34.8)	100.0 (100.0)	100.0 (64.1)	100.0 (35.9)

Sources: Department of Statistics, *Population Census, 1957*; *Labour Force Survey*, 1975 and 1986, *Mid-term Review of Seventh Malaysia Plan, 1996–2000*; *Eighth Malaysia Plan, 2001–2005*; *Labour Force Survey Report, 2005*.

since standardized union-negotiated wages are rare at higher occupational levels.[45] Even in the more regulated government sector, the Equal Opportunities Act of 1967 has not been sufficient to abolish job and wage discrimination. Such discrimination is clearly rooted in the low labour market status of women, which lowers the minimum supply price that women can demand for their labour. Hiring, promotion and pay policies further influence future female labour supply. The outlook for a more equitable access and reward system for female labour is not optimistic, as Malaysian women remain weak politically.

Other Factors

Although workers' organizations are fairly limited in Malaysia, they have had some influence. In post-colonial Malaysia, trade unions have never been particularly strong, with their powers limited by the state through labour legislation and the encouragement of collaborating and in-house (company's) unions.[46] The small trade union membership in Malaysia has been another limitation. Only 11.1 per cent of the 4.7 million workers in the peninsula, and 18.4 per cent of the 3.1 million wage employees were unionized in 1986,[47] with unionization rates declining despite the absolute and relative growth of wage employment. Within the service sector, the largest union membership is in the public sector (45.4 per cent unionized) and financial services (70.0 per cent unionized).

In industries where workers have low labour market status, unions can help improve their labour market status and their bargaining power. Yet, it is precisely these industries which tend to have lower unionization rates because these industries commonly use casual labour, part-time or temporary workers, who cannot easily be unionized and are barely protected under the country's labour legislation. Where workers have higher labour market status, and where the collective agreement covers an industry as a whole, free-riding by non-members occurs as unions in Malaysia cannot enforce close-door policies.

In traditional services, unionization is extremely low in small firms with paternalistic employment relations. Although the minimum wages of workers in some of the "lower" services — specifically shop assistants, employees in the hotel and catering trade, cinema workers, and cargo handlers — are governed by the National Wage Council Act of 1947, enforcement is low.[48] Even union members do not all enjoy the same benefits since collective agreements are negotiated between the unions and individual employers (see Chapter 4). In such cases, firm size and locality are important determinants of negotiated benefits. In small family-run enterprises, downward pressure on wage and non-wage benefits is sometimes mitigated by family or community sanctions.

Framework for Analysis

Supply and demand-structuring factors interact to produce a segmented market. In modern services, hiring policies in both state and private enterprises emphasize academic credentials in their recruitment, promotion and pay policies. In private sector traditional services, historical and cultural influence the organization of work as well as entry, pay and mobility systems. The dynamics of labour market segmentation constantly responds to new conditions, including rules imposed on the labour market. A useful analytical tool to better understand the dynamics of labour market segmentation in Malaysia is the division of the labour force horizontally into segments based on objective criteria such as academic qualifications, occupational level and skill.[49] These segments then meet the labour needs of different industries or sectors.

Horizontal Segmentation

The Malaysian labour market seems horizontally stratified by educational level[50] which is highly correlated with income, employment and occupational status. Although subjective and ascriptive factors supplement education as screening/rationing mechanisms, education remains the most important determinant of occupation and job access to the more prestigious modern sector wage employment. Table 2.9 shows that with the rapid expansion of educational opportunities, the proportion of the labour force without any formal education has continued to decline from to less than five per cent in 2005. In terms of employment opportunities, there seems to be little difference in the way employers view this group compared to those with only basic school qualifications. Although a vocational certificate is supposedly equivalent to the conventional Malaysian Certificate of Education (MCE), bias against blue-collar work, reflected by lower wages and social prestige, has reduced the number of people choosing such training despite obvious shortages of semi-skilled and skilled blue-collar workers.

Interviews with various employers found that most employers assess the upper secondary school certificate in much the same light as the pre-university school certificate; employees with these credentials were usually assigned clerical occupations. Excess supply and credentialism have led to the pre-university certificate being used as a screening device to select workers for "good" modern sector clerical jobs even if the objective skill requirements do not extend beyond the upper secondary school certificate.[51] Hence, only a small proportion actually ended their education at the HSC level as the small pay differentials do not justify the extra two years in school. At the higher end, workers with university degrees or other equivalent professional qualifications are usually assigned to executive positions. They are conventionally defined as "skilled" workers, possibly because they are ascribed greater potential for faster learning of practical skills, by virtue of their higher education.

In light of the foregoing, the Malaysian workforce may be horizontally stratified into the following categories:

(i)   *elite-primary or upper-tier primary "core" workers*, comprising college/ university graduates or holders of professional qualifications. This category of workers is considered "skilled" by virtue of their educational level and sometimes by the artificial restriction of supply (e.g. by professional associations). Elite-primary workers tend to work in core firms, and possess better bargaining power even though management workers in the private sector cannot be unionized. They are often highly mobile within professional markets either as independent self-employed professionals or as executives. However, mobility may become restricted once they acquire seniority and industry, firm or job-specific skills. Self-employment for professionals tends to be better remunerated and relatively secure, unlike conventional informal sector self-employment. During economic downturns, a large proportion of new entrants in this category may be downgraded to clerical positions since downward wage revisions are insufficient to accommodate the excess supply.

(ii) *secondary-primary white-collar workers*, consisting of workers with at least a MCE (Malaysian Certificate of Education, equivalent to British Ordinary level) or HSC (Higher School Certificate, or Advanced (A) level) or their equivalents, but without a university degree. The highest proportion of this group is in clerical positions. Their significant representation in the professional and technical categories is due to their presence as teachers and nurses, who need at least the MCE. In traditional services, such as wholesale/retail establishments, restaurants and hotels, the MCE is generally a sufficient entry requirement, after which training is provided on-the-job. Generally, secondary-primary workers are considered "skilled" workers once they have some work experience. Vertical mobility within the firm depends on seniority, and increasingly, also on self-funded acquisition of additional relevant academic qualifications. Depending on the type of skills possessed, promotions may also be secured through inter-firm or inter-industry movement. The position of this group of workers has been rapidly eroded by rapid growth in credential acquisition.

(iii) *secondary-primary blue-collar workers*, comprising workers with technical qualifications from vocational/technical schools. Depending on work experience, they are usually categorized as semi-skilled or skilled workers.

However, their pay or status seldom matches those of group (ii), causing a severe shortage of this group of workers. It is expected that those with technical qualifications will increasingly be viewed as "skilled" as the wage differentials between them and group (ii) narrow. Promotion usually depends on seniority or additional training, which is either self-funded or firm-funded depending on the nature of skill-upgrading.

(iv) *secondary workers*, consisting of workers with lower-intermediate school education, i.e. holders of the LCE (Lower Certificate of Education) or its equivalent. The majority in this group are production workers, including manual workers, factory workers, and transport workers such as drivers and labourers. Those in sales and service occupations work in the lowest job grades in medium-sized firms, in smaller family-type firms, or are self-employed. They are usually classified as unskilled workers and are in the lowest-graded group in government employment. Their job prospects are limited, and upward mobility is restricted by the small number of openings in higher grades and the bottom-heaviness of the pyramidal occupational structure in firms that have substantial wage employees of this type.

(v) *casual, marginalized, unskilled secondary workers*, consisting of workers with only primary school education or no formal schooling. Small-scale employers do not seem to differentiate between them in their recruitment or pay policies. However, access to wage employment in factory production lines is probably easier for those with primary education; hence, there is a higher proportion in industrial production compared to agricultural occupations. Most production workers are drawn from those with basic or lower secondary education, while those without any formal education are usually self-employed peasants or manual labourers in agriculture. Opportunities for upward mobility are extremely limited. In addition, seniority does not guarantee job security in industries where work conditions imply considerable or rapid job turnover, including production-line workers in the electronics and textiles industries, manual coolies and drivers in the transportation sector.

Category (v) and, to a lesser extent, category (iv), form a pool from which casual, contract or part-time cheap labour tend to be drawn. They are illiterate or semi-illiterate, found in numerous, scattered small operations, and rarely organized or aware of their basic labour rights. As the proportion of workers in wage employment increases with educational level (Table 2.5), workers in categories (iv) and (v) tend to end up as own-account workers (usually self-employed peasants) or unpaid family workers. Category (i) workers invariably become wage employees, while categories (ii) and (iii) are also predominantly wage employees although a significant proportion of (iii) are self-employed in personal services such as repairs and maintenance.

Vertical Segmentation

As discussed above, educational characteristics are not completely dissociated from other characteristics that structure supply, e.g. ethnicity, gender and class. Rather, they have to be studied within the context of such inter-relationships. Exogenous factors can affect the dynamics of these inter-relationships, creating new influences that may reshape traditional structuring factors and their impacts (see the following chapters).

The labour market categories outlined above are horizontally distributed across different industries/sectors according to the hiring requirements of each sector, including the occupational matrices of each industry. Hiring standards are functions of both economic and non-economic factors influencing labour demand. Table 2.8 suggests that elite-primary workers, especially in professional and technical categories, are mainly in community and social services, such as education and health care, and in financial and business services, sectors highly-ranked by the workforce.[52] The highest proportion of elite-primary administrative workers is in finance, followed by manufacturing and construction. Secondary-primary workers, i.e. clerical workers, are concentrated in services, especially finance, community and social services, which all have a high proportion of clerical staff. Secondary workers in sales and service functions are concentrated in distributive and personal services.

Agriculture mainly utilizes self-employed workers or secondary marginalized wage labourers while mining employs secondary production wage workers. Manufacturing and construction mostly employ secondary production workers. The greatest diversity of workers is found in services, where a clear-cut polarization of workers is evident between modern and traditional services, manifested in their significantly different recruitment and reward systems. The broad distinction simplifies analysis of the considerably different factors shaping the segmentation of modern and traditional sector labour markets.

As there are significant differentials in wages and non-pecuniary benefits for similar occupations across different industries, sectors and firm sizes,[53] understanding differential job access to these different segments is important. Where objective endowments (such as educational qualifications or skills) of workers are equal, employers' hiring decisions may be based on non-cognitive factors such as ethnicity, age, gender, work experience, institutional regulations, personality, social skills, attitudes towards authority and responsibility, and quality of education.[54]

Conclusion

As education is the main determinant of employment opportunities in the Malaysian labour market, the framework for labour force analyzing segmentation stratifies the workforce horizontally by educational/skill level, into elite-primary, secondary-primary, secondary and casual marginalized workers. Workers from each horizontal segment are often prevented from moving upwards to other segments unless they gain additional qualifications or new skills. These horizontal segments are then distributed across the various industries, occupational matrices, following varying combinations of objective, subjective and ascriptive criteria.

Access to modern service employment is largely dependent on formal educational qualifications. Educational qualifications horizontally stratify the labour force into occupational categories, while access to education is not equal among ethnic groups, genders or classes. Income is dependent on the service and the occupational category in which a person is employed, and the degree of labour unionization.

While the service sector has a larger proportion of "good jobs" utilizing upper-level elite-primary and secondary-primary workers with high educational qualifications, especially in modern services such as finance, utilities, community and social services (the last two sectors mainly have public sector employment), workers in traditional services such as transport, distributive and personal services, comprise mostly secondary workers assigned to bad jobs in sales, service and manual functions, requiring relatively low-level qualifications. Except for those employed by the public sector and by primary core firms, secondary workers in the service sector are generally less unionized and more vulnerable. Whether the expansion of the service sector expands the middle class or increases income inequality depends, to a large extent, on the growth of private modern services *vis-à-vis* traditional services.

Historically, horizontal and vertical segmentation of the labour force were closely related. The roots of segmentation in the Malaysian labour market by ethnicity, and to a lesser extent, by gender and class, can be traced to the nature of proletarianization under colonialism. The effects of colonial land, labour and educational policies resulted in a population unevenly ethnically distributed by geographical regions, industrial sectors, and occupational categories. Access to education and other skills favoured urban dwellers, usually Chinese and the Malay salariat. Chinese access to better paid occupations and jobs was made easier, by their better educational credentials, as well as the labour market in which more Chinese were employers, and prone to hiring on the basis of kith and kin. Inter-ethnic and intra-ethnic income inequalities generated by these processes — were generally perceived and described in communal terms, culminating in the post-election racial riots of May 1969.

Subsequently, the NEP was launched in 1970, to reduce poverty and inter-ethnic economic disparities. The inter-ethnic redistribution goal of the government was advanced by structural change in the fast industrializing economy, which saw a tremendous decline in agriculture and the rapid growth of manufacturing and services, particularly public services. In spite of such state-directed affirmative action, Malays continued to face barriers to entry in higher-level professions and occupations in the private sector, particularly in Chinese-controlled small-scale enterprises. Historical and cultural differences on the demand side continued to structure labour supply, through education and training opportunities and choices for different ethnic and gender groups. As a result, occupational and industrial labour force segmentation persists despite tremendous narrowing of human resource endowments between ethnic groups.

In implementing the NEP, the government influenced demand and supply structuring factors by promoting Malay economic interests through educational and employment quotas, loans, subsidies, licensing preferences and government-enterprises which acquired equity on behalf of the Malays and generated modern sector employment at all occupational levels. Hence, the NEP's purpose was both horizontal (in the sense of opening up educational opportunities such that the ethnic composition of horizontal strata of the labour force does not reflect differential ethnic access) and vertical (in the sense of reducing barriers to entry into the core-primary segments/industries for traditionally low labour-market status groups) restructuring.

The preoccupation with ethnic segmentation has, however, tended to neglect other issues such as gender segmentation and class segmentation. In addition, the effects of the country's education and human resource policies, with their emphasis on the creation of a middle class, have led to over-production of credentials and under-production of basic practical skills. This problem has been made more acute by the use of education credentials as a screening mechanism in the absence of labour market information and large returns to credentials, and thus, significant wage differentials between skills acquired through informal channels and through the conventional education system.

Segmentation has great relevance for lifetime labour market status and income over lifetimes. Once a career path is determined, mobility tends to be limited to the initial segment to which the worker was first allocated, because of skill-specificity and work habits associated with particular segments. Therefore, subsequent income and promotion prospects are affected by pre-market and in-market segmentation. Barriers to inter-segment mobility can be considerable, and can only be broken down by attending to factors structuring both labour demand and supply.

Subsequent chapters deal with the various ways in which employers and workers deal with structural changes, competitive pressures, and state policies. Recruitment, pay and promotion policies in modern and traditional services are compared and contrasted to show the importance of workers' labour market status and employers' hiring policies on job access and wages.

3

Traditional Services Employment

This chapter reviews the different sources of services employment for secondary labour categories: protected, unionized and regulated wage employment; unprotected wage employment, such as casual or contract work; self-employment; and unpaid family employment in the peripheral segments, including informal sector employment in the squatter economy. The chapter studies how low-status service workers — mainly foreign immigrants, youths, part-timers and women — are allocated secondary employment, and the dynamics of structural changes, ethnic and gender segmentation, and the search of labour flexibility. Employment patterns within the informal sector are also examined. Employment in traditional services is compared to employment in the modern services, discussed in the next chapter, as well as employment elsewhere in the traditional sector.

Traditional Services

Traditional services are often identified with activities which have the following characteristics:

(i)   employment is typically irregular, low-skilled, low-paid, marginal and casual, and working hours are either long and tedious, or short and unstable;

(ii)   subcontracting, self-employment and the use of unpaid or under-paid family labour;

(iii)   most activities are very competitive, consisting of many non-corporate, family-owned sole proprietorships or partnerships using "traditional" management methods;

(iv)   relatively more labour-intensive, with a lower level of technology compared to the rest of the economy, and hence, relatively lower barriers to entry, owing to lower technological, capital and other requirements; and

(v)   lower degrees of regulation of both product and labour markets.

The boundaries between modern and traditional sectors are not always clearly delineated. In many traditional services sectors, modern forms of organization are emerging, often in larger enterprises which are market leaders. Hence, some of the above characteristics have become muted.

Firms in the modern core of traditional services may be considered quasi-modern; while better than their smaller rivals, their terms of employment are not as good as those in modern services (unless these quasi-modern firms are part of a large modern conglomerate). Because of the similarities in their labour processes, particularly in the use of low-wage secondary labour, the modern component of traditional services will be analyzed together with other traditional services. While the modern core of traditional services is usually unionized, the nature of their product and labour markets nevertheless imbue them with secondary status in terms of occupational status, pay, mobility and employment security.

The peripheral sector of traditional services consists of smaller firms in the formal economy as well as enterprises in the informal sector. However, the distinction between these two kinds of firms is not always clear-cut. Wide variations in vulnerability and income exist in the informal economy, depending on the type of business activity.

Based on the above definition, and the general organization as well as characteristics of Malaysian services (Khong, 1991: Appendix 2), traditional services in Malaysia consist of a mixture of producer, distributive, personal and household services such as passenger and freight transport (by road and water),[1] wholesale and retail trade (i.e. petty trade or commerce), the hospitality industry (including hotels, lodging houses and travel agencies), food-catering, household and domestic services, personal services[2] and service activities in the informal economy.

Industrial Profile

The largest source of traditional sector employment has been petty trade, with a workforce of more than 600,000 in the late 1980s, of whom about three-quarters were in retail trade (Khong, 1991: Statistical Annex 6). The second largest source of employment is the food-catering industry, with more than 270,000 workers, followed by personal and household services with 212,000, and the transport sector with 159,000 (after deducting sub-sectors considered modern).

Generally, wage employment tends be more prominent in services which employ many workers per firm, or services which require a substantial amount of start-up capital. Conversely, services which have lower start-up capital costs and lower labour requirements per firm tend to involve a relatively higher proportion of self-employment and unpaid family employment. Non-wage employment is relatively more common in taxi, school-bus and trishaw transport; wholesale and retail of small merchandise (such as groceries and household and personal goods); food-catering in small restaurants, cafes, and hawkers' stalls; and personal, household and domestic services.

Commerce was one of the earliest service sectors, dominated by large British trading houses at the apex of the distribution pyramid and ubiquitous Chinese wholesalers and retailers. The industrial structure of commerce has long been concentrated, and increasingly so, now that small shops are under pressure from modern larger shops and chains, an increasing share of which are transnational businesses.[3] Some small shops, especially in the villages, survive because of their lower operating expenditures, and their indispensability to particular customer niches, e.g. barter customers, or poorer customers who buy in small quantities, and are given purchase credit (on the basis of trust).

Similarly, the transportation sector, one of the oldest services sectors in Malaysia,[4] juxtaposes a core of large, increasingly modern corporations with a decreasing number of small family-style firms outside of Kuala Lumpur, usually Chinese-owned or controlled. These traditionally paternalistic Chinese family firms often recruited on the basis of kinship and familiarity, ostensibly to communicate more effectively with workers. Increasingly, surveying firms are much larger, particularly where financial capital requirements and cash flow are substantial. The industrial structure is increasingly concentrated in the transportation sector.

Bus companies have monopoly or oligopolistic rights to routes allocated by the Road Transport Department through the issuance of operating permits. Where overlap of routes occurs, competition is intense from other licensed companies, unlicensed operators and other road transport vehicles. On the other hand, the freight transport business is less regulated and more disorganized. Stiff competition exists among and between core firms and the multitude of small firms that try to undercut each other through lower prices and operating costs. Over a succession of economic downturns, the industry has become more concentrated, with segmented niches for the big corporate consortium operators, small family-firms and individual owner-operators. Although self-employment, particularly in mini-bus transport and taxi transport, is regulated by the government through the issuance of vehicles' and drivers' permits, lax monitoring has resulted in a rampantly inefficient and irregular system.

In traditional services, the highest proportion of wage employment is found in the hotel and lodging industry, owing to greater labour requirements per establishment. Although the industry is highly regulated,[5] it retains many characteristics of secondary wage labour markets, with a small proportion of elite-primary and secondary-primary labour. With the expansion of large international hotels, the hospitality industry too has become more concentrated and segmented. Larger hotels have been better able to cope with increasing competition and new customer expectations which the small family-run lodging houses cannot afford to cater to. However, the latter have survived on the basis of price competitiveness.

The structure of the travel industry is also very oligopolistic and concentrated. Business is concentrated in the hands of the largest firms because of the finance needed to operate and expand businesses to cater to changes in customer preferences.[6] There are few genuine tour operators, and most registered agencies are merely involved in the competitive ticketing business, where discounting wars[7] exert downward pressure on costs. Two major types of travel agencies exist, one connected to international travel agencies, and the other based on Chinese management and price competitiveness with different labour markets and customer niches[8] although the two are becoming far less distinct.

Occupational Structure

In general, traditional services share one major characteristic: the employment of a large share of secondary workers who bear the risks of the volatility of demand. The secondary labour force can be further sub-divided into secondary manual, sales and service workers, who may be part-time, full-time, temporary, casual, contract or self-employed workers. The degree of self-employment depends on barriers to entry such as financial and skill requirements.

Secondary labour is distributed across different services according to the structure of labour demand, which is dependent on the nature of demand for the service, the level of technology, the degree of external regulation, the relative prices of factor inputs, and the organizational characteristics of the service industry. Thus, the labour-intensive bus transport sector mainly utilizes manual wage labour, while some sub-sectors, such as road-haulage and freight-forwarding, utilize mostly non-unionized contract or casual manual labour. Petty commerce utilizes secondary sales workers who are either wage employees or unpaid or nominally-paid family labour. The labour-intensive hospitality sector mainly utilizes general service labour, while the fast-food industry mainly utilizes much temporary part-time labour. Smaller firms have a greater tendency to have unpaid employees. Family labour, comprising the labour of young children, teenagers and pensioners, is fairly common in small retail outlets and food-catering.[9]

Elite-primary and secondary-primary workers have formed only a small proportion of the workforce in traditional services (Tables 3.1a and 3.1b). They are more prevalent in the quasi-modern core of traditional services that has very segmented workforce with a few white-collar and managerial workers amidst a mass of secondary workers. In general, white-collar employment in these quasi-modern services is not as sought after as better-paid white-collar employment in modern services, unless they are part of a modern conglomerate.

Table 3.1a Occupational Structure by Gender and Average Annual Earnings in Selected Services, 1985, 1992

	1985			1992		
Occupational category	*Distribution*	*Female*	*Av. annual earnings*	*Distribution*	*Female*	*Av. annual earnings*
	%	%	*(RM)*	%	%	*(RM)*
Bus Transport						
Professional/managerial	3.0	5.4	16,471	3.4	10.2	22,171
Technical & supervisory	5.3	4.3	9,761	6.7	3.8	12,574
Clerical & related	8.5	46.1	7,391	9.0	46.8	8,754
General workers:						
ushers & ticket sellers	2.3	32.8	6,674	3.3	34.0	7687
drivers & conductors	70.8	10.6	7,171	69.8	10.2	9,201
others	3.0	8.6	5,324	2.9	10.2	6,830
Other directly employed workers:						
skilled	1.4	0.0	8,923	1.1	0.3	10,591
semiskilled	1.4	2.2	5,790	1.1	0.6	6,501
unskilled	1.5	2.1	4,419	0.8	–	4,208
Workers employed through labour contractors:						
skilled	0.1	0.0	10,872	0.2	0.0	13,325
semiskilled	0.2	0.0	6,433	0.05	–	16,571
unskilled	0.3	1.3	5,859	0.06	–	4,214
Part-time employees	1.5	7.8	1,655	1.1	13.2	3,222
Total distribution	100.0	n.a.	n.a.	100.0	n.a.	n.a.
Total number of workers	26,200	13.1	n.a.	26,818	13.6	n.a.
Road Haulage						
Professional/managerial	3.6	8.6	16,654	4.0	11.4	24,834
Technical & supervisory	2.2	0.9	10,361	1.8	4.7	12,532
Clerical & related	8.2	51.4	6,628	9.2	60.6	7,620

Table 3.1a (continued)

Occupational category	1985			1992		
	Distribution	Female	Av. annual earnings	Distribution	Female	Av. annual earnings
	%	%	(RM)	%	%	(RM)
General workers:						
ushers & ticket sellers	62.4	n.a.	6,880	62.9	n.a.	9,528
drivers & conductors	2.2	9.8	4,521	2.8	5.7	6,292
Other directly employed workers:						
skilled	0.6	2.1	6,726	0.5	1.4	10,647
semiskilled	0.4	2.0	5,784	0.7	4.6	4,883
unskilled	1.3	1.1	4,275	1.3	0.9	4,752
Workers employed through labour contractors:						
skilled	0.1	3.0	8,394	0.4	–	10,296
semiskilled	0.3	0.0	4,912	0.5	1.9	4,184
unskilled	1.1	0.3	4,890	0.4	–	4,049
Part-time employees	3.9	3.5	3,072	2.7	6.6	3,585
Total distribution	100.0	n.a.	n.a.	100.0	n.a.	n.a.
Total number of workers	11,451	0.8	n.a.	47166	7	n.a.
Stevedoring Companies						
Professional/managerial	1.2	7.1	18,634	0.9	9.3	29,277
Technical & supervisory	1.8	0.0	13,629	1.7	0.5	16,784
Clerical & related	0.2	88.3	7,983	2.9	41.4	9,431
General workers:						
ushers & ticket sellers	0.8	0.0	6,970	1.0	0.0	8,831
drivers & conductors	2.1	0.6	7,040	0.8	7.6	8,077
Other directly employed workers:						
skilled	38.3	0.0	9,313	7.7	0.0	12,790
semiskilled	2.1	0.0	7,119	4.5	0.0	7,104
unskilled	28.7	0.0	5,412	16.8	0.0	8,409
Workers employed through labour contractors:						
skilled	1.2	0.0	7,250	7.2	0.0	11,986
semiskilled	2.1	0.0	5,261	11.3	0.0	10,325
unskilled	7.8	0.0	4,068	0.5	0.0	3,075
Part-time employees	6.9	0.5	5,265	42.5	6.0	1,046
Total distribution	100.0	1.2	n.a.	100.0	1.5	n.a.
Total number of workers	8,248	n.a.	n.a.	11,737	n.a.	n.a.
Hotels & Other Lodgings						
Professional/managerial	5.4	22.0	22,466	7.6	29.8	28,687
Technical & supervisory	8.4	27.5	9,968	8.4	27.1	12,792
Clerical & related	10.1	65.7	6,093	9.5	64.3	6,093

(continued overleaf)

Table 3.1a (continued)

Occupational category	1985			1992		
	Distribution	Female	Av. annual earnings	Distribution	Female	Av. annual earnings
	%	%	(RM)	%	%	(RM)
General workers:						
ushers & ticket sellers	0.0	0.0	0	0.0	0.0	0
drivers & conductors	0.6	0.0	5,307	0.9	16.6	7,726
others	52.9	41.4	4,291	54.4	37.9	5,999
Other directly employed workers:						
skilled	5.0	27.6	7,869	6.3	33.2	5,990
semiskilled	6.6	34.5	5,478	3.9	32.9	5,001
unskilled	5.6	38.2	3,995	2.8	35.0	4,134
Workers employed through labour contractors:						
skilled	0.1	50.0	7,875	0.1	46.6	7,350
semiskilled	0.0	0.0	0	0.1	25.9	4,296
unskilled	0.1	100.0	4,615	0.2	42.5	6,050
Part-time employees	1.5	38.1	1,737	3.1	39.6	4,123
Total distribution	100.0	39.1	n.a.	100.0	38.0	n.a.
Total number of workers	29,598	n.a.	n.a.	46,107	n.a.	n.a.
Tourist & Travel Agencies						
Professional/managerial	16.1	31.4	15,266	30.6	34.9	24,519
Technical & supervisory	2.7	50.3	12,503	7.5	59.2	14,562
Clerical & related	55.5	67.7	5,718	19.9	69.1	8,344
General workers:						
ushers & ticket sellers	0.0	0.0	0	0.0	0.0	0
drivers & conductors	6.0	2.8	6,182	4.6	3.7	8,170
others	8.4	22.3	3,792	19.5	30.1	5,987
Other directly employed workers:						
skilled	0.2	26.7	4,533	0.4	30.4	6,696
semiskilled	0.1	0.0	2,000	0.2	2.0	3,800
unskilled	0.0	0.0	0	0.0	0.0	3,000
Workers employed through labour contractors:						
skilled	0.0	0.0	0	100.0	100.0	7,000
semiskilled	0.0	0.0	0	100.0	100.0	3,800
unskilled	0.0	0.0	0	0.0	0.0	0
Part-time employees	2.3	36.9	2,262	31.8	31.8	3,150
Total distribution	100.0	48.8	n.a.	51.3	51.3	n.a.
Total number of workers	5373	n.a.	n.a.	n.a.	n.a.	n.a.

Sources: Department of Statistics, *Census of Selected Services Industries, 1985*; *Census of Selected Services Industries, 1992.*

Table 3.1b Occupational Structure by Gender and Average Annual Earnings in Selected Services, 2003

Occupational category	Share %	Female %	Average annual earnings (RM)
Bus Transport			
Professional/managerial	4.2	17.5	3,292
Technical & supervisory	13.9	6.5	1,663
Clerical & related	11.9	63.1	1,148
General workers:			
drivers & conductors	58.9	2.3	1,360
others	10.4	38.9	774
Part-time employees	0.7	13.0	362
Total distribution	100	14.6	
Total number of workers	18,146	2,650	1,390
Road Haulage			
Professional/managerial	8.5	27.6	4,513
Technical & supervisory	7.0	16.8	2,113
Clerical & related	20.2	45.8	1,424
General workers:			
drivers & conductors	46.8	0.0	1,634
Other directly employed workers	11.6	5.4	814
Part-time employees	5.9	8.8	850
Total distribution	100.0	13.9	
Total number of workers	35,227	4,905	1,728
Hotels & Other Lodgings			
Professional/managerial	12.2	37.6	3,373
Technical & supervisory	20.9	34.1	1,348
Clerical & related	18.8	52.3	900
General workers:			
others	43.0	38.8	736
Part-time employees	5.2	38.7	300
Total distribution	100.0	40.2	
Total number of workers	83,715	33,658	1193
Tourist & Travel Agencies			
Professional/managerial	24.8	4,471.3	38
Technical & supervisory	12.6	2,745.6	48

(continued overleaf)

Table 3.1b (continued)

Occupational category	Share %	Female %	Average annual earnings (RM)
Clerical & related	15.1	4,047.1	157
General workers:			
drivers & conductors	10.6	1,379.2	1
others	8.3	1,031.0	17
Part-time employees	28.5	51.9	3
Total distribution	100.0	2,316.1	
Total number of workers	12,495	289,394	42

Source: Department of Statistics, *Census of Selected Services Industries, 2003.*

Employment Growth

Admittedly, labour productivity is generally lower in traditional services than in modern services. But there is little conclusive evidence that employment in the Malaysian traditional services is only supply-determined, and not also demand-determined. Some traditional services have expanded tremendously, with economic growth, population growth, urbanization, and changes in demand, e.g. most forms of passenger bus transport. Economic growth and better road systems have also increased the volume of freight transport by road, which, together with freight-forwarding, are the largest employers in the transportation sector (Khong, 1991: Statistical Annex 6).

Population expansion and increases in incomes as well as demand have spurred the growth of petty trade. Rising living standards, urbanization and changing lifestyles have restructured the industry, leading to stagnating or declining small uncompetitive outlets, eclipsed by larger chain stores, supermarkets and shopping malls. Similarly, Westernization and rising standards of living have made fast-food chains one of the fastest growing services since its introduction into Malaysia in 1963.[10] Population growth has also increased the demand for personal services. Increased labour force participation of middle-class and upper-class women has brought about increased market provision of services, as well as new opportunities for employment in the informal economy for working-class women and housebound females.

Official promotion of tourism has led to a boom in the hospitality industry.[11] Despite official plans to upgrade the industry as a source of modern employment, efforts have not been too successful because of the nature of the industry, which still largely relies on semi-skilled labour. The number of good jobs in the industry is small and concentrated in large international hotels and in the larger travel agencies, which principally cater for the needs of the internationally mobile.[12]

Segmentation

Ethnic and gender segmentation is more pronounced in traditional services than in modern services (see Chapter 4; also Khong, 1991). However, ethnic segmentation and competition for employment is much less a public issue in traditional services because of the low status and low pay associated with these services. Only where lucrative income prospects are at stake has there been state intervention to redistribute ownership and employment through quota-licensing.[13] However, the size of firms and their regional dispersion make regulation easier to circumvent.

Origins of Segmentation

Ethnically-segmented employment is persistent in traditional services, especially in small and medium-sized firms, which have a relatively more self-employment and family employment. Historically, most small businesses in Malaysia have been owned and operated by Chinese using family labour. Production and supply was dominated by foreign firms or their local Chinese partners (Puthucheary, 1960). Domestic demand also came principally from the Chinese community who were relatively wealthier (Khong, 1991: Statistical Annex 2). Kinship, clan and other cultural ties, rather than objective qualifications such as educational credentials, were important recruitment criteria into the trades and guilds. Interlocking interests through alliances formed through social networks helped reinforce ethnic segmentation in production, consumption and employment.

Ownership of especially wholesale trade and even petty trade has remained ethnically segmented, partly because of the variegated social links between the predominantly Chinese wholesalers and retailers. Ethnic employment preferences in trade, however, cannot be solely attributed to the structure of product demand, which is heterogeneous. Limited labour requirement encourages the use of family and familiar labour. Thus, largely non-Malay ownership and control reflected in employment. Similarly, employment in repairs and maintenance services is overwhelmingly Chinese as skill acquisition is mainly through on-the-job training and apprenticeships but declining Chinese youth employment in such work has seen growing non-Chinese (Indian, Malay and immigrant) recruitment in recent decades. Many of the "old masters" were Chinese, mono-lingual and ethnocentric, and reluctant to accept non-Chinese trainees but the increasingly widespread use of Malay as a common language in recent decades has also lowered such linguistic barriers. Nonetheless, traditional services of employment still tend to have over-representation of: (i) the older generation, (ii) workers educated in vernacular schools and (iii) workers qualified for white-collar employment in modern services, but unable to obtain such employment.

Malay and Indian participation is greater in the newer, more institutionalized services, and in other services where culture, religion, custom and language are not an important part of working life. For instance, in tourism, international hotel chains, with highly-diverse clienteles, have substantial Malay and Indian employment, especially in the lower occupations. Although Malay and Indian participation has grown substantially in the hospitality industry, some ethnic segmentation remains.[14]

In general, women are more prevalent in services where the occupational structure consists of jobs that are historically and culturally-defined as female. Table 3.1 shows women more significant in retail trade, food-catering, hotels and lodging services,[15] tourist and travel agencies, and particularly in laundry services, domestic services and personal services (see Khong, 1991: Statistical Annex 6). In services where they account for a small proportion of the workforce (e.g. transport services), women are mostly in clerical and general job functions, serving as telephone operators, ticket sellers, and clerks. Manual work, requiring brawn or technical skills, in transport services, wholesale trade, stevedoring, repairs and maintenance services have traditionally been the preserve of men.

Dynamics of Segmentation

Although the restructuring of ethnic ownership and changes in the ethnic pattern of market demand have helped reduce ethnic segmentation in traditional services, the greatest impetus for ethnic and gender restructuring has come from competitive pressure on wage costs. As wage employment increases with firm size, efforts to lower wage costs tend to redistribute employment opportunities to the cheaper segments of the workforce, e.g. non-Chinese (including immigrant) labour, part-time labour and/or female labour.[16] The supply prices (wages) of these groups of labour tend to be lower because of their lower labour market status and weaker bargaining power.

Various factors have led to the corporatization of retail and wholesale trade in the form of supermarkets, hypermarkets, large departmental stores and shopping centres, which are urban "catchment areas" for all with the means regardless of ethnicity. This development has led to greater wage employment at the expense of self-employment and family employment. Similarly, the expansion of international/ large and medium-sized hotels in the hospitality industry has led to greater wage employment, and hence, increased proportions of Malays and women in the workforce. Tax-breaks for large hotels meeting the ethnic-employment quota under pioneer industries legislation offer added incentives for ethnic redistribution of the industry's workforce.[17]

Malays, Indians and women tend to be over-represented in the unskilled lower occupational categories. In the hotel industry, this can be partly attributed to their relatively late entrance into the industry from the mid-1970s and their limited experience in an industry where upward mobility depends largely on seniority and possession of industry-specific skills.[18] Moreover, the occupational representation of Malays and women depends on the degree of deskilling and skill-specificity. In the larger hotels, the proportion of de-skilled jobs tends to be greater, which explains the greater proportion of Malay, Indian and female employment in the lower categories in big hotels.

In the transport sector, corporatization and increasing Bumiputera ownership from 17.1 per cent in 1971 to 62.5 per cent in 1981 have raised Malay employment from about a quarter in 1970 to slightly less than half in 1983 (*Fifth Malaysia Plan, 1986–1990*: Table 3-11; *Labour Indicators, 1983*: Table 22). As access to officially allocated resources is institutionally — including licences — is officially rationed, such business practices even extend to the simplest informal services such as hawking, helping to improve recruitment of Malays. Competitive pressures in labour markets and changing ethnic patterns of demand have also ensured growing employment of cheaper non-Chinese workers.[19]

Pricing and Allocation of Wage Labour

Owing to the heterogeneity of traditional services, the pricing and allocation of labour is extremely diverse or segmented. Limited union and state regulations limit institutional pricing and allocation of labour. Nevertheless, market forces do not operate freely, even in the casual and informal labour markets, because of "distortions" due to social, cultural, religious and political factors.

Job Access and Ports of Entry

Secondary-primary and elite-primary workers are often chosen on the basis of educational qualifications, job experience and other subjective and ascriptive criteria. However, unless the firms are industry leaders or part of a larger conglomerate, the level of qualifications needed to meet the screening and rationing threshold is generally lower than those in modern sector services, due to lower pay and insecure employment in traditional services.[20]

With the exception of large hotels as well as restaurants and core firms in the transport sector, unionization is generally low in traditional services. However, ports of entry are still limited to the bottom of the occupational hierarchy, particularly where industry-specific skills acquired on the job are important pre-requisites for job access. Except for core and corporate firms that advertise vacancies through the mass media, recruitment channels in traditional services tend to be informal. Kinship or "inside contacts" are cited by almost all industry sources as important channels of job access.

Blue-collar maintenance or repair workers are usually recruited as apprentices. In the corporate sector, the minimum qualifications are some combination of technical training qualifications and an LCE, although this formal certificate is not really necessary in small firms where on-the-job training is broader and longer.[21] Manual workers are only required to have the most basic education. Sales and service workers generally possess at least a lower-intermediate or middle-intermediate educational level, if employed in the formal economy. In some cases, workers require additional relevant skills. For instance, in the transport sector, bus and trailer drivers must have an appropriate driving licence, and preferably, a Public Service Vehicle (PSV) licence. In addition, work experience or on-the-job training is essential, particularly for driving trailers, a job considered at least semi-skilled.

Quasi-modern core firms in transport tend to have higher hiring standards for operations staff and prefer young male workers (18–40 years of age) with at least a basic or lower-intermediate school education and the relevant driving licence. Freight companies also prefer young male workers because drivers and assistants are required to load and unload heavy cargo. Women are seldom hired, except as clerks, bus conductors or ticket sellers.[22] To lower wage costs, transport firms may resort to inexperienced, but cheaper workers who may not have a PSV licence. In these cases, the firms train the workers and apply for the PSV licence on their behalf.[23]

Secondary sales and service jobs typically involve long working hours (Khong, 1991: Statistical Annex 8). As their jobs are not technically complicated, only a basic school education is needed. Job experience is not crucial, though numeracy and the "gift of the gab" are considered important advantages, if not prerequisites. In smaller retail outlets, kinship helped gain employment[24] as workers with referrals from friends or relatives were favoured but this has become much less of an advantage over the decades. However, in larger firms with more developed management systems, employees are recruited through formal channels.

Sexual-stereotyping persists in commerce, where job functions requiring physical stamina and brawn are performed by men. Wholesalers and large modern retail corporations mostly recruit male workers, who double-up as manual labour. However, the advent of departmental stores and supermarkets has led to feminization of lower sales jobs, where women are preferred due to their relatively lower supply price, i.e. wages they are prepared to accept.

Market segmentation of domestic and international tourism is reflected in labour market structure. Cheap, unskilled and inexperienced casual and secondary workers, particularly women, are mainly recruited by lower-end hotels.[25] Before the 1970s, formal qualifications were not vital for jobs in hotels, including the bigger hotels. However, with the spread of credentialism, work experience must now be supplemented with educational credentials for access to white-collar employment as well as higher service functions, particularly in the larger international hotels.

In hotels whose workers are members of the National Union of Hotel, Bar and Restaurant Workers (NUHBRW), ports of entry for every occupation are at the lowest level of their categories. To deter inter-firm movement, promotion is encouraged from among the rank and file. In domestically-oriented hotels, some intermediate education and working knowledge of languages such as Mandarin, Chinese dialects, English and Malay are often highly valued.[26] International hotels have more stringent entry requirements for secondary-primary jobs, at least an MCE, a good command of English and, another foreign language. Secondary manual and service workers, e.g. chambermaids or kitchen staff, must at least be literate. Work experience is particularly useful for access to employment in the larger hotels. In this sector, workers can work their way up to the top of the occupational pyramid, particularly when supplemented with formal industrial training.

In the travel industry, entry requirements are relatively high. The minimum qualifications for a combined-clerical-sales position, which is considered relatively skilled, are at least an MCE, a ticketing certificate, and preferably, some related work experience. Firms with modern Western-style management generally provide more comprehensive training; emphasize professionalism and consequently, paper qualifications. A greater proportion of elite-primary labour in marketing and planning are employed in these firms. In regulated segments of the tourism industry, access to "informal jobs", e.g. as free-lance tourist guides, is difficult because of the stiff entry requirements imposed by the Tourism Development Corporation (TDC).

Skill-Specificity, Inter-Industry and Intra-Industry Movement and Career Paths

Most secondary labour market entrants begin labour market involvement with similar formal qualifications, but differing subjective and ascriptive endowments. Their first job may ultimately determine their lifetime career paths since many skills are learnt on the job, and they may not qualify for formal training or re-education programmes due to their poor initial educational qualifications. Generally, inter-industry movement is rare because of the constraints of skill-specificity.

Most secondary jobs tend to be dead-end jobs since vertical mobility for most secondary workers is limited without additional qualifications and the occupation pyramid is extremely bottom-heavy, e.g. drivers and manual workers in transport services and sales workers in trade. Work experience is rewarded by seniority based pay, and more rarely, by promotions to relatively higher-paid supervisory positions.[27] Vertical and horizontal mobility are limited by the absence of a training system which equips workers with additional industry-specific or even firm-specific skills. Inter-firm mobility is further discouraged by the practice of rewarding seniority (within a particular firm) with annual wage increments. Turnover is low in the corporate core, where workers enjoy better pay and work benefits. In family firms, non-kin have limited promotion prospects because of nepotism and limited attrition in firms without any formal retirement age. In large corporate firms, where wage employment is the norm, upward mobility for secondary workers is restricted because recruitment into highly-ranked occupations often rewards reputation as well as work experience.

In some traditional services, such as repairs and other petty trades, apprenticeships still serve as ports of entry.[28] Where an apprenticeship offers a narrow range of skills, workers may learn the skills of a trade by moving from task to task within a workshop. It is believed that artisan-employers retain "trade secrets".[29] Such apprenticeship training in many small-scale enterprises is not officially recognized as a source of skill acquisition; this tends to limit the future opportunities of the apprentice unless their apprenticeship is supplemented with formal certification by official training institutes.

Labour turnover is generally high among secondary sales and service workers, who tend to be part-time or temporary workers. In the fast-food and hospitality industries, temporary and part-time workers help absorb seasonal fluctuations in business.[30] As little or no training is offered, employers have few incentives to retain staff through better pay, especially when increasing competition squeezes profits. Moreover, high turnover due to low entry wages helps to keep labour costs low.

In industries which are regulated or unionized, such as the transport and hotel sectors, inter-firm movement is constrained by institutional rules. Nevertheless, high labour turnover rates exist because of competition for experienced labour. Inter-firm movement within the same industry is one way secondary workers may work their way up. Where industry-specific skills are mostly obtained on-the-job, small firms serve as industrial training grounds, and face both inter-firm and inter-industry competition for skilled and semi-skilled labour. Mobility is greatest at the extreme ends of the industry: employees of small firms achieve vertical mobility by moving to larger firms while employees of large firms also try to move in search of better pay and work prospects, within the constraints posed by their industry-specific skills.

With some exceptions, e.g. working for of international firms, even quasi-modern traditional services, such as hospitality services, are not considered as prestigious as modern services. This is because most jobs are perceived as low-status secondary jobs not requiring much formal education. The consequent low pay, in turn, depresses job status further. Moreover, public valuation of jobs is influenced by cultural conditioning, and in many developing countries, personal service jobs are lowly-regarded as "servile jobs". Pay is comparable to other industries only at the highest levels.

Wage Determination and Payment Systems

Secondary labour categories are segmented according to whether they are in core or peripheral firms in traditional services. Pay and other employment benefits are better in larger firms and in firms when product markets are more stable. In any case, the level of pay and benefits of these secondary workers is still not comparable to modern services sectors, especially in the corporate and public sectors. Employees in smaller firms are vulnerable to demand fluctuations in product and profit levels. Differences in the structure of demand are often used to justify pay differentials and vastly disparate entry and promotion systems, even though the basic skills required in some jobs may not be significantly different among the segments.

A major characteristic of payment systems in traditional services, including the quasi-modern core, is income instability because of low basic wages and the high proportion of wage income based from "productivity-related" performance. With the exception of monthly-rated white-collar secondary-primary and elite-primary workers, most secondary workers are either daily-rated or, piece-rated, or some combination of both. Basic wages tend to be low, with commissions, tips and other allowances forming the major components of take-home pay (see Table 3.1). Wage determination in traditional services may be roughly divided into three categories: (i) unionized workers (usually found in core firms), who only form a very small proportion of the workforce, (ii) non-unionized workers — such as shop assistants, cinema workers, harbour workers — covered by minimum wage legislation under the National Wage Councils Act of 1947, (iii) unprotected workers who are not unionized and outside the scope of the country's labour laws, e.g. casual workers, part-time workers, temporary workers and illegal immigrants. Category (iii) is most vulnerable to exploitation, lay-offs and unfair dismissals.

Unionized workers tend to enjoy higher wages and benefits, including automatic annual pay increments, occasional bonuses, paid annual leave, medical benefits, and more secure employment. Firms are inclined to join the unionized sector in booms because union wages serve as a ceiling to wage escalation in tight labour markets. In the transport sector, union-negotiated wages are separately negotiated with each individual firm. The wages of secondary transport employees depend on the number of trips they make, which is directly related to passenger or product volume, traffic density, the technical efficiency of the vehicle, making workers bear the brunt of market uncertainties.

In bus companies, the low basic wages for operations staff are supplemented by variable elements such as the cost of living allowance (COLA), attendance and punctuality incentives, and commissions. Commissions and allowances contribute substantially to take-home pay, sometimes exceeding basic wages. Wage rates and commission rates vary from company to company, even for companies with the same union. Commissions in stage bus companies are calculated as a percentage of ticket sales, which encourages overloading. In long-distance bus transport, where passenger overloading is strictly forbidden, non-basic wage income derives mainly from built-in overtime payments, which are sometimes in violation of legal overtime regulations.

The wage rates of manual workers in road haulage and freight-forwarding firms depend on cargo types. Several types of commission systems exist, either according to the number of trips made, or as a percentage of freight charges. As basic monthly wages are very low, commissions are crucial for a living wage. Although freight-forwarding wages are low, wage costs account for a high proportion of total variable costs, exerting downward pressure on wages and other types of workers' benefits to maintain profitability.[31] When competition is stiff, firms seek to reduce wage costs by using cheaper foreign labour or using two-tier wage systems.[32]

In the secondary non-unionized peripheral segments of the transport sector, such as mini-bus companies, small freight firms, stevedoring firms and miscellaneous transport firms, entry arrangements are highly informal.

For example, mini-bus companies[33] only recruit workers who already possess a Public Service Vehicle driving licence, and no substantial training is provided. Full-time workers in these companies are more protected than casual employees, and enjoy access to medical care, annual leave, bonus payments and employers' contributions to the Employee Provident Fund and Social Security Organization. However, these benefits are indirectly deducted from their basic pay and commissions which tend to be lower than those of the casually employed as well as drivers employed in the unionized stage-bus and express bus companies (Khong, 1991).

With its large number of small and regionally-dispersed distributive outlets, workers in small petty trading firms' are seldom unionized. Only permanent full-time employees of the larger departmental stores, emporiums, supermarkets and hypermarkets belong to the National Union of Commercial Workers. As significant proportions of the employees consist of temporary and part-time workers, the better wages and work benefits negotiated by the union are only enjoyed by a small proportion of sales workers. Although non-unionized shop assistants are technically protected by minimum wage legislation under the Wage Councils Act, many workers not getting the stipulated benefits are unaware of their legal rights, or unwilling to report on employers who break the law, some of whom may be relatives or community leaders.

Competition among the major food chains for market share has led to downward pressure on the wages of the largely non-unionized workers. Low wages are allegedly justified by the low-skill requirements of the jobs, which require only elementary technical competence in terms of just following instructions. Lower wages are also encouraged by the practically unlimited supply of students and other workers searching for supplementary income from temporary and part-time work. As the basic pay is extremely low, workers depend largely on tips and other allowances, such as the uniform allowance and the night-shift allowance, to supplement their take-home income.

In the hotel industry, employment is segmented between core and peripheral firms. Unlike hourly-rated fast-food workers, hotel workers are monthly-rated. The most important components of take-home pay for hotel workers are service charges (calculated on the mandatory service charge tagged onto all bills), tips and other allowances. Since the amount of service charges a hotel earns depends on the volume of business, take-home pay may vary significantly between workers in small and large hotels, despite similar basic pay, because of differences in revenue. A very small percentage of the industry's workforce, comprising non-supervisory and non-managerial full-time employees in the larger enterprises, is organized under the auspices of the National Union of Hotel, Bar and Restaurant Workers. The union negotiates individual collective agreements with each of the large hotels. Incentives for improving incomes largely come from opportunities for internal promotion or industry-level promotion.

Casual Labour and Sub-Contracting

Casual labour, temporary labour and sub-contracting are common in traditional services, particularly where demand fluctuates considerably with economic cycles. The move towards casual, temporary and contract labour is not dictated solely by direct wage costs, but is a strategy whereby employers pass on the costs of business fluctuations and labour management to subcontractors, external workers and temporary labour.[34] In other words, the use of temporary and part-time labour in the fast-food, hotel and restaurant industries is dictated by the seasonality of demand, rather than lower wage costs per se.

Although wage employment is still the most common form of labour organization in the transportation industry, permanent formal wage employment is the exception rather than the rule. Increasingly, firms (including large core firms) wishing to avoid contributions to the Employees' Provident Fund and Social Security Organization, and to pass on the vagaries of the market to labour, prefer to outsource work to daily-paid or piece-rated casual workers, or self-employed workers. Casual labour gangs are commonly used in stevedoring firms, warehouses, and bulk-packaging work in freight-forwarding firms.[35]

Technical change has simultaneously brought about deskilling on the one hand and upgrading of skills on the other, and has redrawn the boundaries between categories of manual labour. There has been a reduction in the role of traditional services as sources of full-time employment for secondary workers, who have been increasingly replaced by machines, temporary or part-time workers, casual and contract workers.

Self-Employment in the Informal Sector

True informal sector employment involves self-employment or "semi-feudal" wage employment relationships, requires little financial or human capital, uses non-labour inputs that are independently sourced from any supplier, and involves marketing to any buyer. Dependent self-employment produces goods or services which are tied to larger enterprises through sub-contracting such arrangements. True self-employment is more prevalent in sub-sectors where the technical and financial capital requirements are small. Job access in the informal sector is through: (i) general criteria such as skill or job experience; access to capital through own resources, or with family, community or state support; and access to markets; (ii) specific criteria such as access to particular types of work through inter-personal networks, which themselves reflect kin, clan, community or ethnic affinities.

The informal sector provides employment for the aged, youth, unskilled foreign labour and rural-urban migrants who cannot otherwise be absorbed into factory employment. Work in the informal sector helps to supplement low family income.[36] Where entry is regulated by the state through licences or permits, loopholes in the system result in indirect access (e.g. through bribery), and these economic costs are passed onto workers and consumers in line with the relative bargaining strength of each group and existing institutional rules.

Own-account working and unpaid family services employment have been most prevalent in some segments of transportation, retail trade (particularly food), catering and personal services (Khong, 1991: Statistical Annex 6). Unpaid family employment is common in the retail and food-catering trades which rely on the use of the cheap unpaid family labour of children and the elderly to compete against larger firms. Although Malaysia encourages the development of small-scale enterprises, official strategies for this purpose have been haphazard, partly because of the state's active encouragement of export-oriented industrialization sector and modern services.

Owing to structural changes, several kinds of differentiation have existed and evolved over time within the informal sector. Members of the informal sector are constantly moving; once a particular group has gained upward and outward mobility into the secondary sector of formal employment and, more rarely, the primary sector, others from the constant stream of rural-urban migration and foreign immigration move in to take their place. However, in some informal sector employment, where the technical and capital requirements for self-employment are relatively substantial, entry is limited to those endowed with financial or human capital. Although informal employment in traditional services has low status, competition for access (through licences or permits) occurs particularly in sectors that offer good self-employment income relative to secondary wage employment. In such instances, the cost of entry is relatively high.

With the exception of jobs considered masculine (especially in transportation and some services such as repairs and maintenance), informal employment has a higher female participation because personal and domestic services conform to the traditional ideology of women's role in family and society. Ethnic and gender segmentation is encouraged by differential labour status, vastly differing supply prices, and other factors that serve to structure labour demand, such as custom and religion. The supply price of non-Chinese labour in the informal sector tends to be relatively cheaper, and thus paid lower wages.[37]

Self-Employment in Transportation

Traditional road transport such as trishaws, which do not require much capital investment are more conducive to informal self-employment because of the few barriers to entry. However, development and urbanization in Malaysia have led to the demise of such forms of transport while motorized alternatives conducive to self-employment — such as taxis, school-buses and mini-buses, for those with enough initial working capital and social capital[38] — have expanded instead.

Owing to the numerical discrepancy between the numbers of Public Service Vehicle licences, taxi drivers' licences and vehicle permits issued, the system has been rife with irregularities Owing to ethnic preferential policies, the issue of mini-bus and taxi permits has been politically sensitive.[39] It has been alleged that 90 per cent of all new permits go to Bumiputeras, of whom the most influential are not interested in becoming owner-operators.[40] They then lease out (*pajak*) their permits to others, usually non-Bumiputeras, to considerable gain.

The three types of leasing or *pajak* arrangements that exist involve (1) leasing the vehicle permit only (the most common form of leasing), (2) leasing the vehicle only, and (3) leasing the vehicle with the permit. The prices for such permits vary according to how lucrative the routes are. The lease is for an indefinite time period, although a permit has to be renewed every seven years. Some permits change hands several times because mini-bus transportation was a very lucrative and profitable business, where the initial investments (for the permit and the vehicle) could be recouped within a year. Those only leasing permits will have to come up with the capital to buy or hire a bus. They then either become operators (as drivers or conductors) themselves and hire conductors, or work out arrangements for others to operate the vehicle. Many casual employees are Indonesian workers hired on a daily contract basis, who are not entitled to any protection under the Employment Act.[41]

Employment in this sector is highly informal. The educational level of workers is very low (primary or lower-secondary education) because education does not play any job rationing role. Casual workers are free to move from "employer to employer", although there is an implicit understanding among mini-bus operators on "going wages". Labour turnover is high, mainly because take-home pay changes according to commissions, which depending on revenue, which in turn depends on passenger routes allocated by the authorities. Wage employees rarely progress to become self-employed owner-operators because of the prohibitive costs of *pajak* and vehicle purchase.

A slightly cheaper variation for the self-employed is employment as taxi drivers. The *pajak* system is also widespread in this sector, and harder to monitor since there are far more taxis than mini-buses. Licences are issued with ad hoc restrictions on supply by the Road Transport Department. The ethnic distribution of taxi operators is a politically sensitive issue, with more operating permits issued to Malays, even though the proportion of non-Malay taxi drivers is relatively high partly, because non-Malay taxi operators operate taxis using permits issued to Malays. With the exception of limousine taxi firms which employ drivers, most taxi firms lease out their vehicles (not the taxi operating permits) for substantial profits. Technically, the operating permits could not be leased out and second drivers were only permitted if the first driver was more than 50 years old and the second driver was a relative of the first. However, the issue of more than one permit to individual applicants has been rampant. It has thus been possible for the taxi driver not to be the car owner and the car owner, not to be the owner of the operating permit.

In reality, lessees are not really self-employed, but are dependent workers who hire the means of transportation for a period of time, usually daily or monthly. After every rota or day, the lessee has to relinquish the vehicle to the leaser. Some enterprising individuals may share the cost of leasing between two or three persons, although only one of them will be the direct lessee. In addition, "tea money" is almost always a pre-requisite for securing the deal.[42] Another variation closer to the mini-bus *pajak* system is the monthly leasing of both vehicle and permit. In this case, the lessee is responsible for vehicle repairs and maintenance. Another less popular practice is leasing the permit only, with the driver leasing the vehicle from elsewhere.

Barriers to entry occur in the form of the substantial start-up capital needed to pay for the security deposit and tea-money, and the need for referrals from friends or family already in the business. The fare charged per mile is officially fixed by the government, but only city taxis usually follow this rule. Long-distance taxis generally do not follow the prescribed fares and monitoring them is harder. In freight transport, the *pajak* system is less important, but exists nevertheless. However, *pajak* is checked by the greater difficulty in obtaining a Public Service Vehicle "E" driving licence compared to a taxi driver's or a mini-bus driver's licence.

The most common form of true self-employment (not dependent self-employment) in the transportation industry is offered by school-bus transport. Compared to taxi and mini-bus transport, the school bus transport system presents fewer opportunities for *pajak* exploitation. The school bus permit is not issued until the applicant shows proof that he has the means to buy a bus, and that he has the relevant driver's licence. The vehicle permit is tied to the ability to buy a vehicle within a year of permit issue; otherwise, the permit is revoked. The market is also less regulated; the applicant can specify his own route although this route may not usually be followed. Fares are supposedly fixed by the Ministry of Transport, but in reality, are subject to demand and supply forces because of the sustained demand for school transport. The checks on prices come in the form of competition from rival school buses, although there are informal understandings about the level of undercutting.

This form of self-employment features a higher proportion of women drivers because of the relative flexibility of work schedules around school hours. Operators may either work one shift or combine shifts. Income varies with vehicle size and the number of passengers it can accommodate as well as the type of passengers and distances covered. There are, of course, economies of scale in the operation of big buses. However, it takes a long time to recoup the initial cost of the bus purchase because the number of passengers is limited by strict restrictions on overloading.

Petty Trading and Hawking

An ubiquitous form of truly informal economic activity is petty trading and hawking,[43] because of the relatively small capital requirements and flexible nature of the job. There are relatively few barriers to entry. Legal hawkers and petty traders have to be registered with the municipal authority. The ethnic composition of petty traders has changed with the ethnic composition of urban centres. In 1970, Malays accounted for only 4.4 per cent of licensed hawkers in Kuala Lumpur, while Chinese accounted for 80.8 per cent and Indians for 14.8 per cent.[44] By 1989, the ethnic composition of licensed hawkers in Kuala Lumpur was 36.6 per cent Malay, 56.2 per cent Chinese and 7.2 per cent Indians. Owing to the ethnic distribution of customers by location, some degree of ethnic segmentation by locality exists. Hawkers plying areas near government offices and Malay residential areas are predominantly Malay, while the ethnic composition of hawkers is more diversified in more cosmopolitan areas.

A few studies (Rokiah and Fauzi, 1986; Nor Aini, 1989; Junaenah Solehan, 1987; SERU, 1979; Lam, 1977) indicate a low level of formal educational qualifications among hawkers and petty traders, as in other developing countries. Most are secondary labour categories, having either no formal schooling or only primary school education. SERU (1979) found men dominant among Malay traders. Most traders were younger than 40 years of age and three-quarters of those surveyed in the two studies were married. Business is not passed on inter-generationally because the next generation benefits from the increased standard of living, e.g. in the form of human capital investments, provided by their parents' hawking activities.

Historically, the main barrier to entry for licensed traders has been capital. Where the supply of hawking licences or plots is limited and revenue is attractive, start-up costs are increased by the additional costs of bribes to secure licences. Other capital outlay depends on the trade, e.g. the food-catering business is the easiest to penetrate as it requires small capital outlay and demand is very elastic. The slim profit margins must be compensated for by large turnover volumes to earn a comfortable net income. Food-catering is also more labour-intensive, with long hours needed for preparation[45] and sales. Women are more commonly found in food-catering, whereas men are more present in high-risk, high-profit merchandising.

At present, as part of the government's encouragement of small-scale enterprises, hawkers and petty traders are able to obtain loans from commercial banks that are guaranteed by the Credit Guarantee Corporation's Loan Fund for Hawkers and Petty Traders. First implemented in 1986 as the Special Loan Scheme for Hawkers and Petty Traders, the scheme was designed to help hawkers and petty traders obtain loans from participating commercial banks. The scheme is only open to licensed hawkers and petty traders who are members of recognized trade associations. However, not many have taken advantage of the scheme because of lack of information among the poorly-educated hawkers.

In non-food trades, a good example of simple self-employment is provided by a cobbler, who only requires a small capital outlay and easily-learned skills. Other activities such as trading textiles/clothing, pirated items, electronic goods, counterfeit luxury items and household goods, usually require more capital for the purchase of stock. Products and services in the informal sector are usually sold at lower prices than those in the formal sector, which helps to keep living costs, and thus wages, down. Lowly-paid or unpaid labour in the informal sector thus indirectly subsidizes labour elsewhere in the economy.

Petty trading can be quite lucrative relative to secondary wage work in the formal or modern economy, even if the skills involved are low-status.[46] Self-employed traders and hawkers in large metropolitan cities earn more than the poverty-line income, particularly in stable markets such as for food-catering. In poorer regions, petty trading is very competitive because many sell the same product or close substitutes. Petty trading is often a family venture. Outsiders are seldom employed unless labour requirements cannot be met by family members. Outsiders are usually already known and trusted by the employer or are highly recommended by those trusted. Employment is ethnically segmented because of the ethnic pattern of demand and the use of family labour and community-related hiring patterns.

Domestic and Other Personal Services

Structural change in the economy's labour market has resulted in a rise in market provision of domestic services. With more women entering the labour market and the break-up of extended families, women's tasks in the home are replaced or complemented by domestic appliances, family labour, cheap labour recruited from outside the family, purchased products and services. Choosing from among these alternatives depends on the relative prices of the substitutes. In developed countries where labour is expensive, many household functions have been taken over by machines (e.g. washing machines), marketed services, launderettes, restaurants and day-care centres. However, in developing countries with large pools of cheap, e.g. foreign labour available, such labour are preferred as substitutes because they are cheaper and can perform a wide range of functions, as cooking and childminding.

Until the last quarter of the last century, immigrant Chinese women in the cities found jobs as maids; over time, a group of "specialized skilled middle-aged Chinese maids" had evolved.[47] When supply dwindled with the end of such immigration after independence, and new demand for maids emerged among the nouveau riche and the upper-middle class, the void was filled by the urban poor and then by young village girls. As demand continued to rise with the increasing number of middle-class working women, supply fell due to competing demands from export-oriented manufacturing and new service employment. Also, the ethnically-segmented market (for cultural reasons) and the dwindling supply of Chinese maids due to the out-migration of Chinese women to Singapore, Chinese maids' bargaining power increased briefly until it was diluted by employment of women from other local ethnic groups (especially Indians and Malays) and foreign workers, particularly Filipino and Indonesian maids.

In domestic services, no special qualifications are needed except of the ability to cook, clean and look after children. Full-time maids do not have fixed working hours although they are usually given a day off every week. Housebound women may also offer services to other families as child minders. Again, ethnic differentials in pay are common because of the ethnically segmented customer market. The supply of Chinese women willing to be child minders is small, while the demand is high due to the higher number of middle-class working Chinese women who can afford child minders. Recent decades have seen the proliferation of child care facilities, including kindergartens, and other related services. Wages — that vary with locality, work experience and ethnicity — are the only compensation derived from their work. They get no other non-pecuniary benefits, and most employers do not contribute to the Employees' Provident Fund (EPF) or the Social Security Organization (SOCSO).

Apart from helping out in small manufacturing or repair workshops, housebound women without formal education may resort to contracting or putting-out opportunities in embroidery, tailoring, laundry and food preparation, or work as sales agents for directly-marketed home products, all of which require only limited capital outlay. Other feminized services with a high representation of women are laundry and cleaning services, beauty and hairdressing services, and tailoring. Under the putting-out system, "materials" are provided by the employer, who may himself be a subcontractor. For instance, women may be contracted to sew buttons on uniforms, or they may be given patterns to sew according to instructions. They are piece-rated, but the rates vary with locality and ethnicity, which is used to signal skill. The proportion of direct employment is small while the proportion of females employed is large because the putting-out system is conducive to the use of otherwise housebound female labour. The putting-out system is also fairly common in food-catering and tailoring, where women predominate, although the masters of the crafts are mainly male. Thus, a salaried master tailor engages in a job which involves designing, measurement and cutting patterns, while the more tedious parts of the process, such as sewing, are done by cheaper labour, including women or apprentices, either in-house or after subcontracting out. In the beauty and hair-care industry, workers are mostly wage employees and own-account workers.

Although apprenticeships used to be the only channel through which particular crafts were learnt, e.g. in tailoring, beauty and hair-care, repairs and maintenance services, the move has increasingly been towards skill acquisition through formally and institutionally-run courses, which are shorter in duration than apprenticeships system. After completing these courses, workers can immediately become self-employed or wage employees at the going market-wage. This formal acquisition of skills in special schools has reduced ethnic segmentation in the acquisition of practical skills because skill acquisition is no longer tied to apprenticed employment in small enterprises which are largely Chinese-owned and controlled.

Conclusion

This chapter has focused on the employment of secondary labour, either as wage employees in the quasi-modern core of traditional services, or in wage employment, self-employment and unpaid family employment in the peripheral segment of traditional services. All traditional services, including services in both the formal and informal sectors, seem to share an occupational structure where secondary and casual labour categories feature prominently. Although ethnic segmentation, and, to a lesser degree, gender segmentation of the workforce persist, they are not vehemently contested because of the low status and pay associated with these services. In areas where income and/or labour status are significantly better, ethnic rivalry is keener, especially if the state plays an active role in the distribution of income-generating sources such as operating permits in passenger and freight transport. Owing to the unequal distribution of income, those with sufficient capital may gain access to licences through indirect and illegal means, boosting the price of entry into informal self-employment. Due to loopholes in institutional arrangements, the higher costs are usually passed onto workers since consumers usually have some degree of protection in the form of state regulation of fares and rates. The end result of competition in a regulated product market, but unregulated labour market is greater downward pressure on wages to reduce costs.

Job access does not depend on formal qualifications, but on job experience and acquired "industry-specific or job-specific skills", and a combination of extra-economic factors such as kinship, clan and other social ties. Traditional firms coming under modern management use a combination of institutional and informal rules established within the wider industry in their recruitment, promotion and pay policies. Self-employment depends on the availability of financial capital. Some types of self-employment require considerable start-up capital even if the technical competence required is minimal, e.g. in transportation or in petty trading of expensive merchandise.

Although white-collar secondary-primary labour is not common in traditional services, the multitude of small firms in this sector (largely Chinese-owned and managed, with Chinese dialects as the main mediums of communication) is a shrinking option for white-collar employment for some workers whose educational qualifications have been rejected by modern services, for instance, workers educated in Chinese schools and whose English or Malay is not up to the standard required in the more prestigious modern sector services. Ethnically-segmented employment by small firms has been increasingly broken up by changes in demand, labour supply changes and the cost implications of ethnic discrimination. Competitive pressures to lower labour costs have reduced barriers to entry for cheaper non-Chinese labour, e.g. foreign, Indian and Malay labour, even in small Chinese owned firms. Economic, social and political changes have resulted in many small businesses being replaced by better-organized larger firms where job access is through formal channels. In these quasi-modern firms, educational qualifications and ascriptive principles have become rationing devices for jobs which actually do not require much formal schooling, but rather on-the-job training. Ethnic hiring (in the form of wage and job discrimination against non-Chinese labour) has become less important to such firms compared to the relentless pressure for lower labour costs.

The skills associated with secondary employment are often poorly compensated, not because the job is low-skilled (with respect to technical competence), but because these skills have come to be economically defined as low-skilled due to the potentially unlimited labour supply, even in the short-run. Unlike employment contracts where output is not specified, "simple metering" of output in some sectors leads to flexible compensation systems where a substantial proportion of income is based on factors beyond the workers' control, e.g. volume of sales, mileage and number of trips. Basic wages also tend to be daily-rated or hourly-rated. There are wide dispersions in wage rates and non-pecuniary benefits, particularly in non-unionized firms. Pay and other work benefits depend substantially on firm size and locality.

Ports of entry for blue-collar employment are usually at the bottom, with limited vertical mobility. The jobs are usually dead-end jobs, except in some industries, such as hotels and tourism, where vertical mobility can occur through industry-wide transformation. Inter-industry mobility is limited by industry-specific skills learnt on-the-job. Intra-industry movement is limited by the ports of entry situated at the bottom of each category, and seniority-related automatic annual increments negotiated by unions for those working in unionized firms. Promotion to better positions is rare because the nature of the secondary-labour occupational pyramid is essentially bottom-heavy.

Market structure is very concentrated in some traditional services, with the core firms, usually market leaders, generating a disproportionate amount of the industries' revenue and profits. Although they employ elite-primary and secondary-primary workers, the wages and non-pecuniary benefits for these workers are often less favourable than the wages of their counterparts in modern services, except for highly-specialized jobs requiring substantial experience. Permanent workers, including secondary workers, in core firms are usually unionized and better paid than workers in peripheral firms. However, the terms and conditions of employment for secondary workers in core firms are still less favourable than for similar jobs in modern services, particularly government services. Wage employment, even in core firms, bears the characteristics of secondary employment, i.e. low status, low pay, and little vertical mobility.

Even core firms resort to the use of cheaper, non-unionized, part-time, temporary and casual labour, to whom the risks of economic uncertainty can be easily transferred. The easy availability of cheap secondary labour, especially marginalized, casual and temporary labour, often holds back technical upgrading in traditional services, and continues to exert downward pressure on wages in the face of unlimited supplies of labour untrained in any basic industrial skills. The technical change that has occurred has involved both deskilling and reskilling. This facilitates the use of unprotected temporary, casual and contract labour to complement the concept of labour flexibility preached by the government and some captains of industry. Although some informal sector workers (including family labour) and employees in small non-unionized firms in some services in the formal sector may technically be covered by the country's selective minimum wage legislation, difficulties in monitoring many scattered firms have resulted in many unreported violations.

Urban informal sector employment serves as a sponge in absorbing excess labour since entry into the less capitalized informal sector is easier than entry into the formal sector with its many institutional rules. As employers in the formal economy are, by nature, more selective and prefer the young, marginalized older workers and married women with few educational qualifications have to seek non-wage incomes in the informal economy. Except for capital requirements and customary rules, there are few barriers to entry in to petty trading and hawking, the most ubiquitous informal economic activities. Again, barriers to entry largely involve capital requirements, which depend on the type of activity; however, this type of entry barrier can overcome with financial aid from the state. Where profit margins are small, sales volume must be large to make ends meet. However, increasing competition among those selling similar products or close substitutes has led to slimmer profit margins and lower net incomes. Nevertheless, income from self-employment in such cases generally exceeds the poverty-line income. Informal sector employment may involve: (i) full-time employment, (ii) part-time employment, to supplement household income, which would otherwise be insufficient since many household heads who hold jobs in the formal economy also need supplementary secondary wage employment despite the low pay, (iii) transitional employment while awaiting job opportunities in the formal economy. By providing goods and services at lower prices, often by extensively using lowly-paid or unpaid family labour, the informal economy indirectly subsidizes lowly-paid secondary workers in the formal economy, involving a vicious circle of causation.

Women are typically crowded into services historically stereotyped as feminine, e.g. secretarial and clerical occupations, housekeeping and other personal and domestic services. With its flexible work schedule, the informal sector makes it easier for women to carry out dual roles as housewife and income-earner more easily. The dynamics of labour organization in personal services have evolved and changed with structural changes in the economy. As more services are provided by the market, the demand for older services will be replaced by demand for newer services.

Where demand for and supply of labour is still segmented, job access and pay often depend on one's labour market status, particularly the subjective and ascriptive aspects. Pay differentials arise from the different labour status and socio-economic standing of ethnic segments, reflected in the minimum supply prices (wages) of workers as well as employers' ability to pay. Unlike modern services, where government requirements have led to economic premiums for some types of Malay labour, Malay labour generally costs relatively less compared to Chinese labour in non-regulated services, reflecting their differential supply prices and the segmented nature of both labour supply and demand.

4

Modern Services Employment

This chapter discusses the impact of services market structures and historical and socio-cultural conditioning on the modern service labour market in Malaysia. Various mechanisms of labour recruitment, compensation and mobility are examined, highlighting similarities and differences in the internal labour markets of public and private modern services. The origins of segmentation in modern services are analyzed, and contrasted with the dynamics of segmentation, which have evolved over time to accommodate changes in the political, social and cultural environment. Also examined are the effects of technological change and new forms of labour management on the employment structure in an open economy.

Modern Services

For the purposes of the study, in contrast to traditional services discussed in Chapter 3, modern services are those activities that:

(i)   have a high component of wage employment, especially protected wage work (protected wage work refers to employment in the unionized sector or employment covered by the country's labour laws);

(ii)   have modern organizational management;

(iii) utilize a higher level of technology relative to the rest of the economy;

(iv)   require substantial capital, meaning finance;

(v)   have highly structured product and labour markets; firms are usually large, with well-defined internal markets where institutional rules govern the employment and compensation of labour; labour markets tend to be institutionally regulated, often resulting in higher barriers to entry;

(vi) offer better pecuniary and non-pecuniary terms of employment, such as better pay, promotion prospects, stable working hours, paid annual leave, employment security, employee perks above the statutory minimum, such as medical benefits, housing and car loans at subsidized rates, and clearly defined working hours; and

(vii) employ significantly more elite-primary and secondary-primary labour.

By this definition and considering the characteristics of Malaysian services (Khong, 1991: Appendix 2), modern services in Malaysia comprise services such as finance and business services, and all government services, including government-owned transport and communications services, such as railway and postal services, government-operated community and social services, and the quasi-privatized utilities, telecommunications and air transport services.[1] The structure and organization of employment in the recently-privatized services combine characteristics of public sector employment and employment in large institutional private services.

Public sector services are of two types: (i) services that use a relatively high proportion of secondary and manual labour, e.g. rail transport, port activities, public utilities, (ii) services that utilize a high proportion of elite-primary and secondary-primary workers such as professional/technical, administrative and clerical labour, e.g. health, educational and administrative services.

Private modern services may be divided into stable and unstable segments. The stable component of private modern services may be sub-divided into the large institutional, regulated and unionized services, such as financial services and the non-unionized professional and business services, mainly consisting of a multitude of small and medium-sized firms, which are largely self-regulated. The unstable segment consists of independent, self-employed secondary-primary workers in the insurance, brokerage and real estate business. Independent self-employed professionals enjoy many benefits usually associated with stable formal-sector employment because of their status and skills. Usually such workers do not immediately start their careers as independent professionals, but make the choice to do so in mid-career after obtaining valuable on-the-job training and experience besides cultivating business contacts. Their skills and experience make it easier for them to be re-absorbed into wage employment should the need arise.

In contrast, secondary-primary workers in the insurance or brokerage sectors experience the uncertainties normally associated with traditional informal self-employment. In addition, recent encouragement of labour flexibility may have led to a secondary segment in the modern services workforce, linked to the traditional sector via subcontractors, and thus subject to the same vulnerabilities as traditional informal employment.

The institutional and regulated segments of modern services — such as government services, quasi-government firms such as public enterprises (including "non-financial public enterprises" once known as off-budget agencies),[2] newly-privatized services, and the banking industry, are characterized by internal markets with well-defined rules for recruitment, pay and mobility. These internal markets are less affected by conditions in the external labour market.

State intervention in the allocation of labour in the finance sector occurs through the central bank and other government regulatory bodies. With the exception of stock-broking and other securities, overseen by the Securities Commission since the early 1990s, all financial institutions come under the jurisdiction of the central bank (see Khong, 1991: Statistical Annexes 9 and 10). Through the Banking and Financial Institutions Act (BAFIA) of 1989 and various amendments to the relevant financial legislation, the central bank had increasingly tightened regulatory control over financial services until the 1990s, when its role was diminished by financial liberalization as well as some proliferation of authority. After the 1997–98 financial crisis, however, its role was greatly strengthened briefly until the authorities re-initiated liberalization initiatives once again.

Commercial banks are the oldest and largest employer in financial services, followed by insurance companies, finance companies, and merchant banks. According to central bank data, employment in the sector continued to grow rapidly from the 1960s until the mid-1980s until the banking crisis of the late 1980s. The non-bank financial sector grew rapidly in the early and mid-1990s until the 1997–98 financial crisis adversely affected employment throughout the financial sector. Bumiputera employment generally grew faster than non-Bumiputera employment, while insurance services employment probably grew more slowly than the rest of the financial sector. Although some blurring of the demarcation among their services has increased competition, the finance sector is still hierarchically ranked by market power, financial strength and growth prospects. Although the stock-broking industry is outside the central bank's regulatory powers, corporatization of the industry has involved a greater degree of regulatory co-operation between the Kuala Lumpur Stock Exchange (KLSE), the Securities Commission (SC) and the central bank, Bank Negara Malaysia (BNM). In the professions, small sole proprietorships or partnerships are more common because of the smaller start-up capital required.[3] The market structure is characterized by oligopolistic competition among a multitude of small- and medium-sized firms on the one hand, and concentration of business in the hands of the largest market leaders (usually large transnational partnerships or joint ventures with foreign companies) on the other.[4] Core or primary firms (market leaders) and small secondary firms cater to different market niches. Sometimes, change in industrial structure is brought about by external forces. For instance, corporatized firms in the securities industry caters to big corporate or institutional customers, while smaller firms cater to individuals and small businesses. Increasingly, however, business is concentrated in big firms due to global economic trends and the ability of big firms to marginalize small ones on the basis of their financial strength, their better international connections, and the cumulative advantages of large firm size.

Unlike the institutionalized industries, the stable, but non-unionized segments of private modern services, consisting of smaller, regionally-dispersed firms, employ a relatively smaller proportion of wage employees[5] who is distributed across core firms (usually market leaders) and small secondary firms. The market for these professions is comparable to closed craft guilds in which professional associations or governing bodies regulate the supply of professional workers to maintain the prestige and standards associated with their calling, thus justifying income differentials between members and non-members. Wages, career prospects and other terms and conditions of work in non-unionized professional and business services vary with whether workers are employed by core firms or secondary firms. The terms and conditions of work differ between these two segments, mainly because of the effects of firm size and market share on firms' abilities to pay. Because of the high incomes, career prospects and status offered by modern services, the sector has been the subject of contentious professional employment "restructuring" under the NEP.

Occupational Structure

As part of its modernization effort, Malaysia has been trying to enlarge modern services employment because of the greater proportion of elite-primary and secondary-primary occupations in these industries. The vast majority of the modern services workforce has consisted of these two labour categories, much higher than for the urban economy and especially for the whole economy. The proportion of elite-primary professional and technical workers has been greater in the public sector compared to private modern services, mainly due to the government's dominant role in the health and education sector. The proportions of secondary-primary clerical as well as administrative and managerial workers are much greater in private modern services than in the public sector. The public sector also accounts for a significant proportion of secondary manual labour.

Owing to their rather similar occupational structure, the labour markets for private modern services and government services affect each other in two different ways. Firstly, although employment growth and wage determination in each sector may be determined by very different factors, these two sectors employ and compete for the same type of labour. In tight labour markets, the public sector's hiring and remuneration levels impinge on the private sector, although the converse is not true. Secondly, the two sectors are disjoint in the sense that non-competing groups exist within each labour category, segmented by ethnicity and, to a lesser degree, by gender. Although similarly qualified in the educational sense, these non-competing groups are allocated to private modern services and government employment according to the respective hiring standards of each sector, which may change over time.

The structure of labour demand shapes future labour supply and the education choices made by individuals. Initial access to various sectors generally determines subsequent labour market status. After a particular point, inter-sectoral movement is constrained by work attitudes or traits associated with particular sectors, and by the costs of movement, since the points of entry into particular occupations are usually at the bottom of that occupational category.

Employment Growth

At its peak, public sector employment amounted to 896,335 in 1985 (Khong, 1991), i.e. accounting for over a quarter (26 per cent) of non-agricultural employment, compared to 1,857,000 in private modern services in 1987; 1985 and 1986 years of unusually slow economic growth. The freeze on government employment since 1982 and privatization from the mid-1980s has kept public sector employment under 900,000 since then. With the rapid growth of private services since then, the share of public services has declined significantly in the last two decades.

The size of public sector employment has no easily identifiable link to income and population growth (Edgren, 1988; Heller and Tait, 1984). While total government employment per capita tends to increase as per capita income rises, state and local government expenditure per capita as well as general public sector employment may not be significantly influenced by population size.[6] Historical developments in the public sectors of developing countries suggest that public sector employment has been used as a job creation strategy when the pace of development in the modern sector is insufficient to absorb the supply of educated youths (usually graduates) who have certain expectations of the types of jobs they would be willing to accept.[7] In other words, public sector employment may be politically-motivated. In addition, the state is not neutral in its relations with all segments of society; hence, vested interest groups or coalitions of groups vie with one another to influence government decisions in their favour.[8] Correspondingly, the preferences of potential employees are governed by prestige, historical and cultural factors, employment security, as well as wages.[9]

The public sector has always been an important source of non-agricultural employment. Despite its comparatively large size, owing to the economic importance of Malaya to the British, public sector employment as a proportion of total employment continued to grow after independence in 1957, and especially after the launch of the New Economic Policy (NEP) in 1970 before being reined in from the early 1980s. During the years of easy oil and commodity revenues in the 1970s and in the early 1980s, public sector employment burgeoned. In 1980, the government embarked on a large-scale recruitment drive called *Operasi Isi Penuh* ("fill up [vacancies] operation") to fill about 42,000 vacancies. By the time rapid expansion stopped with an official austerity drive (*Jimat Cermat*) from June 1982 following the April 1982 election and the end of the oil and commodity boom, 159,246 employees had been added to the public sector.

The rapid growth of the Malaysian public sector in the 1970s was largely due to efforts to rapidly increase Malay modern sector employment through public sector expansion. Rising public revenues coincided with the emergence of an educated Malay middle-class, whose job expectations had been raised by earlier government successes in opening up urban job opportunities. Because of the development of vested interests and changes in the structure of labour supply, increases in public sector employment were almost irreversible, particularly when the rest of the economy could not be transformed quickly enough to absorb the excess supply of educated labour.

Public sector employment, encompassing federal, state, local and statutory bodies, employs four major categories of workers. Category A comprises workers with at least a university degree; Category B consists of workers with at least a HSC [Higher School Certificate or Advanced (A1) levels] or a diploma; Category C are holders of the MCE [Malaysian Certificate of Education or Ordinary (O) levels] or its equivalent; and Category D comprises industrial and manual workers who usually have less than the MCE. In the classification adopted for this study, Category A (and, to a lesser extent, B) can be categorized as elite-primary workers, category C (and occasionally, B as secondary-primary workers, and category D as secondary workers.

All government employees are subject to the same set of work rules and procedures. Enforcement and implementation of the NEP led to public sector employment growing at an annual average of 7.3 per cent between 1970 and 1982, before budgetary constraints forced an austerity drive that slowed down subsequent employment growth (Table 4.1).[10] The largest increases were

Table 4.1 Malaysia: Public Employment as Share of Non-agricultural
Labour Force, 1957–2004

Year	Public sector employees	Total employed labour force	Non-agricultural workforce	% share of public sector in total employment	% share of public sector in non-agricultural employment
1957	200,000	2,126,000	881,000	9.4	22.7
1970	396,600	3,396,000	1,620,000	11.9	24.5
1980	740,000	4,816,900	2,905,900	15.4	25.5
1990	850,200	6,686,000	4,948,000	12.7	17.2
1995	872,000	7,915,400	6,486,700	11.0	13.4
2004	681,200	9,986,000	8,510,200	6.8	8.0

Sources: 1957–85 figures are from Supian (1988); later figures are from *Economic Report, 1988/1989*. Non-agricultural workforce is calculated from Ismail (1986: Table 14), *Economic Report*, and *Population Census, 1957*. Calculated with data from *Malaysia: Yearbook of Statistics, 2006*.

registered by employees in categories A and B in line with the NEP's aim of creating a Malay middle class.[11]

Private modern services have also grown more rapidly in terms of output and employment since the mid-1980s. The growth of private modern services is linked to structural changes in the economy, i.e. to service a modernizing economy where per capita income and business output are increasing rapidly. Table 4.1 shows that the number of full-time employees in the finance and banking sector increased from only 5,147 employees[12] in 1957 until the late 1980s before declining, especially from the late 1990s.[13]

From its original role of financing the trade of Malaya's open economy, the banking industry has expanded its role to include consumer retail banking to finance house and motor vehicle ownership, and loans to entrepreneurs. Financial intermediaries — such as merchant banks, discount and brokerage houses — offer specialized consultancy services to the expanding corporate sector and capital market. The general insurance business flourished with the increase in business activities and personal asset ownership, while the life insurance business expanded rapidly rising standards of living. Except for those without any formal collateral or credit-standing, improved security-awareness led to a movement away from traditional forms of savings and consumer loans such as the "tontine" and pawnbrokers.[14]

Segmentation

The workforce in Malaysian modern services is characterized ethnic segmentation, with political and economic power influencing the distribution of employment in modern services, albeit differently, over time (Chapter 2). The colonial legacy of an ethnic-quota system left government services with a significant Malay workforce. With the NEP, Malay representation in public services was further increased. In contrast, non-Malays were over-represented in private modern services. Over time, segmentation in modern services has evolved in response to the changing economic, social and political environment.

Ethnic Segmentation

In the colonial era, peasant Malays, isolated in villages with their own vernacular and religious education, lacked the education opportunities that could open access to modern sector employment. As part of the politically expedient deal between the Malay ruling class and the British colonialists, compliant members of the Malay "aristocracy" were co-opted into the lower rungs of the colonial administrative machinery, the Malay Administrative Service (MAS). Selection into the more prestigious Malayan Civil Service (MCS) was never really meritocratic.[15]

In line with official policy, other ethnic communities who settled in the Malay states had little formal right to administrative positions and political influence. The MAS was protected in two respects: firstly, access was limited to Malays, and initially, only to the elite. Secondly, while Malay officers were offered some protection, position and status, they were given little real power, as noted in Chapter 2.[16] While Malay officers could technically be promoted to the MCS, the highest Class 1A positions were not within reach, ostensibly due to their limited education and ability.[17] Limiting employment in the MAS to the aristocracy was justified on the grounds that the MAS opened special opportunities in the colonial government for Malays, and thus partially restored the traditional privileges and role of the Malay ruling class.[18]

As independence became imminent, the colonial government accommodated the demands of various Malayan ethnic groups for employment opportunities in the civil service.[19] The government historically justified its restrictive hiring policy towards non-Malays in the higher echelons of the administration with the claim that it was that Malays could only in the public sector hold their own against the other ethnic group. In protest, non-Malay university graduates had protested to the British Parliament in 1911,[20] leading to the formation of the Straits Settlements Civil Service (SSCS) in 1933, into which non-Malays could be admitted. While similar to the Malayan Administrative Service in its bias against non-British officers, the SSCS required higher minimum educational qualifications for admission, but officers in the SSCS were not eligible for promotion into the Malayan Civil Service.

Under the Malayanization scheme introduced in the 1950s, British expatriate officers were replaced by promoted Malay officers as places in the bureaucracy were opened to non-aristocratic Malays and other ethnic groups. It was not until 1953 as decolonization seemed imminent that the administrative branch of the civil service was finally opened to non-Malays,[21] but with a quota of four Malays for every non-Malay. Qualified Malays were given preference over other applicants as selection was based on minimum entry qualifications, and not on the highest level of educational attainment of applicants. Tilman (1964) suggests that the heavy Malay representation in government services requiring a liberal general education background encouraged Malay University students to seek such an education. In contrast, non-Malays aspiring to a government service career were better off taking the engineering, medicine, sciences or some professional qualification as non-Malays had better chances of finding employment in the technical and professional services where there was a shortage of qualified Malays (Tilman, 1964).

With the implementation of the NEP, much larger numbers of Malays gained opportunities — at home and abroad — for university studies, especially for professional and technical courses; hence, even the professional and technical services have become increasingly Malay. Although there is now even greater Malay representation at the higher levels of the public sector, Malay ethnic preference remains entrenched though some middle and upper-class Malays who benefited from the NEP's pro-Malay educational and employment programmes now privately agree to some erosion, if not the elimination of their privileges.

Ethnic segmentation in private modern services can be traced to the inter-relationships between the structure of the product market, and the structure of labour demand and supply. Historically, private modern services were concentrated in urban centres where non-Malays lived. These urban non-Malays had better access to urban schools providing English medium education which equipped them for jobs in the private sector which the British and, to a lesser extent, the Chinese, owned and controlled (see Puthucheary, 1960; Tan, 1982; Lim, 1980). Rural Malays had little access to bank credit, relying mostly on informal credit from suppliers, middlemen and other informal creditors such as pawnbrokers, who charged exorbitant interest rates and required substantial security. Malays comprised only 5.1 per cent of the 5,147 employees in banks and financial institutions in 1957, the year of independence, Chinese 49.3 per cent, Indian 40.8 per cent and others 4.7 per cent, also reflecting the tendency for British employers to hire ethnic Indians and "Others", mainly Eurasians, who also had relatively greater English medium education compared to Chinese.

Some existing commercial banks were founded before the Second World War by Chinese capital to serve specific sub-ethnic or dialect communities. Others were set up in the 1950s and early 1960s after independence before affirmative action initiatives began in the banking sector. Ethnic segmentation in bank staffing reflected the ethnically-skewed nature of bank customers, and consequently, the ethnically-segmented nature of bank products market. This affected employment patterns because the working languages of many small-scale businessmen were Chinese dialects, rather than English or Malay. These community banks relied on good faith and personal relations as well as what would now be called "social capital" for business. Malay participation in the banking and financial services had increased significantly by 1983 (see Table 4.2), and is believed to have greatly increased further since then with the further consolidation of the industry under Malay control since then.

Table 4.2 Ethnic Distribution of Bank Employees by Control, 31 March 1983

Ethnicity of bank ownership	*Malay*	*Chinese*	*Indian*	*Others*	*Total*	*Number*
Malay-controlled Banks						
Malayan Banking	52.0	40.7	6.7	0.6	100.0	5,186
Kwong Yik Bank	49.9	45.0	4.5	0.6	100.0	706
Chinese-controlled Banks						
Overseas Chinese Banking Corp.	25.7	66.0	7.1	1.2	100.0	1,197
Development & Commercial Bank	36.2	61.0	2.8	0.0	100.0	937
Public Bank	37.7	58.6	3.3	0.3	100.0	n.a.
Indian-controlled Bank						
United Asian Bank	28.0	15.8	55.6	0.6	100.0	1,387

Source: Unpublished statistics from the Malaysian Commercial Banks' Association.

Besides the British-owned banks, the banks which later merged to become the United Asian Bank were seen as the banks for Indians, with larger proportions of Indian employees; the Overseas Chinese Banking Corporation, the Overseas Union Bank, Public Bank, and Development and Commercial Bank, had large Chinese clienteles, and much a larger proportions of Chinese employees with a working knowledge of Mandarin Chinese and typically, a few Southern Chinese dialects. With NEP ownership changes proceeding fastest in the banking sector in the 1970s, the government-controlled banks, as well as banks with substantial Malay ownership, e.g. Bank Bumiputra and Malayan Banking and Kwong Yik Bank (a Chinese bank later taken over by Malay interests), soon recruited a larger proportion of Malay employees, together with the rest of the banking sector to comply with NEP ethnic employment requirements. Similarly, finance companies' historically large Chinese clientele is reflected in the significant dominance of ethnic Chinese employees.

Ethnic identification remains strong today after more than half a century of affirmative action efforts since the early 1950s, and three and a half decades since the NEP began. There has been a significant ethnic redistribution of ownership in the banking sector, as it soon became the sector in which Malay ownership advanced most over the 1970s. This was facilitated by close government regulation as well as the periodic bank failures which have allowed government bail-out operations to be used to advance Malay ownership. This happened with the banking failures of the 1960s, when Malayan Banking came under government ownership and Bank Bumiputra was set up by the government to advance the Malay position in banking.

The advent of the NEP in the 1970s saw greater encouragement of both government and later private Malay ownership of banks. The bank failures of the mid-1980s offered another important opportunity for closer government regulation, but it also coincided with a time when the government was withdrawing from public ownership of economic assets, allowing politically influential bankers to enhance their positions. The 1997–98 financial crisis provided yet another opportunity, but this time accompanied by a reversal of the earlier privatization policy. A 1999 proposal by the then Minister of Finance to consolidate the entire banking sector (including finance companies and merchant banks) into six banking groups met with fierce public opposition, which led the Prime Minister to compromise with ten groups instead, just before the general election when the ruling party took a battering (Jomo, 2001). Developments since then have seen the consolidation of the banking sector around fewer politically-connected groups. All these changes in ownership and control were accompanied by very significant advancement of Malay employment in the banking sector, with corresponding marginalization of the ethnic Indian presence, and significant reduction of the ethnic Chinese presence. The recent downsizing of employment in this sector over the last two decade has adversely affected all ethnic groups, albeit consolidating the new pattern.

In the less regulated insurance services, the influence of the ethnic patterns of demand on the ethnic pattern of employment in the industry is striking. Owing to Islamic teachings, which discourage interest-based financial arrangements, the insurance industry is largely non-Malay. Apart from religion, the relatively greater wealth and income of Chinese — including greater ownership of businesses, houses and motor vehicles — also implies greater general insurance coverage needs.[22]

Professional and business services have been under close government scrutiny for their ostensibly slow progress in meeting NEP ownership and employment targets. In 1985, Malays accounted for only 11.5 per cent of the private sector accounting workforce, 27.0 per cent of the private legal workforce and 34.7 per cent of the architectural workforce (Khong, 1991: Table 5.5). Ethnic segmentation has been mainly due to the lack of skilled professional Malays caused by a lag in the supply of Malay professionals, many of whom were absorbed into government services or the public sector. Supply was further restricted by the educational preferences of many Malays for the liberal arts, with a government career in mind; many had historically been unable to infiltrate the private sector with its cultural barriers to entry.[23]

Unlike other private modern services, the air transport and telecommunications services have a relatively high Malay presence as these industries were government owned until 1985 and 1987 respectively. Telecommunications has a significant proportion of Indians who have historically been over-represented from the outset under colonialism in the Public Works Department, Telecoms Department and other public utilities departments, while air transport has a significant proportion of Chinese and Indians because of the greater technical requirements of the industry.

Dynamics of Ethnic Segmentation

Post-1970 developments saw more pronounced ethnic preferences in public sector employment recruitment as the very nature of public sector employment has changed, with the expansion of education opportunities for all, especially Malays, and not just the better off.[24] Rapid economic and population growth necessitated a tremendous increase in the provision of basic services, which expanded public sector employment and fitted well with the government's aim of using public sector employment as a redistributive mechanism.

The Malay position in the public sector was significantly advanced during the 1970s. Their share of new public sector jobs increased from 67.6 per cent in the 1970–77 period to 82.7 per cent during 1977–80, before declining to 72.4 per cent in the 1980–85 period, after which the public sector has experienced much expansion of employment. As Table 4.3 shows, Malays accounted for

Table 4.3 Malaysia: Malay Share of Government Jobs Created, 1970–94

	1970–77	*1977–80*	*1980–85*	*1985–90*	*1991–94*
No. of government jobs created	162,200	91,800	161,300	88,800	67,269
No. of Malays employed	109,600	75,900	116,800	65,200	52,218
Malay share (%)	67.6	82.7	72.4	73.4	77.6

73.4 per cent of the fewer government jobs created during 1986-1990 and 77.6 per cent during 1991–94. Malay participation is even higher in the armed forces and police and in public enterprises, with 79.6 per cent in 1980, and as much as 94.0 per cent in MARA (Majlis Amanah Rakyat) (Khong, 1991). Public sector employment (including in public enterprises) has often been obligatory for the mainly Malay recipients of government scholarships for tertiary education. Non-Malays find their way into public sector employment, mainly into the professional or technical services, at a slower rate than before, as the supply of qualified Malays in these areas gradually rose and the public sector expansion of the 1970s and early 1980s gave way to consolidation and even some down-sizing especially following privatization for over a decade from the mid-1980s.

In pursuing the NEP's goal of greater Malay participation in managerial occupations, the government provided greater education and employment opportunities, especially to Malays. Private investments in higher education also escalated. However, demand could not keep pace with the over-expansion of supply, especially the supply of generalist liberal arts graduates, for whom the major demand came from the public sector. With the downturn in government revenues due to the oil and primary commodity price slumps in the early and mid-1980s, the ability of the government (already the country's largest single employer) to act as employer of last resort, particularly for Malay graduates, was constrained.[25] Private modern services, the most dynamic sector in terms of income and skill generation, were exhorted to take up the slack, by recruiting for the educated middle-class, especially Malays. Private modern services found such ethnic restructuring harder when overall growth was slow, especially when employment was shrinking. After a decade of rapid growth and affirmative action during the 1970s, ethnic Malay employment in modern private sector services had risen considerably by 1980 and has continued to increase since then (Tables 4.4a, 4.4b and 4.4c).

Table 4.4a Employment Distribution and Average Annual Earnings in Professional Services and Stock-broking Houses by Occupational Status, Gender and Ethnicity, 1985

Occupational group	Total	Male strata	Female strata	Female %	Bumi %	Bumi strata	Non-Bumi strata	Average annual salary (RM)
Stockbroking								
Professional	14.9	19.9	8.0	22.2	27.2	12.4	16.0	46,300
Technical/supervisory	4.7	5.5	3.7	32.4	30.0	4.4	4.9	17,865
Clerical	73.6	66.7	83.4	47.0	31.2	70.7	75.2	6,542
General & manual	6.1	7.3	4.4	29.7	60.4	12.5	3.9	4,681
Part-time	0.6	0.6	0.6	40.9	72.7	1.4	0.2	3,273
Total	100.0	100.0	100.0	41.5	32.5	100.0	100.0	12,961
N = absolute numbers	3,590	2,100	1,490	n.a.	n.a.	1,162	2,428	n.a.
Accounting								
Professional workers	19.2	24.2	14.6	39.1	8.0	13.2	19.9	19,135
Technical/supervisory	9.7	11.5	8.0	42.6	6.9	6.5	11.5	10,443
Clerical	56.8	41.2	71.6	64.9	10.3	50.1	57.2	6,374
General & manual	3.9	5.7	2.3	30.0	27.8	27.3	9.3	4,174
Part-time	2.0	2.1	1.9	53.6	15.0	2.9	2.2	2,507
Total	100.0	100.0	100.0	51.6	11.6	100.0	100.0	9,282
N = absolute numbers	9,436	4,565	4,871	n.a.	n.a.	925	7,061	n.a.

Working proprietors and active business partners = 730, of whom only 5.5% were women.

(continued overleaf)

Table 4.4a (continued)

Occupational group	Total	Male strata	Female strata	Female %	Bumi %	Bumi strata	Non-Bumi strata	Average annual salary (RM)
Law								
Professional workers	7.3	9.2	5.5	40.1	10.0	2.7	8.9	23,230
Technical/supervisory	0.2	0.3	0.1	25.0	10.5	0.1	0.2	13,083
Clerical	69.6	49.8	87.2	66.3	26.7	69.0	70.3	6,306
General & manual	8.5	13.8	3.7	23.1	34.6	27.4	19.2	3,763
Part-time	1.2	1.5	1.0	44.7	18.0	0.8	1.4	2,979
Total	100.0	100.0	100.0	52.9	27.0	100.0	100.0	7,441
N = absolute numbers	11,350	5,343	6,007	n.a.	n.a.	2,733	7,373	n.a.

Working proprietors and active business partners = 1,485, of whom only 9.0% were women.

Occupational group	Total	Male strata	Female strata	Female %	Bumi %	Bumi strata	Non-Bumi strata	Average annual salary (RM)
Architecture								
Professional workers	15.7	20.1	5.6	9.3	32.2	13.9	15.5	37,321
Technical/supervisory	47.5	52	37.3	23.6	34.6	48.5	48.8	10,712
Clerical	15.7	4.4	41.8	80.2	28.5	13.4	18.0	7,646
General & manual	7.0	7.3	6.4	27.3	43.0	18.7	13.2	4,297
Part-time	5.2	4.3	7.3	42.4	39.4	5.6	4.5	4,166
Total	100.0	100.0	100.0	30.1	34.7	100.0	100.0	13,912
N = absolute numbers	4,181	2,922	1,259	n.a.	n.a.	1,205	2,264	n.a.

Working proprietors and active business partners = 349, of whom only 1.7% were women.

Table 4.4a (continued)

Occupational group	Total	Male strata	Female strata	Female (%)	Average annual salary (RM)
Engineering					
Professional workers	27.0	36.4	6.5	6.6	35,353
Technical/supervisory	44.5	45.7	41.7	26.5	11,984
Clerical	14.7	3.4	43.2	83.4	8,428
General & manual	6.9	7.3	5.7	23.7	4,673
Part-time	3.3	3.6	2.6	22.2	3,217
Total	100.0	100.0	100.0	28.3	17,340
N = absolute numbers	7,620	5,462	2,158	n.a.	n.a.

Working proprietors and active business partners = 192, of whom only 0.5% were women.

Sources: Calculated from the *Census of Selected Service Industries, 1985* and *Census of Professional and Institutional Establishments, 1985*; Bumi and non-bumi figures are calculated from Birks and Hamzah (1988: Statistical Annex 6a and 6b).

Table 4.4b Employment Distribution and Average Annual Earnings in
Professional Services and Stock-broking Houses by
Occupational Status and Gender, 1992

Occupational group	Total	Male strata	Female strata	% Female	Average annual salary (RM)
Stock-broking					
Professional	14.7	18.8	9.6	28.4	69,488
Technical/supervisory	12.1	11.8	12.3	44.3	26,450
Clerical	57.3	51.8	64.2	48.9	11,181
General & manual	7.1	8.8	4.9	30.8	8,576
Part-time	0.9		1.5	63.9	5,967
Total	100.0	100.0	100.0	473.6	23,691
Numbers	6,104		2,664	n.a.	n.a.
Accounting					
Professional workers	10.2	14.1	7.1	38.5	37,497
Technical/supervisory	11.4	12.5	10.5	45.5	12,494
Clerical	50.4	33.3	64.1	70.6	7,313
General & manual	3.0	4.9	1.6	28.9	5,406
Part-time	2.3	2.0	2.5	60.3	2,810
Total	100.0	100.0	100.0	55.5	11,312
Numbers	12,794	5,666	7,104	n.a.	n.a.

Working proprietors and active business partners = 1,023, of whom only 8.5% were women.

Law					
Professional workers	9.5	11.6	7.9	49.2	29,952
Technical/supervisory	0.3	0.4	0.2	43.6	15,400
Clerical	65.6	44.4	80.8	71.9	8,321
General & manual	7.9	14.1	3.5	25.5	5,074
Part-time	2.9	3.5	2.6	50.9	2,764
Total	100.0	100.0	100.0	58.4	9,063
Numbers	19,239	8,059	11,230	n.a.	n.a.

Working proprietors and active business partners = 2,329, of whom only 15.7% were women.

Architecture					
Professional workers	17.9	21.6	9.9	17.9	41,959
Technical/supervisory	42.3	46.8	32.8	25.1	13,461
Clerical	16.3	4.4	41.3	81.8	9,988

Table 4.4b (continued)

Occupational group	Total	Male strata	Female strata	% Female	Average annual salary (RM)
General & manual	5.8	5.9	5.6	31.3	5,456
Part-time	4.7	4.4	5.4	40.9	4,083
Total	100.0	100.0	100.0	36.9	16,206
Numbers	5,126	3,460	1,661	n.a.	n.a.

Working proprietors and active business partners = 419, of whom only 2.4% were women.

Engineering

Occupational group	Total	Male strata	Female strata	% Female	Average annual salary (RM)
Professional workers	29.5	37.7	9.5	9.3	49,008
Technical/supervisory	41.6	44.3	35.1	24.5	18,351
Clerical	15.4	4.1	43.3	81.7	12,337
General & manual	6.7	6.6	6.8	29.6	7,132
Part-time	2.4	2.2	3.4	40.1	4,310
Total	100.0	100.0	100.0	29.1	25,075
Numbers	11,630	8,275	3,386	n.a.	n.a.

Working proprietors and active business partners = 257, of whom only 0.2% were women.

Sources: Calculated from the *Census of Selected Service Industries, 1992* and *Census of Professional and Institutional Establishments, 1992*; Bumi and non-Bumi figures are calculated from Birks and Hamzah (1988: Statistical Annex 6a and 6b).

Table 4.4c Employment Distribution and Average Annual Earnings in Professional Services and Stock-broking Houses by Occupational Status, Gender and Ethnicity, 2003

Occupational group	Total	Male strata	Female strata	Average annual salary (RM)
Stockbroking				
Professional	41.0	41.3	40.7	59,047
Dealers	17.4	20.7	13.7	55,600
Clerical	7.2	7.3	7.1	26,474
General & manual	27.6	21.4	34.3	18,891
Part-time	6.7	9.2	4.0	15,219
Total	0.2	0.1	0.3	6,067
Numbers	100.0	100.0	100.0	41,994

(continued overleaf)

Table 4.4c (continued)

Occupational group	Total	Male strata	Female strata	Average annual salary (RM)
Accounting				
Professional workers	33.7	40.9	29.8	45,764
Technical/supervisory	27.1	27.5	27.0	20,968
Clerical	30.2	20.2	35.6	15,392
General & manual	4.7	7.1	3.5	11,145
Part-time	4.2	4.3	4.2	6,162
Total	100.0	100.0	100.0	26,542
Numbers	17,536	6,131	11,405	
Law				
Professional workers	17.1	23.9	14.2	43,855
Technical/supervisory	2.5	3.1	2.3	26,043
Clerical	66.8	41.0	77.8	15,897
General & manual	9.9	25.3	3.3	11,586
Part-time	3.7	6.8	2.4	4,923
Total	100.0	100.0	100.0	20,098
Numbers	26,915	7,997	18,918	
Architecture				
Professional workers	25.9	30.9	18.0	58,027
Technical/supervisory	45.5	53.0	33.5	25,844
Clerical	19.1	6.4	39.4	17,177
General & manual	4.5	5.0	3.8	10,682
Part-time	5.0	4.8	5.3	7,404
Total	100.0	100.0	100.0	30,921
Numbers	8,480	5,221	3,259	
Engineering	Total	Males		
Professional workers	37.7	45.3		
Technical/supervisory	38.5	41.9		
Clerical	16.8	5.2		
General & manual	4.9	5.5		
Part-time	2.1	2.1		
Total	100.0	100.0		
Numbers	15,617	10,647		

Source: Calculated from the *Census of Selected Service Industries, 2003.*

Trends suggest that progress on ethnic restructuring of employment depended on the structure and pace of overall employment expansion the nature of state intervention in labour markets, and the transformation of demand.[26] Recognizing the links between ethnic ownership, control and employment, the government sought to hasten the pace of employment redistribution in the corporate sector by redistributing corporate ownership through government investments on behalf of the Malay community. The country's largest banks were increasingly government-controlled from the 1960s and 1970s, while Malay trust agencies also have significant equity stakes in a number of others. Ethnic restructuring of bank ownership sometimes changed the ethnic nature of the bank's clientele.

Other methods of forcing the pace of employment restructuring have included direct ethnic restructuring of demand and the labour market by the central bank by regulating the direction of lending and employment itself.[27] Malay representation in financial institutions has improved substantially from 5.1 per cent in 1957 (see Tables 4.1 and 4.2). Reaching 43.2 per cent in 1980, the share of Malay employment exceeded the 37.1 per cent share for all private modern services. The share of Chinese in financial sector employment did not decline significantly to 45.0 per cent in 1980 from 49.3 per cent in 1957. The most drastic change occurred among Indians, whose share dropped from 40.8 per cent in 1957 to just 10.8 per cent in 1980, mainly due to the growth of Malaysian banks, the reduced share of British banks and the declining role of the English language in banking services. As Table 4.5 shows, these trends continued until 1994, soon after which the 1997–98 financial crisis and ongoing technological changes led to significant contraction of financial services employment.

Although finance companies recorded great improvements in Malay employment,[28] Malays remained under-represented in finance companies,

Table 4.5 Financial Institutions: Share of Employment by Ethnicity, 1980–94

Type of financial institution	1980		1994	
	Bumi	Non-Bumi	Bumi	Non-Bumi
Commercial banks	41.4	58.6	54.0	46.0
Merchant banks	49.3	50.7	58.2	41.8
Finance companies	31.4	68.6	53.1	46.9
Insurance companies	33.5	66.5	44.2	55.8
Total	13,894	21,937	52.3	47.7

as in the insurance industry, sectors not subjected to as much employment and clientele regulation as commercial banks and merchant banks.[29] Instead, the greatest level of Malay representation was to be found in the relatively new merchant banks which first grew in the 1970s. This is partly due to the nature of merchant banking, which is more cosmopolitan and specialized, involving direct contacts with generally better-educated corporate and institutional customers who conduct their business in English. At least 30 per cent of merchant bank's business was derived from fee-based activities such as consultancy, portfolio management and underwriting. Also, as merchant banks only emerged in Malaysia from the 1970s, greater Malay ownership was assured from the outset through government nominee companies.

Historically, financial institutions were much preferred employers, who associated the finance sector with comfortable working conditions, decent remuneration, employment stability and security.[30] With increasing government pressure to ethnically restructure employment in these services, ethnic competition for financial sector jobs (especially at the clerical and junior management level) increased substantially. Financial institutions' employment policies have been relatively easy to monitor as these institutions have had to submit annual reports on the ethnic composition of their workforces. While there is no official penalty for not complying with the ethnic quota of at least 30 per cent Malay employment, there is a general suspicion that if the institutions are not seen to comply, then their applications for licences to open new branches or gain other concessions from the authorities are less likely to be favourably considered. Personnel managers at Chinese banks who were interviewed claimed that they tried to comply with the ruling as much as possible. However, because the quota is an across-the-board quota, Malays were usually hired to fill the lower level occupations, with limited access to upper level occupations in Chinese-controlled banks. Occupational concentration of Malays into secondary manual and non-clerical categories became widespread as large employers tried to comply with the NEP employment requirements.

Central banks pressure on financial institutions to ensure Bumiputera employment at every occupational level has also succeeded. This was reflected in increased employment of Bumiputera supervisors and senior managers, either through new recruiting or internal promotion. However, Malay supervisors and managers tend to be placed in non-technical, non-income-generating and non-critical administrative positions, e.g. public relations, government relations, personnel management, allegedly because of their relevant financial and technical expertise. This resulted in intense competition for experienced and qualified Bumiputera managers. Birks and Hamzah (1988) found that Bumiputera senior managers and technical professionals could command an economic rent of 20 to 50 per cent because of the short-term supply shortage.

To discourage staff-poaching within the industry, the central bank imposed a severe penalty from 1988 on inter-firm staff poaching of supervisors, i.e. those earning over RM1500 a month.[31] Non-Malays responded to increasing infiltration of the occupations which they historically dominated by creating new niches for themselves, by re-skilling themselves with higher professional qualifications or professional and technical skills in newly-developed services such as computing, consultancy, marketing, as well as new money-market and credit-market instruments.

As Malay employment is less significant in the less regulated professional and business services, their occupational crowding in secondary-primary or lower secondary jobs (e.g. clerical and general manual work) in these private services has been less pronounced. Malays are under-represented in professional and supervisory/technical positions, in the accounting, legal and architectural professions and in stock-broking,[32] but their representation increases inversely with occupational status. The bigger firms (such as the largest partnerships) have been trying to recruit Bumiputera experienced staff or even trainees, but complained of undersupply. In bigger firms, employment restructuring has not been simply due to the need to comply with regulations, but has also been due to pragmatic business considerations and the fear of adverse political interventions.

At present, segmentation in demand continues, with Malay firms servicing the government state owned enterprises and private Malay-controlled firms. The increasing involvement of the public sector in corporate business and construction projects from the 1970s led to a rising proportion of corporate work going to Bumiputera firms or firms deemed to have complied with the NEP objectives. To circumvent the ethnically-biased award of business contracts and tenders by the public sector or government-controlled enterprises, the ownership of medium-sized and large professional firms have become more ethnically diversified. Small firms less able to compete with larger ones for big projects continue to cater to their own niche markets, without facing great pressure to restructure in the short and medium term.

Other forces blurring the ethnic division of labour include the national language policy, ownership restructuring (through corporatization), and monitoring of joint ventures between Malays and non-Malays. In the legal profession, Bahasa Malaysia has increasingly become the language of the courts. Implementation of the language policy has rendered a significant number of senior non-Malay lawyers ineffective in court. Corporatization of

Table 4.6 Malaysia: Share and Growth Rate of Female Employment in the Government Sector, 1957–94

Year	Number	Male (%)	Female (%)	Average period	Annual growth rate for males	Annual growth rate for females
1957	119,010	86.3	13.7			
1962	157,400	81.1	18.9	1957–62	4.4%	12.8%
1966	183,730	80.6	19.4	1962–66	3.8%	4.7%
1980	488,729	73.0	27.0	1966–80	7.0%	9.5%
1985	709,184	70.7	29.3	1980–85	-0.9%	1.5%
1988	704,945	69.2	30.8	1985–88	-2.9%	2.9%
1994	677,394	61.8	38.1	1988–94	-2.2%	2.9%

Sources: Calculated from Norma (1988: Tables 4, 9) and the Public Services Department Central Staff Lists.

Table 4.7 Malaysia: Percentage Share of Women in Government Employment, 1980, 1994

| | 1980 | | | | | 1994 | | | | |
| | Women | | | Men and Women | | Women | | | Men and Women | |
Group	Number	Female	% Female	Number	Share	Number	Female	% Female	Number	Share
A	9,461	7.2	28.7	32,929	6.7	32,901	12.7	41.9	78,361	11.6
B	8,579	6.5	31.9	26,926	5.5	99,226	38.4	52.9	189,053	27.9
C	69,317	52.5	39.5	175,282	35.9	60,833	23.6	41.8	145,536	21.5
D	44,597	33.8	17.6	253,592	51.9	65,314	25.3	24.7	264,446	39.0
Total	131,954	100.0	27.0	488,729	100.0	258,276	100.0	38.1	677,396	100.0

Source: Calculated from Norma (1988: Table 7) and the Public Services Department Central Staff Lists.

the stock-broking industry has also helped increase Bumiputera employment, in "Ali-Baba" partnerships,[33] Malays are merely "fronts" in partnerships between Malays and non-Malays.

Gender Segmentation

Despite some similarities with ethnic segmentation, occupational segmentation by gender has not generated sufficient political will for comparable affirmative action measures. In both public and private services, women tend to be concentrated in occupations mirroring their traditional social roles. Although education has increased the supply of qualified women, they are still under-represented in high-level occupations. In turn, the structure of labour demand serves to structure women's choice of training.

Historically, upper-level occupations in the public sector were closed to women in the colonial administration that also discriminated against the locals and the "lower classes". When the public sector was finally opened to women, they were largely concentrated in certain "feminine" professions such as teaching and nursing. Gender wage and job discrimination occurred in tandem. Gender wage discrimination for those in the higher salary scales, not abolished until 1969,[34] both reflected and reinforced the ideology of women's inferior status even if they were already in some positions of prestige and power.[35] Before 1966, women public sector employees were employed on a temporary basis, especially married women who had to be appointed on a month-to-month basis. Women officers who married while still on probation were required to retire unless their services were deemed indispensable. Only in 1971, two years after the principle of equal pay was finally implemented, did the government finally confer permanent status on women staff.

After independence, the female share of employment in the public sector sharply increased from only 13.7 per cent in 1957 to 38.1 per cent in 1994, and has continued to grow much faster than male employment until the mid-1980s, and continued to increase its share of total public sector employment at least until the mid-1990s (Table 4.6). The rapid growth of female employment in the public sector, particularly in education, medical and health services, and social welfare services, has not arisen from deliberate government policies to redress gender imbalances in public sector employment, but has partly been the result of the expansion of services in which women have long been over-represented.[36] Thus, the government has given the impression of being an "equal opportunity" employer (in terms of salary scales and access to higher category jobs, i.e. jobs in categories A and B) without threatening male-dominance in the more prestigious posts (see Table 4.7).

Compared to government services, job and wage discrimination are more conspicuous in private modern services. Historically, banks and financial institutions were the preserve of male workers, with women accounting for only 1.5 per cent of all employment in the banks and other financial institutions in 1957 (Table 4.2), although they comprised 24.5 per cent of the 5,147 employees then. Although women are proportionately represented in total private service sector employment, they are concentrated in clerical occupations. Generally, women tend to be better represented in the upper echelons of the newer financial services which do not already have a large pool of male workers from which to promote senior executives, e.g. in merchant banking (Khong, 1991). More women are employed in accounting and legal services than in the traditional male fortes of engineering and architectural services.[37] Women's promotion prospects are limited in the male-dominated professions as recruitment and promotion policies for upper positions tend to favour men, who are believed to take less (contingency or sick or maternity) leave[38] and have fewer career interruptions in their employment histories because they do not have dual career/home roles.[39]

Interviews with bank personnel managers confirmed that females were preferred for jobs that do not require much decision-making, such as research or counter work, which involves directly dealing with customers. The issue of female concentration in stereotypically female job functions has never been taken up, either by the central bank, which regulates everything, or by the union. Unless employers' hiring practices change, it is possible that the relative decline in clerical jobs and the increase in supervisory and technical jobs may limit opportunities for female advancement in financial services.

Internal Labour Markets

Apart from using internal labour markets to justify their recruitment, pay and promotion policies, employers generally rely on such markets to ensure upward mobility and deter "quitting" by workers on whom they have invested time and money for industry and firm-specific training. Although public and private modern services largely employ the same categories of labour, internal labour markets in these two sectors have distinct recruitment and pay policies.

Similar labour categories are employed in different modern services based on different criteria. Workers are thus allocated to different sectors/segments based on: (i) their labour market status, (ii) their minimum supply price; (iii) employers' hiring preferences, which may reflect the pattern of demand, and ownership, firm size, and external regulations (by government legislations, or professional associations or unions). Once a worker's labour market experience is established, mobility between firms and sectors is limited by the costs of moving between alternatives after a particular stage in a career. These costs include sunk investment costs in industry or firm-specific skills, the opportunity costs of losing one's seniority, or one's pensionable status in the case of public sector employment.

Recruitment, Job Access and Career Paths

Job access to modern institutional services is strictly determined, with the pricing and allocation of labour governed by a set of administrative rules and procedures. There are limited ports of entry and considerable barriers at non-entry points. Formal rules of internal markets are generated not so much by skill specificity, on-the-job training or customary law, but rather by the need of the firm to define rules in order to legitimize its treatment of different segments. Depending on their functions, these rules may be rigidly or loosely defined, and changed with political and economic conditions in the country.

For all components of the public sector, the rules governing employment practices and wages are based on the Cabinet Committee Report of 1977.[40] Malaysian's civil servants' terms and conditions of employment depend on the type of occupation and job description. Government employment is characterized by strict mobility paths for occupational categories A, B, C and D, where movement between categories is strictly controlled because the categorization is based solely on educational qualifications (see Tables 4.8a, 4.8b and 4.9). Theoretically, job access is dependent on educational qualifications, and, to a lesser extent, skill, work experience, and a good command of Malay.[41]

Table 4.8a Malaysia: Civilian Public Employment by Salary Groups, 1957–90

Salary group	1957	1970	1982	1987	1990
A	3,100	5,700	44,800	57,900	63,650
B	6,100	6,900	36,200	42,900	48,500
C	75,700	127,800	229,200	242,300	248,120
D	109,300	130,000	337,700	358,100	334,460
Total	194,200	270,400	647,900	701,200	694,730

Sources: Figures for 1957–82 are calculated from Supian (1988) while 1987 figures are from *Economic Report, 1988/1989*; *Sixth Malaysia Plan, 1991–95*: Table 17-2.

Table 4.8b Malaysia: Civilian Public Employment by Occupational
Category, 2005

Administrative and Legal Services	303
Senior management	774
Management and professional	217,324
Support	813,518
Total	1,031,919

Source: Ministry of Finance, Malaysia. *Senarai Perjawatan 2005*: Appendix D-3.

Table 4.9 Malaysia: Civilian Public Employment by Salary Groups, 1957–87

Salary group	1957 (%)	1970 (%)	1982 (%)	1987 (%)	1970–82 AAGR (%)	1982–87 AAGR (%)
A	1.6	2.1	6.9	8.3	18.7	5.3
B	3.1	2.6	5.6	6.1	14.8	3.5
C	39.0	47.3	35.4	34.6	5.0	1.1
D	56.3	48.1	52.1	51.1	8.3	1.2
Total	100.0	100.0	100.0	100.0	7.6	1.6

Note: AAGR – average annual growth rate.
Sources: Figures for 1957–82 are calculated from Supian (1988), while the 1987
figures are from the *Economic Report, 1988/1989*.

Category A, and to a lesser extent, category B occupations, are the objects
of ethnic resentment in times of high unemployment.[42] While objective job
requirements, such as minimum educational qualifications, are clearly stated,
the public sector's internal labour market rules do not elaborate how prospective
workers are chosen from a pool of workers with similar objective competencies.
It has been suggested that the level of educational attainment does not increase
the probability of being picked because this would be unjust, given the
historically uneven economic and educational development among different
ethnic groups. The government has never publicly acknowledged whether the
ethnic quota system (four Malays to one non-Malay) in operation during the
late colonial era still exists today, although it is more explicit with respect to
other criteria.[43]

All private financial and business services, except merchant banks, architectural and engineering firms, have occupational pyramids where the largest
category of workers comprises clerical workers, followed by supervisory and

professional workers. However, some other services have more supervisory and technical staff than clerical staff because of their more specialized roles and functions, which require support staff who are suitably qualified and experienced.

The basic criteria for non-unionized entry-level elite-primary jobs are based on the highest level of educational attainment[44] (including a good command of English), initiative and innovativeness, social and business contacts and, to a lesser extent, work experience. Besides these hiring standards, there may be ethnic and gender requirements. Work experience and social/political business contacts are particularly decisive in the recruitment of middle and upper-level elite-primary workers to take advantage of other externalities.[45] However, a survey by the Malaysian Employers' Federation found that, in general, firms which can afford training costs do not stress experience as much as paper qualifications in their recruitment policies.[46] Such firms provide on-the-job training for inexperienced elite-primary workers during the probationary period, which may last three to six months.[47] Once the probation is over, wages may be significantly increased to ensure loyalty and commitment.

Entry ports for elite-primary workers in the professions are governed by professional associations.[48] To obtain membership in the relevant associations, newly-qualified professionals have to go through a period of apprenticeship. During this practical training, apprentices are only paid small allowances, effectively the cost of industrial training is borne by the apprentice. In contrast, apprentices in large core or primary firms are better off in terms of training facilities and career exposure. These firms do not charge a rent (e.g. through lower apprenticeship allowances) because they want to retain the best apprentices, and also their image as "market leaders". Qualified elite-primary workers may end up either practising their trade in a specialized professional firm or applying their skills in management or executive functions in immediately after qualifying, or after a brief stint as a practising professional in a specialized firm. Others become life-long public sector employees, or join private industry after working for a brief period in the public sector.

The minimum qualifications for entry-level secondary-primary occupations is at least a MCE, while the minimum education level for secondary occupations is at least an LCE.[49] Subjective characteristics, such as ethnicity, gender and age, have an important impact on the probability of selection from a pool of applicants who have equal objective qualifications.[50] Further screening devices in the recruitment of entry-level clerical staff include good grades (although exceptional grades can be a disadvantage[51]), relevant subjects studied, the school from which the applicant graduated, the ability to function in a few languages and dialects, and a knowledge of computing. At interviews, applicants are further judged by ascriptive factors such as personality,[52] "attitude" and other factors deemed desirable for enhancing productivity and firm-loyalty. Credentialism has raised the minimum threshold needed for job access to highly sought after firms/industries, e.g. merchant banks, large domestic banks, and market leaders in the insurance, stock-broking and other business and professional services.

Unless special skills are required, ports of entry into secondary-primary and secondary occupations in the financial and professional services are usually at the bottom of a particular job classification. Several reasons contribute to this strategy, such as the lower wages of inexperienced staff, the opportunity for the firm to mould the right "attitude" for these jobs, and union policy which favours internal promotion as a means to fill vacancies in the upper levels of each job classification. Firms are inclined to follow union preference because promotion is one incentive used to motivate employees and to deter quitting. The union also discourages the labour-divisive practice of recruiting overqualified staff for lower-level jobs. Credential bumping is unfair to the less-qualified whose qualifications are perfectly adequate for their jobs, but are passed over in favour of applicants with more than the necessary qualification or skills for the job. Also, it is in the firm's interest not to recruit overqualified staff since they are more likely to leave when the economic situation improves subsequently, thus imposing replacement costs on the employer.

Staff are commonly recruited through advertisements, although firms normally have many KIV (keep-in-view) applications from those who write or phone in independently of advertisements. Advertisements are important for the recruitment of professional staff as well as higher clerical and supervisory positions because advertisements provide a larger and more diversified pool of workers for the selection process. On the other hand, the recruitment of messenger boys and clerical staff is generally done through employee referral, i.e. recommendations from present employees. Employee referrals usually provide a good and costless screening process for employers satisfied with their current employees.[53]

Skill Specificity, Inter-Industry and Intra-Industry Movement and Career Paths

Labour turnover is generally at the bottom of each occupational hierarchy because firm-specific skills increase in importance away from the lowest level. Once a career path has been established, mobility is limited by a person's labour market experience, industry-specific or job-specific skills, and the costs of skill-retraining. In elite-primary and secondary-primary occupations, job-specific skills and responsibilities constrain inter-industry movement and, to a lesser extent, inter-firm movement.

In banking, inter-industry movement among clerical staff is rare because the remuneration package and career prospects in the industry are considered relatively good.[54] Some inter-firm movement occurs, particularly from non-unionized firms to unionized ones, or from small firms to large firms, because of workers' search for better pay and career prospects. The collective agreement[55] ensures automatic pay increases every year for unionized secondary-primary and secondary workers. Clerks may achieve upward mobility, either by gaining seniority in the original firm, or by moving to another firm with better promotion prospects fairly early in their careers. In services where employment is less structured or less institutionalized, for example, in the insurance and stock-broking industries, the possibility of upward mobility is higher and a significant number of clerical staff has managed to work their way up to managerial and supervisory positions with the help of some additional industry-specific training.

Promotion to clerical and other support occupations often depends on factors such as seniority, ability and "attitude".[56] Internal promotion is one means used by firms to recover their investments in training inexperienced clerical workers recruited with only basic general skills. The costs of investing in industry-specific skills are shared between the firm and the worker; typically, the cost of acquiring general skills is wholly borne by the worker while those for firm-specific skills are wholly borne by the firm. Large firms emphasizing both industry-specific and firm-specific training conduct their own in-house training schemes and serve as training grounds for apprenticed professionals and support staff.[57] Therefore, such firms have an incentive to retain these workers with better remuneration or promotion prospects. Firms with limited promotion prospects, e.g. non-prestigious foreign-incorporated banks[58] and small start-up firms in the insurance and professional services, are often unable to retain staff who leave for better-paid and more stable and senior jobs within or outside the industry.

In medium and small modern service firms, upward mobility is typically achieved through inter-firm movement if there are no institutional constraints. In large firms, upward mobility is largely internal. Mid-career hire of support staff is uncommon in private modern services except for new small firms which cannot afford to train all support staff from scratch, and thus poach some staff from larger firms. Large firms seldom resort to poaching staff from smaller firms, except in extremely tight labour market situations. After a few years, inter-industry movement becomes rare because the industry-specific skills learnt on the job become a valuable asset in services. Firms serving as industry-training grounds may not recoup their training costs, as experienced professional staff leave to start up their own businesses, experienced support staff join start-up firms where they can go to the top of their occupational category, and both professional and support staff leave for better job prospects in smaller firms.[59]

Even if employers do not provide industry-specific skills, it is still in the interest of the worker to invest in those skills that are a necessary condition for career advancement.[60] The training costs may be reimbursed, either directly by the current employer or indirectly by a future employer through higher pay and better promotion prospects. As for employers, investing in industry-specific skills is considered worthwhile for improving employees' productivity, securing workers' loyalty (to deter quitting) and to comply with external regulations.[61] As a firm's long-term returns to investment in training is highly vulnerable to employee quitting, some regulatory bodies, such as the central bank or the Kuala Lumpur Stock Exchange, have tried to mitigate this by imposing penalties on poacher-firms. Some firms which invest in expensive industry-specific training, attempt to minimize potential losses by "bonding" the employee for a certain number of years for certain amount, length or costs of training.[62]

It could be theorized that in non-institutionalized services with a concentrated industrial market structure, workers prefer the stability of large core firms and attempt to move to such firms early in their career. However, workers are also attracted by the greater opportunity for faster advancement in rapidly growing smaller firms. Among institutional services, inter-industry movement for upper-level elite-primary workers is determined by the trade-off between the lower wages, greater employment security and lower work-intensity in the public sector and the higher wages, lower employment security and higher work-intensity in the private sector.

In general, inter-industry mobility is constrained by industry-specific and firm-specific skills. Inter-firm intra-industry and inter-firm inter-industry movement are determined by the way workers rank a firm or industry, e.g. by pay levels,[63] working conditions, employment security, career prospects, (ethnic/foreign/domestic) ownership,[64] historical and cultural prestige, and work intensity. Thus, within financial services sector, banking is ranked over insurance or securities industry, and within banking, merchant banking ranks over commercial banking, which in turn, is preferred over finance companies. Conversely, firms rank workers, with highly sought-after firms imposing stricter hiring standards; e.g. merchant banks almost never recruit school-leavers, even for lower clerical positions.[65] Where few barriers to inter-firm intra-industry mobility exist, two possible scenarios exist as to who bears the burden of training costs: (i) firms at the bottom of the hierarchy of capital often serve, as the initial work-socialization ground for new labour market entrants, and thus indirectly train workers for firms at the top, (ii) conversely, small start-up firms poach experienced staff from well-established firms higher up in the capital hierarchy.

In the public sector, horizontal mobility between governmental departments may take place without involving any upward mobility while regulations governing promotion in the public sector are decidedly vague. Promotion for elite-primary and secondary-primary workers is at the discretion of senior officers who deal with the Public Services Commission, without clearly defined yardsticks. Many non-Malay workers believe that promotions favour Malays because of the predominance of Malays in decision-making positions. Meanwhile, Malay workers perceive promotions as being based on "political loyalty", and various types of favouritism or cronyism, e.g. place of origin, since top positions are political appointments. In addition, the upper strata of the Civil Service was dominated in the 1960s, 1970s and even 1980s by members of the old aristocracy and, to a lesser extent, by the new Malay elite.

Wage Determination

The public sector has set up several pay-review commissions which have reviewed wages and terms of employment every few years.[66] Wage determination and non-monetary employment benefits are neither directly related to productivity nor to demand or supply, but are often related to other factors, especially the government's desire to secure political support, e.g. before general election.

However, the remuneration principle revolves round the idea that an employee should be paid according to the work they do, so that remuneration increases with responsibility.[67] However, the Cabinet Committee Report (1977: 7–14) admitted:

> The principles governing the structure and scales of wages and salaries are largely arbitrary ... and as it is difficult to evaluate the different qualities of different jobs, a set of criteria based on the differing values of basic qualifications, scarcity of post or of qualified personnel, job content, should be agreed upon and thereupon the final say should rest with an independent body whose assessment will be final and binding ... qualifications must be taken into consideration where they are relevant to the jobs, but they must not override the principle of rate for the job.

On wage revisions, the Committee said:

> with such a huge group, not only must the effect of economic forces on wages be considered but the effect of wages on the economy must be also be given due consideration.... Economic and social forces must

influence increases in wages and salaries but the basis for computation of these increases is not one of mere proportion but one that takes into consideration the complex interplay between incomes and costs.

Cabinet Committee Report, 1977: 17–8

Since Malaysia's public sector employment as a proportion of non-agricultural employment has declined significantly from over a quarter in 1980 (Table 4.1), the significant breakpoint in the Heller-Tait measure of public sector influence on economy-wide wage determination,[68] the Committee believed that the government had the additional responsibility of considering the socio-economic and political environment when deciding on wage revisions. The factors allegedly determining salary revisions include: (i) wages, productivity and economic growth,[69] (ii) the government budgetary position, (iii) inflation, (iv) income distribution, (v) the country's savings and investment.

While the above criteria for the determination of wages and wage differentials for and between occupations or jobs are clear, they can be circumvented since "the present government wage structure has no less than 200 separate allowances, some of which are logical while others possess no logical basis whatsoever" (Cabinet Committee Report, 1977: 8). Workers with similar qualifications can obtain very different wages and subsequent wage increases, depending on the job grade they are initially placed in. Unlike the private sector, where employees are expected to display some initiative, jobs in the public sector are formally spelt out so that employees know their duties and responsibilities. Positions in the bureaucracy seem fixed from the time they first join the bureaucracy, as initial entry point determines subsequent job prospects. Once formally in the public sector's internal labour market, possible progress up the hierarchy is constrained.

The elite-primary professional and managerial occupations are far better paid in the private sector than in the public sector. However, personal accountability and responsibility are also greater in the private sector.[70] The differential between public and private sector wages becomes greater as one moves up the job hierarchy, encouraging movement from the public sector to the private sector, except during economic slumps. In secondary-primary as well as secondary manual and general occupations, the public sector pays better than the private sector. Unskilled workers and clerical workers in the public sector still command higher wages than they would in the private sector, especially in manufacturing.[71] In tight labour markets, public sector wages serve as a ceiling in wage negotiations for secondary-primary or secondary workers in the private sector, and is one indirect way in which the government can restrain wage increases in the private sector.[72]

The government is explicit in not condoning a wage war between itself and the private sector for upper-echelon employees:

> there is no way in which the public sector can match salaries in the private sector. In fact, it is more for the private sector to follow the guidelines from the government, which is the largest single employer in the country. Experience has shown that any increase in the pay of government executives as a means to induce them to remain in the service will only be met by a corresponding or greater increase in the offer made by the private sector for these executives.
>
> Cabinet Committee Report, 1980: 15[73]

Instead, non-wage considerations — such as prestige, subsidized car and housing loans for all employees; security of office; and steady salary progression regardless of public sector productivity — are important inducements for retaining elite-primary workers. Employment and income security associated with public sector employment are particularly important factors during recessions when the non-unionized private sector may indiscriminately fire workers in the name of economic efficiency and organizational restructuring. The value of employment security in the public sector can be observed from the quit rates of doctors, which are high in good economic conditions and low during economic slumps, when the security of government employment provides a welcome respite.

Wage determination for secondary-primary and secondary workers in the banking industry (and to a lesser extent, the insurance industry) may be divided into primary core firms and secondary firms. The primary core consists of merchant banks[74] and unionized firms, including the commercial banks and bank-owned finance companies which come under the ambit of the NUBE (National Union of Bank Employees — for clerical and lower general occupations), the ABOM (Association of Bank Officers of Malaysia — for Internal Officers and Class 2 Officers) and the employers' association, the MCBA (Malayan Commercial Banks' Association). The collective agreements cover wage rates, wage increases (at least inflation-indexing), overtime rates, bonus payments,[75] annual leave, medical care and maternity leave, car and housing loans, uniform allowances, and procedures for appealing unfair dismissals. Negotiation deadlocks are settled in the Industrial Court.

Although the NUBE is one of the most organized unions in private modern services, negotiations with the employers' association have sometimes been difficult, particularly in a recession when financially-weaker members of the MCBA are not exempted from the wages and benefits negotiated under the broad NUBE-MCBA umbrella.[76] Given various amendments to the Trade Unions Ordinance, the Employment Act, and the Industrial Relations

Act, Industrial Court settlements have usually not been in the union's favour. Interference by the central bank complicates matters and ties the hands of the union.[77] However, the central bank's attempts to limit wage competition and job-hopping in the industry, by imposing strict fines, have been largely ignored in tight labour markets.

In the primary-core firms, wage discrimination is not a problem since the collective agreement ensures that workers in the same job category are equally paid, irrespective of the qualifications of the worker. Salary points are fixed to the respective job grades and movement from one grade to another is by promotion. However, because the union has no real control over the particular job classification into which new workers are recruited, firms can still engage in discrimination through the job classification of new recruits. It is in the firms' interest to maintain a hierarchy based on qualifications to minimize their wage bills and ensure worker loyalty. Although the collective agreement is meant to serve as a standardizing influence, top firms outside the union use the agreement as a minimum benchmark for recruiting and retaining desirable workers.

In the insurance industry, salaried workers are covered by the collective agreement between the employers' association, SOMIA (States of Malaya Insurance Association) and the NUCW (National Union of Commercial Workers). However, the benefits of unionization are only enjoyed by employees in a number of insurance firms and brokers. The NUCW is divided, not least because of the confusion about where its jurisdiction lay when it was first registered as a union. Pay and non-pecuniary benefits in the unionized insurance sector are inferior to those in the organized banking for similarly-qualified workers. Because the insurance industry is not as prestigious as banking, credentialism is less significant as a rationing device.

In the non-unionized, non-institutionalized professional and business services, wages are determined by supply and demand in the nation-wide labour market, and by some informal "collusion" among the industry's market leaders, whose salaries act as ceilings. While wages for elite-primary professional/technical employees in the core firms are comparable to other modern services, pay for inexperienced secondary-primary support staff is not. Wages depend on qualifications, work experience, firm size and market share, and regional location. For instance, engineering and architectural firms, which tend to be larger and located in urban areas, tend to pay better than other professional services. Smaller peripheral professional and business firms deter valued elite-primary workers from quitting by compensating for the initially poorer remuneration package with the possibility of achieving partner status in the near future. In the case of experienced secondary-primary support staff, wages are increased to comparable levels with other modern services.

Technical Change and the Restructuring of Segments

Computerization has led to reorganization of the occupational structure and ethnic restructuring in modern services. Jobs are increasingly found in more specialized fields where labour cannot be economically substituted with computers. More importantly, computerization has created its own manpower requirements, thus also affecting the ethnic redistribution of the workforce. With the enforcement of ethnic employment quotas at all occupational levels, non-Malays have built new niches for themselves in technical fields, such as computing, as Malays fill more administrative positions.

In addition to improving labour productivity, technical change has also changed occupational structure in modern services. Technical change has encouraged labour flexibility, and increased the proportion of vulnerable workers through the substitution of permanent staff with contract/temporary staff, and the substitution of computers or temporary staff for part-time or full-time workers in some operations.

Self-Employment in Private Sector Services

Self-employment may be roughly divided into self-employment of elite-primary workers (such as independent professionals and consultants) and self-employment of secondary-primary workers. The greatest number of self-employed secondary-primary workers is to be found in the insurance industry and, to a lesser extent, in stock broking and real estate. Unlike independently employed elite-primary professional workers, the nature of self-employment for secondary-primary workers is highly unstable because their income depends largely on sales volume, which is vulnerable to economic cycles. Most of these occupations act as sponges during economic downturns because of the low barriers to entry in terms of human or financial capital.[78]

Agency Workforce in Insurance Services

With the exception of general business insurance, fire insurance, house and motor insurance, the marketing of insurance generally has been brought to the clientele. Therefore, insurance firms find it more practical to have an independent sales force, with commission payments having the added advantage of not imposing fixed variable costs on firms. Agents are paid commissions based on the volume of business secured (policies sold), with firms thus saved from making contributions to the Employees' Provident Fund and Social Security Organization. New agents begin at the bottom of the hierarchy unless they have some sales or marketing experience, in which case middle management hire is possible. Barriers to entry come in the form of Malaysian Insurance Institute (MII) certification or some other acceptable qualifications.

Business in the insurance industry is competitive, with thousands of agents selling similar policies. Commission rates vary from firm to firm, and agents occasionally change companies if they cannot meet their sales targets, or if offered higher commissions elsewhere. An agent with a good sales record has the opportunity of being directly employed as a group sales manager. However, owing to employment and income insecurity, few agents regard their jobs as ensuring long-term employment. Due to flexibility of working hours, the insurance business is also seen as a good source of supplementary part-time employment. However, the proportion of female insurance agents was small, ostensibly due to cultural taboos attached to door-to-door sales jobs for women. Nevertheless, the industry is not exempt from the general pattern of greater part-time employment among women than men.

Over time, the emphasis has been on greater professionalism, which, in the Malaysian context, means training qualifications. The stress on professionalism and continuity, the need for greater scrutiny and control of an industry racked by intense rivalry, increased awareness and sophistication of new and existing clients about the greater range of available products, together generate greater incentives to internalize the agency workforce. However, the incentive for these agents to remain self-employed is greater because of the level of their commission earnings. The alternative appears to be a flexible wage system, i.e. with a proportion of wages varying with productivity (sales), reflecting the secondary nature of the job.

Independent Employment in Brokerage

Another common source of employment for workers whose incomes derive almost entirely from commissions is stock-broking. Traditionally, three types of broking licences are issued to owners or partners of brokerage firms, salaried dealers who are employees of the firms, and self-employed remisiers affiliated to broking firms. Competition between remisiers and salaried dealers is intense. Unlike salaried dealers, remisiers work on a commission-sharing basis. Like most independent professionals, most remisiers do not start their careers immediately as remisiers, but have some working experience and/or paper qualifications. The major job prerequisites are sufficient start-up capital, and good business and social connections. Traditionally, the sizeable capital requirements, their limited historical experience of business and proportionately less Malay interest in investing in the stock market have limited Bumiputera participation as remisiers.

Remisiers with large sales volume may informally employ assistant remisiers to assist in clerical and business-generating functions. Because of their educational qualifications, work experience and relative wealth, remisiers share the status of elite-primary workers with independent professionals. However, being self-employed, they also bear the full brunt of stock market busts. Although direct employment by firms offers greater job security, the trade-off is much lower income. Inter-firm movement is restricted by the Kuala Lumpur Stock Exchange. In addition, horizontal mobility among dealers and remisiers is constrained by the difficulty of obtaining a stock broking licence.[79]

Greater Labour Flexibility

As in many parts of the world, modern sector employment in Malaysia has been undergoing significant changes. Internal hierarchies have been restructured and internal labour markets dismantled in favour of labour flexibility, implying greater instability and insecurity for employees.[80] With technical change and more educated clienteles, firms are increasingly attracted to employing contingent or part-time labour services. In the absence of strong unions, the abundant supply of some types of labour compared to others also leads to multi-tiered wage systems, which results in workers performing similar duties receiving different wages and working conditions, depending on when and how they are hired. Even where unions exist, labour and wage systems have become more flexible, especially with significant downsizing of banking.

Even the public sector is not exempt from such trends, as evidenced by the move towards privatization from the mid-1980s, only partially reversed since the 1997–98 crisis. Like the myth of lifelong Japanese employment (which applies to employees in the biggest firms, i.e. about one-third of the Japanese industrial workforce),[81] the structured internal labour market in government employment only provides stable and secure employment for permanent employees. Casual workers are not protected by the provisions of the Employment Act, 1955; temporary workers or contract workers are provided for under the rules of the pay review commissions, but are not entitled to pension privileges and subsidized housing or car loans. Probationary periods in the public sector may last from one to three years, during which workers may be easily fired. While the government does not directly employ casual labour, casual labourers work in many of the lowest occupations, employed by labour sub-contractors.

To avoid the political furore of restructuring and rationalizing the huge public sector workforce in favour of labour flexibility, privatization was introduced, ostensibly as a move towards liberalization of the economy.

However, privatization does not necessarily ensure the dismantling of internal labour markets. In many cases, the heavily structured labour force, characteristic of public sector employment, has been retained.[82] In others, there has been substantial rationalization of the workforce, especially in state-owned companies.

Generally, privatization allows greater flexibility in hiring and firing to absorb economic fluctuations and uncertainties. Just as the expansion of the public sector was the result of deliberate government policies, privatization became the vehicle for dismantling an increasingly unmanageable large public sector amid ballooning public expenditure. Layoffs in privatized firms are politically more acceptable since private companies are perceived to be running on profit-maximization principles. Consequently, rationalization of some heavily overstaffed departments can be conducted with the economic justification. Privatization also encourages the practice of using casual and contract labour (secondary labour) to serve as buffers against economic fluctuations and to off-set the long-term employment costs associated with maintaining a large primary core.

Conclusion

The Malaysian modern services labour market has clearly been structured and restructured by various historical and cultural factors. Historical demand patterns affect workers' expectations and shape their investments in training. However, their training and skill are, in turn, used by employers to justify existing employment patterns. Non-competing groups exist within each labour category, segmented by ethnicity, gender or class. External forces, such as ownership restructuring, changes in demand and government-directed ethnic employment quotas, continue to transform ethnic segmentation.

Although the public sector and private modern services mostly utilize similar labour categories, segmentation leads to wide variations in entry, pay and mobility systems. Internal labour markets are common in institutional services because of the costs of skill-specificity and the need for firms to justify their differential treatment of workers. Rules and regulations governing job access, promotion and pay in these internal markets may only be changed exogenously with changes in the political and economic climate. For instance, prevailing labour market conditions do not affect the internal labour market in the public sector, although they affect the private sector to some extent, particularly with respect to wages. Public sector labour policies have affected the workings of the external labour market since it is the largest employer of modern sector labour.

In the internal labour markets, the occupational hierarchy is resistant to change. Ports of entry for each category are generally at the bottom of an occupational category. Only at the non-unionized upper occupational levels is external or outside hiring less resisted. At the middle and lowest occupational levels, firms are inclined to accede to the unions' encouragement of upward mobility from within the internal labour market, as a means to retain workers for whose training the employers have invested. Firms intending to secure returns to their training investments often attempt to improve wage and promotion prospects, for example, by absorbing professionals as partners in the firm. As for workers who move, they normally do so early in their career to avoid the higher opportunity costs and sunk costs associated with skill-specificity.

In the public sector, labour market segmentation is reinforced and internalized through rigid adherence to rules used to justify and perpetuate existing inequalities. The rules and regulations may be loosely or rigidly defined and implemented according to the objectives of the government's public sector employment policies. Similarly, in private modern services, the labour market structure changes in response to exogenous forces. The labour market for modern private sector services is structured, especially in the primary and unionized core, where specific rules allocate labour in these firms. However, weak Malaysian unions and strong state intervention mean that external labour market conditions impinge upon internal labour market conditions more than suggested by traditional internal labour market theories. Wage determination and promotion are sometimes decided through employer-union-government negotiations.

Wages, employment security, and other working conditions are generally better in the core than in the periphery. During economic expansion, secondary periphery firms face pressure to match employment conditions within the core because of difficulties in retaining skilled workers. However, during slumps, safety nets do not exist for workers in the secondary periphery, particularly secondary-primary and secondary workers with general skills. The most vulnerable workers in modern services are self-employed secondary-primary workers and non-permanent workers in the public and private sectors.

Skill-specificity is a two-edged sword; when demand for a particular type of skill weakens, workers concerned are in a poorer bargaining position because their specialized skills limit the type of work to which they can move without accepting a reduction in benefits or wages. On the other hand, general skills are transferable, although during expansionary times, their value is limited by specialized needs and labour demand of employers. In the Malaysian context, there is generally a large supply of workers with general skills, but a shortage of labour with specialized skills. This is particularly relevant when discussing the contentious ethnic restructuring of employment forced on private modern service institutions. In general, there is an ample supply of Bumiputera workers with general skills, but severe shortages of those with specialized skills and experience. Owing to greater competition for general clerical and administrative jobs between Bumiputera and non-Bumiputera workers, the response of the non-Bumiputeras has been increased investment in technical and scientific skills, which are in greater demand due to technical changes in modern services. In addition, non-Bumiputeras also contribute to credentialism by pursuing even higher academic qualifications, which they hope will give them an added advantage in the competition among themselves and against other ethnic groups.[83]

Historically, the labour market for modern services was segmented by ethnicity and gender. The labour markets for these services were affected by the patterns of segmentation of demands, influenced in turn by segmentation in the rest of the economy. Thus, after more than thirty years of NEP affirmative action, the labour market for modern services remains segmented. The colonial crowding of Malays and Indians in public sector employment has given way to predominantly Malay over-representation. The occupational concentration of non-Malays, especially Indians, in the more technical and scientific occupations in the public sector has given way to Malay crowding. Malays are still under-represented in the less regulated non-institutionalized private modern services (such as professional services), and are crowded into the lower occupational categories more and less the regulated and unregulated services.

Small unregulated firms face less pressure to conform with the general directive of ethnic restructuring since they employ few workers. With the official preoccupation with ethnic restructuring, other labour issues — such as female participation and worker rights — have been given short shift. Although women, like Bumiputera workers, tend to be crowded into stereotyped clerical and general/manual occupational categories, there is little external pressure to improve their distribution within the occupational hierarchy. By tightening regulations, the government , creates openings in structured labour markets even if the objective is to close the gap between non-competing segments. With forced restructuring, new structures emerge to replace the old, as previously non-competing groups look for ways to create new niches for themselves.

5

Conclusion:
The Anatomy and Dynamics of
Labour Market Segmentation

Although the Malaysian economy has been undergoing rapid change since independence, its experience of structural change does not closely follow the three-stage model of economic growth, i.e. that of extractive industries leading to manufacturing and then later to services. As this study has shown, the service sector has always been significant from the early stages of economic development. The sector's importance expanded rapidly with the more interventionist role taken by the state with the launch of the NEP in 1970, which also redefined the nature of segmentation in the Malaysian labour market.

Given the historical and contemporary economic, social and political inequalities in the country, ethnicity, class and gender determine the level and types of skills; the more urbanized Chinese tend to be more middle-class and have better access to better urban schools and other related facilities, and are thus more likely to possess higher education qualifications. Similarly, their longer history of involvement in trade and artisan activities provides established informal training channels for skill acquisition through the apprenticeship system. Gender is still important in determining educational opportunities and choices of skill-acquisition for women. Their lower market status and lower "offer price" are often due to the prevailing view of women's contribution to family income as supplementary.

Segmentation tends to evolve from the structure of labour demand, which is affected by: (i) the structure of the product market, (ii) ownership of the production unit, (iii) the industry's market structure, (iv) the relative

133

costs of inputs, including different types of labour, (v) technological choice, (vi) externally-imposed human resources regulations and policies by the state or unions or professional associations, (vii) the state's economic and political policies. These factors are not mutually exclusive; the product market structure; industrial market structure, relative costs of inputs, the state's industrial policies (in terms of tax breaks and subsidies) and labour legislation affect the choice of technology through the firm's ability to pay, while segmentation of the market for some services is related to ownership segmentation. Moreover, product market segmentation (e.g. by ethnicity, class and gender) and industrial market structure (e.g. by firm size) encourage labour market segmentation in terms of different conditions for entry systems, pay, job security and career prospects.

However, the structure and level of labour demand may not be alone in determining employers' hiring practices, which may also reflect imperfect information and employers' preferences among similarly qualified workers. A worker's job opportunities are determined by: (i) supply factors, including labour market status and access into different labour markets segments, (ii) demand factors, i.e. employers' hiring practices, influenced by information and employers' preferences. An employer's demand is determined by: (i) their ability to offer remuneration, career prospects and non-pecuniary benefits, (ii) the minimum offer price (wage) of the desired worker. Hence, the real wages reflect the relative bargaining power of employers and workers. The labour market status of workers, and hence their relative bargaining power, may be directly strengthened by trade unions, professional associations, legislation, and, in the Malaysian context, "artificial shortages" of particular ethnic groups of workers owing to state interventionist labour policies.

The Malaysian service labour market clearly exhibits these characteristics and the reviews in Chapters 3 and 4 reveal that segmentation changes over time due to structural changes. The Malaysian labour force has long been segmented by ethnicity, religion, language, custom, class and gender. Such segmentation is reflected in employment in the services sector. Malay over-representation in community, social and personal services was due to their greater participation in public sector employment, where they accounted for much more than two thirds of the government workforce and over half the total labour force. The Chinese's long involvement outside of the commanding heights of capitalism is reflected in their concentration in wholesale/retail and finance/business services, where they long accounted for half of the commerce and almost half of the financial services workforce, although they now account for less than a third of the Peninsular Malaysian workforce. The Indians were historically concentrated at the lower end of government services, as reflected in their over-representation in transport, storage and communications, higher than their share of the labour force. Similarly, the occupational crowding of women, the lower classes, immigrants and particular ethnic groups in the lowest occupations has persisted, due to unequal access to education and skill acquisition, and/or protracted structural impediments to labour demand.

Chapter 2 discusses differential access to educational qualifications by ethnicity, gender and class, and cultural prejudices about the behavioural patterns associated with each group. It also illustrates the consequences of imperfect labour market information and the disadvantages of using educational qualifications as indicators of skill/technical competence. Once access to education is more widespread, without a corresponding increase in job opportunities for educated labour, credentials rather than technical competence, will be used as a rationing and signalling device. Credentialism is particularly rampant in modern sector services, which have the greatest proportion of good jobs.

With the NEP's aim of redistributing "good jobs" (through employment quotas) to the Malay middle-class within the context of an oversupply of qualified non-Malays (who have historically had better access to educational opportunities), "artificial shortages" of Malay professionals have pushed up their demand prices. At the same time, the greater-supply of non-Malay, especially Chinese professionals have threatened their hold in traditional niches in the modern sector. In response, they segmentation by equipping themselves with newer or higher qualifications that allow them to move out of administrative and older service occupations, into newer occupations such as computing, consulting, accounting and technical functions.

Modern services are produced with a greater proportion of elite-primary and secondary-primary workers, while traditional services use a greater proportion of secondary workers as well as casual, part-time or temporary workers, from less regulated markets. Yet, the preceding chapters show greater ethnic and gender segmentation in traditional services, and greater ethnic competition in modern services. The reasons are simple — modern services, largely unionized, have a greater proportion of higher status jobs offering stable, higher and regular income for workers.

Ethnic and gender segmentation are more persistent in traditional and informal sector services. The Chinese are over-represented in such services, possibly because of the informal processes of skill acquisition through apprenticeships and on-the-job training, processes not controlled by institutional regulations. Chinese ownership and control of small-scale private services have perpetuated their over-representation in the workforce because they often employ workers (including unpaid or nominally-paid family members) or recruit trainee apprentices through informal channels, on the basis of kinship, clan or ethnic considerations. In such services, a working knowledge of Chinese and Chinese dialects is essential for communication since many older generation workers, including "master craftsmen", are not fluent in other languages.

However, the growth of wage employment, especially in industry and services, resulted in rising wages with full employment, and consequently, less negative discrimination in efforts to lower overall wage costs a la Becker (1957). Thus, in recent years, the proportion of relatively cheaper Malay, Indian and immigrant workers has been rising generally, e.g. in the transport industry, while the proportion of female workers has risen in the wholesale and retail sector (with the growth of departmental stores and supermarkets). Hence, reduced discrimination in traditional services has come about without direct state intervention in the form of positive discrimination in the labour market, but rather through capitalist competition, reducing discrimination's costs.

The structural change associated with industrialization or skills hierarchy, has been modified by the growing importance of services. New structural changes associated with the services labour market have developed through the interaction between developments in economic structure and technology on the one hand, and the pattern of labour market behaviour on the other. For instance, the services sector is often more conducive to individualistic or small-scale production, and demand is highly variable. Primary firms may transfer risks associated with demand seasonality, particularly in industries not requiring great "skill" or high technology (e.g. fast-food industries, transportation industries and the "lower" occupations in tourism), directly to a flexible workforce comprising part-time, casual or temporary employees, or indirectly — via subcontracting — to the secondary sector, where labour is even cheaper and less organized. Secondary workers in the primary and secondary sectors thus have the degree of flexibility required.

The experience of the Malaysian labour market supports the claim that the rise in services employment increases inequality by raising the proportion of jobs at each end of the spectrum (see Bluestone and Harrison, 1982; Harrison and Bluestone, 1988; Loveman and Tilly, 1988). Traditional informally-organized services employ a lower than average proportion of elite-primary professional/technical and administrative/managerial workers, and a high proportion of secondary-primary or secondary sales, service and production workers and manual labour. With the exception of the emerging quasi-modern "traditional" services, all these jobs are low-skilled, low-income jobs with few prospects for career advancement. Even among quasi-modern services, the probability of upward mobility is limited by the "bottom-heaviness" of the occupational pyramid.

In contrast, the proportion of professional/technical staff in modern finance/business and community/social/personal services (mostly in government) far exceeded the economy's average share. This should come as no surprise since the government is still the largest employer of white-collar workers in Malaysia and employs disproportionately more professional/technical staff. Malaysian private sector services largely comprise of personal and low-value added services, where production is organized along informal lines. The informal service sector, while rarely officially enumerated, is nevertheless increasingly sanctioned in view of urban unemployment problems. While the growth of the labour-intensive service sector has been seen as a solution to excess supply of unskilled labour, this cannot be a long-term solution because the nature of the service sector in developing countries is such that it will accentuate an already highly-segmented urban labour force, and perpetuate urban poverty.

While it is true that the Malaysian service sector can be distinguished into skilled and unskilled jobs (encompassing the above definitions of skill), the destruction and re-composition of skills continue to change the dynamics of segmentation, occupational/skill classification and authority in the workplace, constructing new barriers to inter-segment mobility. New working-class occupations — such as clerical work, lower service occupations and retail trade occupations — have been increasingly standardized, rationalized and degraded, and, in the process, open to secondary labour categories. However, technological changes also create new niches for different segments of the labour force to defend their positions as skilled workers and recipients of higher pay. For instance, computerization in the Malaysian modern sector services in the period of the NEP have reconstructed and "re-segmented" the workforce such that non-Bumiputeras retained their share of elite white-collar employment with newer professional and technical qualifications as Bumiputeras secured administrative occupations. Such skill-reconstructed segmentation by gender, ethnicity and class is obvious in clerical work, which has been increasingly feminized. Thus, women and Bumiputeras have displaced men, usually non-Bumiputera men, in less skilled jobs.

Notes

Chapter 1

1. Murthi (1988: Table 2) has shown that the size of the Malaysian service sector varies considerably depending on the definitions used. In its narrowest definition (i.e. excluding construction, utilities and public administration), the service sector contributed 29.1 per cent of GDP in 1986, while the definition used in this book brings the share up to 42.4 per cent.

2. The importance of the tin mining sector has declined enormously — its contribution fell from 6.3 per cent of GDP and 23.9 per cent of export earnings in 1955 to 4.4 per cent and 5.2 per cent respectively in 1982. Employment plummeted from more than 200,000 persons in the early twentieth century to fewer than 30,000 in 1982. However, it is the agriculture sector which has witnessed greater decreases in terms of contribution to GDP, export earnings and employment.

3. The *National Accounts of the States of Malaya, 1955–1961* showed that out of the service sector's 41.9 per cent share of the real GDP in 1955, modern non-government services — such as finance and business services — accounted for only 1.4 per cent. The largest services then were public administration and defence services (7.2 per cent), petty commerce (13.7 per cent), and other community, social and personal services (15.2 per cent).

4. Although per capita income in Malaysia increased from $1,934 in 1955 (in 1986 prices) to $4,098 in 1986, an increase of 112 per cent, the share of the service sector in national output increased by only 0.5 per cent while the share in employment increased by 73.8 per cent.

5. A UNIDO study (1985: 68) found that the manufacturing sector was more dependent on its own intra-industry transactions for its output growth, while the service industry was more dependent on the manufacturing sector than on intra-industry activities for its output growth. Murthi (1988: 186) found that 43.1 per cent of total domestic intermediate service inputs went into manufacturing, and 40.5 per cent into the service sector itself.

6. These services showed relatively low output growth, possibly because the demands of a growing urban population are met not only by an expanding government sector, but also by informal sector services, which go largely under-enumerated.

7. Like the banking and finance industries in the U.S., labour productivity has

grown slowly in the modern financial and business services because of a spate of rapid recruitment in the late 1970s (particularly in the then relatively labour-intensive banking sector) when banks expanded their branch network all over the country even when business was not expanding so quickly in these areas. More importantly, these services started off at a high productivity level, so opportunities for improvement were less. The commerce sector experienced low productivity growth due to the combined effects of over-expansion of hotels (labour-intensive) and the generally sluggish productivity of wholesale/retail businesses. Labour productivity grows slowly in private sector personal services (comprising small-scale, family-organized and labour-intensive services) because of the nature of labour organization and the little investment in productivity-enhancing techniques.

8. Relative productivity is defined as the percentage share of GDP divided by the percentage share of total employment. A ratio greater than unity denotes positive relative productivity, while a ratio of less than unity, but greater than zero, denotes negative relative productivity.

9. See Heller and Tait (1984) and Bacon and Eltis (1979). One reason why the Malaysian government service sector was relatively less productive than other sectors was the policy of rapidly expanding government employment during the first decade of implementation of the New Economic Policy (NEP).

10. However, the increasing tendency towards labour-intensive export-oriented manufacturing industries will lower manufacturing's productivity.

11. Owing to the way output in government services is measured by multiplying employment with wages, the high growth rates in productivity in government services and the transport and utilities services (which have substantial government employment) were probably due to the 1979–80 pay hike.

12. The mining sector was forced to lay-off approximately one-fifth of its workforce in 1985 when production controls were initiated after the bottom fell out from the tin market in late 1985 and tin trading was suspended on the London Metal Exchange and the Kuala Lumpur Tin Market. The price of tin ore plummeted and marginalized many of the labour-intensive gravel-pump mines.

   Being extremely export-oriented and therefore subject to world's economic conditions, the manufacturing sector — especially the labour-intensive, assembly-type industries found in the Free Trade Zones where wage competition is part and parcel of product and price competition — is prone to layoffs, especially in the wake of stiff wage competition from other countries where wages and conditions of employment are even more flexible. See, for instance, the recent boom in the Thai manufacturing sector that displaced the relatively more wage-expensive countries such as Singapore and Hong Kong. It must also be borne in mind that many foreign investors in the Free Trade Zones used the recession as an opportunity to restructure their global production and shift their labour-intensive operations to other locations with cheaper and more docile labour force, or to win concessions from their workers in existing factories.

13. Operating expenditure in 2003 was estimated at RM84,163 million, while development expenditure was estimated at RM83,315 million.

Chapter 2

1. *Bumiputera*, sometimes abbreviated as "bumi", translates literally as "sons of the soil" and includes the Malays and other indigenous groups, mainly from Sabah and Sarawak on Borneo Island. See Snodgrass (1980); Winstedt (1966); Gullick (1964).

2. Comprehensive accounts of Malaya's history are found in Emerson (1937); Gullick (1964); Winstedt (1966); Wang (1964). Cham (1977), Stenson (1980), Li (1982), Hua (1983), Lim (1984) and Jomo (1986) trace the economic history under British colonialism, providing insightful analyses of the causes of ethnic and class stratification in present-day Malaysia.

3. The basic organizational unit of production was the family, although some communal activities were organized on a village basis. Slavery, debt-bondage and corvee labour were common, with the ruling aristocratic class extracting the latter from commoners.

4. British Malaya covered the Straits Settlements (SS) of Singapore, Penang and Malacca, which came together under British rule by 1824; the Federated Malay States (FMS) of Perak, Selangor, Pahang and Negri Sembilan, formed in 1896; and the Unfederated Malay States (UMS) of Perlis, Kedah, Kelantan, Trengganu (which passed into British hands in 1909) and Johore which finally accepted a permanent British advisor in 1914.

    The fiction of nominal Malay rule in the FMS was maintained by never formally annexing these states. With the exception of Johore, the UMS comprised former vassal states of the Siamese Empire, and were turned over to the British gradually under a series of treaties with Siam (now Thailand). Except for Johore, the UMS contained less land resources suitable for plantation agriculture. The British thus concentrated their investments on the West Coast states and Johore, with the result that the northern former UMS Malay states remain the poorest regions in Peninsular Malaysia today.

5. Long before British intervention in the Federated Malay States, tin mining was a largely Chinese enterprise; with more than 40,000 workers involved in gravel-pump mining in Perak. By 1911, Chinese comprised 96.2 per cent of the 189,100 tin mining workforces in Malaya.

6. Eventually, strong competition for labour from outside the British realm necessitated "protection" measures for Chinese workers to ensure continuous supply. New steps were taken to regulate the employment conditions of indentured labourers, but these laws were more breached than honoured (see Wong, 1965: 74).

7. The Malays were mostly encouraged to remain as rice growers.

8. "Dialectical (*sic*) specialization in the different trades was, and generally is a feature of the Chinese commercial class" (Hua, 1983: 54). For instance, Siow (1983: 179–83) identified the following dialect groups with specific occupations; Straits Chinese Hokkiens were usually traders; Henghua Hokkiens were trishaw-peddlers; Engchoon Hokkiens were rubber dealers and shopkeepers; Teochews were involved in agriculture; Soon Tuck and Tong Koon Cantonese were domestic servants;

Hakkas were textile merchants; Tai Pu Hakkas were pawnbrokers; Kai Yin Chew Hakkas were in the tin-mining business; Hainanese were in the rest-house and food-catering services businesses.

9. See Stenson (1980) for a comprehensive history of Indians in Malaya.

10. This contrasted sharply with granting land to Malay peasants. Once virtually free, land was made scarce by a combination of legal, economic and environmental conditions (Jomo, 1986).

11. "Kanganies" or supervisors were sent back to their villages in India to recruit additional workers for their employers. Assisted immigration refers to the immigration of Indian workers whose passage was subsidized by the Tamil Immigration Fund, to which all employers of Indian labour had to contribute. Assisted immigration was banned by the Indian government in 1938.

12. For instance, upper-class Indians have been (decreasingly) prominent in the legal and medical professions.

13. The colonial government enacted a series of land acts to prevent smallholders competing against plantation capital on the basis of lower labour and administrative costs. For example, the alienation of new land became a state right whereas land rights had previously been usufructuary. A "no-rubber" restriction was placed on land alienated to the Malays under the Malay Land Reservation Act of 1912. Also, land which was once relatively freely available became increasingly difficult to obtain, particularly with higher application premiums for rubber land.

14. The Malay school system was designed "to make the son of the fisherman or the peasant a more intelligent fisherman or peasant than his father had been" (Gullick, 1964, citing an official report).

15. Until today, guilds, clan associations and chambers of commerce are still powerful influences in traditional small Chinese businesses. Apart from being an avenue where employers met to discuss acceptable terms of employment for non-family employees, these associations also provided quasi-welfare benefits such as death-benefits and old-age relief funds. However, some changes, such as the pooling of capital of various clan and dialect associations in the 1980s, have developed after independence in response to the changing political and business environment.

16. Chinese labourers on estates were generally employed through contractors, and were thus not involved in the labour movement.

17. Indians accounted for quarter of total trade union membership in 1986, significantly higher than their 14.6 per cent share of all wage employees in the country. Until today, the National Union of Plantation Workers (NUPW), with a membership of well over a hundred thousand until the 1980s, was for many decades the biggest private sector trade union. While the plantation labour force is now more diverse, Indians still form a major component of the estate workforce. However, Indian prominence in the national union movement as the ethnic block with the largest membership and leadership has been gradually eroded by the rapid proletarianization of the now much larger Malay labour force.

18. This did not occur due to British altruism, but rather because the Indian government had representatives inspecting the conditions of Indian labourers in Malaya, before allowing massive Indian emigration to continue. Widespread exploitation

of Indian labour led to the Indian government stopping the assisted emigration of unskilled labourers in 1938 (see Li, 1982).

19. We are grateful to Vijayakumari Kanapathy for helping to update the information in this section.

20. The first population census of the Straits Settlements (SS) in 1871 indicated that 52.0 per cent of its population were Malays. But the mass immigration of Chinese and Indians resulted in Malays being outnumbered (25.0 per cent) by 1931. Similarly, in the Federated Malay States (FMS), the proportion of the Malay population fell from 56.0 per cent to 37.0 per cent in 1931. Similarly, in the population outnumbered the local Malay population, with immigrants concentrated in developed the FMS and the SS. See Snodgrass (1980: Table 2.1) for details of changes in the population structure.

21. An "unpaid family worker" usually works as part of a family work group. While unpaid in the sense that they do not receive a *formal wage*, they receive a share of the output or proceeds of the output as part of family consumption. Social reciprocities — with respect to the family, households, kith and kin, and community — were important in pre-industrial production relations, usually motivated or sustained economic considerations. Today, these have often been replaced by capitalist forms of control, such as labour contracts (Standing, 1983b).

22. This tradition dates back to the Straits Chinese merchants who later co-operated with imperial interests during the colonial era.

23. See Khong (1991: Statistical Annex 1). In the 1967/68 Socioeconomic Survey and subsequent labour force surveys, the Chinese consistently had lower open unemployment rates than either the Malays or the Indians, due to their generally higher education level and fewer barriers to employment for them in the private sector where there was much more significant Chinese ownership and control. Initially, these hiring biases were justified by ethnically-structured demand in product markets and other social barriers such as language and customs. However, ethnic hiring practices were reinforced over time such that ethnic-occupational or ethnic-industrial identification became self-perpetuating even when the original barriers no longer existed (see Waldinger, 1985).

24. Low unemployment in one ethnic segment co-existed with higher unemployment in another without generating any appreciable interchange of labour. Inter-ethnic inter-occupational and intra-occupational wage differentials generally reflected social and economic differences between ethnic groups (see Mehmet, 1972). Historically, the Chinese had more skilled human resources, and fresh skilled supplies were provided either through immigration, apprenticeships, trade guilds or through extended family arrangements. Tamil Indians and the Malays tend to be far more unskilled. Although supply and demand forces operate within each market segment, they are subject to institutional and customary rules governing recruitment, pay and promotion.

25. For instance, 40.5 per cent of the 1986 rural workforce were in agriculture, 14.8 per cent in manufacturing, 38.3 per cent in services, compared to 4.1 per cent, 20.2 per cent and 67.0 per cent respectively for the urban workforce. The rural

economy in Malaysia remains poor and relatively underdeveloped; 83.1 per cent of all poor households were rural, where the incidence of poverty was 24.7 per cent in 1984 (*Fifth Malaysia Plan, 1986–1990*: Table 2.1). See also Khong (1991: Statistical Annex 2) for inter-ethnic and inter-regional differentials in household income.

26. Lee (1986: 395–401) found that private sector firms emphasized academic record, English proficiency, past relevant experience and affective skills more than mere academic record alone. Ethnicity is also less important than gender or family background. On the other hand, public sector recruitment emphasized minimum educational qualifications, Malay proficiency and ascriptive factors, especially ethnicity. In the public sector, pay depends on educational qualifications, and promotion on seniority and ethnicity.

27. Moreover, in many professional occupations, entry has been restricted by institutional rules requiring certain educational or professional credentials, ostensibly to ensure professional standards. But this requirement also serves to protect the interests and privileges of the educated through control over supply, and hence access to professional advancement.

28. These were absorbed into the colonial bureaucracy because of their potential political power.

29. See Bilton, Bonnet and Jones (1987: 304–54) on educational and social inequality, and the social distribution of achievement within an educational system.

30. See Khong (1991: Appendix 3.1) for a brief explanation of the Malaysian educational system.

31. See Tables 2.1 and 2.2. Also Khong (1991: Statistical Annex 2).

32. In reality, the poor of each ethnic group became poorer and the fruits of rapid economic growth went to the elites of each ethnic group (see Jomo and Ishak, 1986).

33. The successor to the New Economic Policy, announced in 1991, was the National Development Policy, which sought to promote growth while retaining a more muted commitment to inter-ethnic redistribution.

34. A survey covering 50 per cent of the graduates of each of the five local universities in 1982/83 found two-thirds on government scholarships, of which four-fifths were awarded to Malays (Mehmet, 1988: 117–8). Four-fifths of them wound up in government employment because of the standard practice of government "scholarship bonding". Chua (1989) reports that during 1980–84, more than 90 per cent of government-sponsored students overseas were Malays.

    Private investments in university education have also escalated since the mid-1980s because of the historically high private returns to tertiary education, offering upward social and economic mobility.

35. This mismatch could be adjusted in three ways: (i) a decline in relative wages, (ii) credential bumping and upgrading by employers, (iii) new labour market entrants adjusting their expectations downwards for acceptable jobs and earnings; (i) and (ii) have already occurred. Khong (1991: Statistical Annex 4) showed a significant fall in real wage differentials between clerical workers and general and factory workers between 1971 and 1986. Middle and lower secondary school-leavers have adjusted

their expectations. But upper secondary school-leavers and university graduates have faced the greatest mismatch problems, particularly during the mid-1980s' economic recession. To secure "white-collar jobs", they had to accept lower-level occupations and/or settle for wages even lower than the starting wages of factory hands, with the hope of better pay and promotion prospects once the economy recovered from the recession (*New Straits Times*, 1 December 1988).

36. At one point during the 1985–87 recession, the number of unemployed college graduates numbered about 15,000, soaring to 35,000 in 1989. This generated tremendous political concern because of the potential implications since 75 per cent of the unemployed graduates were Malays (*Labour and Manpower Report, 1985/1986*: 19; *Far Eastern Economic Review*, 22 June 1989).

37. See Khong (1991: Appendix 3.1) for an explanation of the Malaysian educational system.

38. Educational opportunities are essentially class-biased although primary and secondary school education is nominally free to everyone, Hoerr (1973) has shown that substantial out-of-pocket expenditure was incurred. Meerman (1979) estimated that out-of-pocket expenditure for schooling came to about 13.0 per cent of average household income in the lowest income decile; the relative burdens of these costs are higher for lower income groups.

39. Only 7.3 per cent of all secondary school enrolments in 1980 and 6.2 per cent in 1985 were in the vocational/technical stream. Of the 808,200 new entrants in the labour force during 1981–85, approximately 79,640 had some kind of technical training, while 123,000 had university/college education from local and foreign universities. This left three-quarters of new labour market entrants without any training or tertiary education (calculated from *Fifth Malaysia Plan, 1986–1990*: Tables 4.5, 4.10, 19.3).

   Official reluctance to increase the number of vocational and technical schools, despite persistent complaints of shortages of skilled manual and technical workers, could also be due to the relatively greater cost of vocational schools *vis-à-vis* ordinary schools (ILO, *World Labour Report*, Volume 3: 17–20, 107). At the same time, continuing mismatches and the low status of vocational training demand for vocational/technical training schools reinforced by the occupational wage differentials between blue and white-collar workers.

40. This concern may have been better met by redistributing income and wealth, not only on ethnic grounds, but across classes. Intra-ethnic income inequality has been greatest among the Malays since 1957, and particularly so after implementation of the NEP (Jomo and Ishak, 1986).

41. Modern sectors such as banking and finance, professional services, manufacturing and the petroleum industry have higher occupational-wage differentials at least twice as high as differentials in more traditional sectors such as transport, petty commerce and personal services.

42. In 1983, women formed between 71 and 79 per cent of the workforce in the textile industry and between 87 and 94 per cent of the workforce in electronics factories. The skills required in these assembly operations are related to nimble and quick fingers, from a young age, women have been socialized into domestic roles and

skills, e.g. needlework, which bear similarities to chipboard-assembly. These skills are not genetically inherited, but socially inculcated (Khong, 1986).

43. For instance, in the colonial era, clerical occupations were the domain of men and were highly-regarded white-collar occupations dominated by men. Over time, as educated men move into the higher white-collar occupations once held by British expatriates and the Malay aristocracy, and their places was increasingly taken over by women, the prestige and general skills associated with clerical work were eroded. Another example is the downgrading of some manufacturing jobs as these jobs become feminized, e.g. in the textile industry.

44. Although illiteracy has fallen substantially since 1970, 33.9 per cent of the 1980 rural female population were illiterate compared to 16.2 per cent of rural men; 29.2 per cent of the total female population were illiterate compared to 13.2 per cent of men (Khong, 1986: 13).

45. Anand (1983) found female mean incomes lower than male mean incomes for every occupation. Even if *wage rates* were similar for men and women for the same job actual wage income may be considerably different since women tend to work fewer hours due to family and housekeeping commitments. If and when they leave the labour force for such reasons, such breaks in their employment history further lower their wage rates and wage earnings.

46. Statutory minimum non-wage benefits have been set under the Employment Ordinance (1955). However, the Ordinance only clearly covers non-casual workers earning less than RM1,250 a month; industrial relations laws are unclear on the status of sub-contract, temporary and probationary workers if a prior written employment contract does not exist.

    The Trade Unions Act (1959) governs the formation of unions, their form of organization and financial controls. The Trade Disputes Ordinance (1949) severely curbs the right of workers to strike, especially those in "essential services", which is loosely defined. In addition, the Employment Ordinance (1955) provides for summary dismissal of workers on potentially spurious grounds such as misconduct. In 1965, arbitration was made compulsory. In 1971, amendments to the Industrial Relations Act of 1967 limited the right to strike by designating various issues non-strikable, strengthened the power of management by no longer requiring employers to state reasons for dismissal, bolstered "responsible" unions and fragmented labour unity. Under provisions of the Employment Ordinance, officers of the Department of Labour are empowered to decide on matters relating to conditions of employment and wage advances; their decisions can only be reversed by the High Court. This exposes workers to the whims and fancies of officials. Union leaders have also been detained under and intimidated by the Internal Security Act under which a person can be jailed indefinitely without trial. In addition, "management functions" pertaining to promotions, transfers and redundancies legally are considered prerogatives not subject to collective bargaining, and a federation of unions can only be formed if it consists of unions whose membership is confined to a particular trade or industry. Malaysian labour laws also allow the formation of in-house unions even when a national union already exists in the industry.

47. Calculated from the *Labour and Manpower Report, 1985/86*: Tables 4.18 and 9.14; the *Labour Force Survey, 1986*, unpublished statistics.

48. Random inspections are conducted; but in most cases, inspections cover less than five per cent of all firms. The onus is on the employee to report any abuses. Employers' non-compliance is usually attributed to illiteracy or misinformation on the part of both employers and employees since these are low-skilled sectors. Also, the presence of unpaid family workers suggests that, sometimes, low money wages may be compensated for by paternalistic benefits.

49. It is possible to further divide the segments into smaller sub-segments based on the "quality" of qualifications/skills. Although labour segmentation according to "maximum qualification attained" is of rather dubious value, it is widely practised in the private sector, which views it as meritocracy in practice and uses it as an indicator of other desirable qualities such as individual motivation.

50. See Khong (1991: Appendix 3.1) for an explanation of the Malaysian education system.

51. Before the expansion of educational opportunities, which resulted in excessive credentialism, even a Malaysian Certificate of Education (upper secondary school certificate) and a sound knowledge of English would have been at least equivalent to the Higher School Certificate. This suggests that job access in modern private sector employment depends on maximum attributes while pay depends on objective job requirements (i.e. minimum attributes). In government employment, job access does not depend on the maximum attributes possessed by applicants, but the minimum objective requirements of the job and some intangible factors, while pay depends on qualifications necessary for the job.

52. The ranking is based on a combination of factors which reflect historical, social and cultural precedents, economics (e.g. in terms of pay, promotion opportunities, and non-pecuniary benefits such as housing or car loans, medical benefits, working hours, annual paid leave). For instance, although the best hospitality firms (such as international five-star hotels) pay very well, the sector is still regarded with some social and cultural reservation. On the other hand any form of government employment was well-regarded even if economically less beneficial.

53. See Mazumdar (1981), Wong (1983) (cf. note 50), who found that earnings are higher in modern sectors and tend to increase with firm size. In many instances, firm size is correlated to industrial category, e.g. more traditional services and the informal sector are more likely to have smaller units of production. Also, small firms, especially Chinese firms, are less likely to be unionized, suggesting a larger dispersion of earnings between them and the larger unionized firms, and greater intra-sectoral occupational wage differentials.

54. Employers rank secondary school graduates and university graduates according to grades obtained and schools/universities attended. Schools are ranked according to geographical location and the performance of students in the country's major examinations. In the case of universities, local and foreign universities are ranked according to the quality of education offered (usually proxied by admission standards). Usually, foreign university graduates are preferred (especially among the Bumiputera students) since they are presumed to be more conversant in English,

the main language of business. This was confirmed by Khong's interviews as well as reports, which indicate that graduate unemployment is highest among graduates of lower-end American and Malaysian universities.

Chapter 3

1. Although some transport sectors such as bus companies and freight-forwarding firms exhibit substantial wage employment, the type of wage employment is of the secondary variety. This excludes the public-sector components of transportation, such as rail and air transport.
2. Excluding community and social services, e.g. education and health services.
3. The major reason for the continued survival of small shops is credit facilities of 30–45 days to trusted customers from suppliers, and the cost-advantage of doing business in rent-control premises. Also, their fewer lines of goods, higher margins on loose items, greater customer loyalty (niche markets), home delivery and wider network of suppliers able to supply smaller quantities, and use of unpaid family labour contribute to their viability in the face of stiff competition from big firms able to take advantage of scale economies.
4. The early service sector was developed to facilitate the development of the tin and plantation economy (Kaur, 1985).
5. The product market and, to a lesser extent, the labour market, attract some degree of state intervention because of the importance attached to tourism as a source of foreign exchange, and what the government views as modern service employment.
6. Under the Tour Operating Business and Travel Agency Business Regulations, 1985, a travel agency must have at least RM30,000 worth of capital if it intends to become an inbound-tour operator (catering to foreign tourists bound for Malaysia), another RM30,000 if it is also an outbound-tour operator (catering to Malaysian tourists bound for abroad), and another RM30,000 if it also acts as an airline or railway ticketing agent. Firms involved in all three aspects of business would require a capital base of at least RM100,000. Out of 1,091 travel agencies in 1989, 37.1 per cent were registered as all three, while 23.6 per cent were ticketing agents only. As mainly tour retailers, small ticketing agencies employ very few workers per firm.
7. The bulk of a typical ticketing agency's revenue is derived from commissions on the sale of tickets.
8. The preferences of the outbound tourist market have changed as younger professionals usually prefer greater professionalism and customer choice instead of only seeking price competitiveness.
9. In the early 1950s, most of the Chinese distributive outlets were family firms, using immigrant labour (usually relatives) from China. No wages were paid, although board and lodging were provided. Workers were also given a little pocket money and "ang-paus" (or money-gifts) during festive seasons, and were occasionally provided free passage to China.

10. With more women going out to work, the need for fast and convenient food supplies has increased. Western-style fast-food is preferred due to the massive promotion campaigns stressing cleanliness, comfortable environment, wholesomeness and associated middle-class Westernization compared to the cheaper, but "low class" hawker stalls.

11. Tourism-related business has been actively encouraged since the Ministry of Tourism was set up in 1986 to enhance the efforts of the Tourist Development Corporation (TDC), incorporated in 1972. Tax packages were revised under the Promotion of Investment Act, 1986, to include tourism as a priority area. The tax rebates and subsidies tend to benefit larger firms rather than smaller ones.

12. Malaysian guests are more common in small-to-medium hotels (20 to 250 rooms), while larger hotels cater to international tourists and business persons with greater spending capacity. Medium-sized hotels cater mostly to ASEAN tourists and organized group tours.

13. Ethnic competition occurs among the self-employed for access to business licences issued on the basis of race and political patronage, e.g. in taxi and mini-bus permits, freight-forwarding (freight brokers, not customs brokers).

14. Malay-owned travel agencies cater mostly to government and public sector businesses. Indian agencies mainly handle tours to India, while the growing market for tours to China (since limitations on travel by Malaysians to China were completely lifted in 1990) and other foreign tours are handled by Chinese-Malaysian travel agencies.

15. Unlike elsewhere, women are not significantly over-represented in the hotel industry because of the cultural stigma associated with women working nightshifts. Under the country's labour laws, women were forbidden to work after 10 p.m. but the regulation was changed in the early 1970s to allow women to work around the clock, e.g. in the Free Trade Zones.

16. Between 1970 and 1980, the female workforce went up from 12.0 per cent to 18.6 per cent in wholesale trade, while female employment in retail increased from 18.7 per cent to 26.5 per cent (Department of Statistics, *Population Census*, 1970, 1980).

17. Employers have been forced by the nature of the industry to expand recruitment to other ethnic groups to cope with labour supply disruptions during various ethnic festivals in a multiracial country.

18. On-the-job training and work experience feature prominently in promotion policies in large hotels.

19. Because of low pay in the sector, Chinese lorry drivers are more likely to be self-employed after gaining some work experience. They either own their lorries or lease them from other firms, and independently solicit for cargo from their contacts within the transport business or through transport agents. However, opportunities for such self-employment are dwindling due to the concentration of the industrial structure where firms are more likely to outsource their work to larger units.

20. Clerical work in some transport segments is regarded as low-skilled pen-pushing or paperwork. Workers often learn their jobs by trial and error.

21. These workers, accounting for a small percentage of the firm's workforce and constitute a fixed cost to the firms, are usually monthly-rated.
22. Even if women are hired, they generally earn less than men in similar jobs; this is not necessarily due to differentials in wage rates, but to shorter overtime hours, owing to family commitments and restrictions on night-time work for women under the Employment Act. In unionized firms, where basic wage rates are the same for men and women, the major differences in take-home pay are due to overtime allowances.
23. PSV licences are relatively easy to obtain, and often, licences were reputedly obtained through bribery in the past.
24. It is unusual to employ non-family members. However, during busy seasons, seasonal contract workers may be temporarily employed. In family shops, ethnic segmentation of the labour force is still common, because of employer-provided meals and religious restrictions on food consumption, and because of communication difficulties between workers and customers, workers and employers, and among workers.
25. Although the proportion of skilled manpower used in small hotels also tends to be smaller, nevertheless, wages and salaries form a disproportionately higher amount of departmental expenses in small hotels (see Damis, 1987). Self-employment and unpaid family workers also tend to increase in smaller hotels. In "no-frills" lodging houses, family members are used for many of the job functions, which are internalized and not contracted out or substituted with machinery, e.g. laundry.
26. Customer expectations have thus been used to justify ethnic recruitment bias.
27. For instance, the number of supervisory positions in transport and petty trade, such as ticket inspectors, station masters, warehouse supervisors and departmental heads, are limited.
28. Even small retail commerce businesses have traditionally provided informal entrepreneurship training for workers. This includes informal training by accumulating knowledge through practice — learning by doing — e.g. of distribution channels, identifying suitable locations, buying and stocking a variety and sufficient quantity of goods, determining price mark-ups, giving out credit and loans, negotiating with suppliers and customers, and maintaining the business operations. Thus, it is a skilled trade in some aspects.
29. This practice of not sharing all the knowledge of a trade is supposedly due to the fear that the apprentice will otherwise compete with the master and is believed to be associated especially with Chinese apprenticeships.
30. Temporary and part-time workers comprise school or university students, housewives, laid-off workers and other transitional workers. Temporary and part-time workers are not covered by the collective agreements with unions or labour legislation.
31. Freight transport has long been controversial, with rampant corruption involve firms and those responsible regulating the industry. Bribery results in an inefficient system, in which a vicious cycle of recouping the cost of bribes through overloading leads to further bribery. Also, competition has led to pressure to overload and decrease wage costs through recruitment of secondary workers.

32. This is the same excuse used in the plantation and construction industries where employers resort to cheap foreign labour because of alleged shortages of local workers. However, this shortage is actually often artificial, age brought on by the reluctance of employers to pay decent wages to attract the needed supply of workers.

33. Mini-bus companies were introduced to reduce the practice of *pajak* (leasing) associated with the old system of granting mini-bus permits to individuals.

34. In his survey of 3,000 manufacturing establishments, Standing (1989: 14) found that the major reasons for hiring temporary or casual labour were fluctuations in demand due to market uncertainty, labour shortages and the desire to pay lower wages.

35. Bulk-handling (such as for packaging, storing and delivering raw and processed materials) provides the main source of income for freight-forwarding firms.

36. In the literature on the informal sector, there is sometimes some confusion between those in informal housing ("squatters") and informal economic activities. The two, while closely connected, are not synonymous with each other; workers living in squatter areas may hold secondary jobs in the formal economy and supplement their incomes with employment in the informal sector.

37. Non-Chinese tend to live in lower-cost areas and their customer market may be restricted to non-Chinese customers who are generally less well-off. Chinese labourers are more expensive; their reputation as reliable workers and the higher standard of living among Chinese contribute to higher wage expectations among Chinese workers.

38. Here, "social capital" refers to social contacts that facilitate business success, e.g. by easing entry into an otherwise closed community.

39. A vehicle-permit holder need not be the owner of the vehicle nor the vehicle driver, even when the permits are issued to individuals, rather than companies.

40. An individual issued an operating permit may not use his permit because: (i) he already holds a full-time job, (ii) he cannot afford to buy or lease a vehicle, (iii) he has been issued more than one permit and cannot use them all. In 1982, 33.8 per cent of all mini-bus permits were issued to individuals who had been given two to five permits each while individuals issued single permits accounted for 62.0 per cent of permits.

41. These foreign workers have no choice but to work for cheaper rates because of their illegal status. Also, they tend to be willing to work for lower wages because their cost of living in illegal squatter areas is much lower.

42. "Tea money" is a common way of doing business in many developing countries, e.g. for successful applications for loans and licences, and for facilitating business deals.

43. Hawkers are those involved in the petty trading of food, whereas petty-traders sell non-food items and services. However, the terms hawking and petty-trading are sometimes used interchangeably.

44. Within informal activities, there is still some degree of ethnic segmentation — Chinese squatters are more prone to be involved in informal economic activities as petty traders or hawkers. Informal economic activities with no regular

income are not regarded as work and have very low prestige — even low-income self-employment in agriculture or low-paid factory jobs are preferred. However, this attitude is changing as increasing rural-urban migration results in longer transitional periods between informal and formal jobs.

45. Sometimes, this may mean working from 8 a.m. to 11 p.m., from preparation to final sales and cleaning or packing up, if the food is not cooked on site. (Unpaid family labour is usually utilized in food preparation.) It is not unusual for petty traders and hawkers to work seven days a week since some may get the most customers on week-ends.

46. Not surprisingly, unemployed graduates in the mid-1980s and 1998 recessions were asked to become hawkers and petty traders. However, there are few graduate hawkers because informal activities require some practical skills not taught in the classroom.

47. Previously, job opportunities for Chinese women outside agriculture and mining were limited 80.4 per cent of female service employees in 1957 were domestic workers (*Population Census, 1957*: Table 14).

Chapter 4

1. Although some parts of transport and communications services and hotel and tourism services have been defined as modern services, they were considered in Chapter 3 since the modern sector components (based on organization of production and labour) are fairly small.

2. Public enterprises refer to firms in which the government has at least a 51 per cent stake (Rogayah, 1995). These firms are bound by the Companies Act of 1965, not by Parliamentary statutes. As such, their finances and management are autonomous. The government retains control over company policy, and often has a role in their finances by serving as guarantor of last resort for large external debts incurred by these enterprises. Ismail (1986) estimated the existence of more than 900 public enterprises, of which only 23 were directly under the control of the Ministry of Public Enterprises then.

3. Professions, such as engineering or architecture, which involve higher start-up capital costs, tend to have more large partnerships or private limited companies rather than sole proprietorships.

4. The industrial structure in the professions is very concentrated. The Big Four (joint ventures between local partners and the largest accounting firms in the world) enjoy a huge portion of the lucrative audit market for multinational companies and publicly-listed Malaysian companies. The biggest law firms, such as Skrine and Co., Shearn and Delamore, and Shook Lin and Bok, dominate large volumes of the legal business. Comparable structures can be found in the architecture and engineering firms.

5. See Khong (1991: Statistical Annex 6) for a comparison of the modes of labour organization in modern services.

6. In general, employment in general administration, defence and policing should be less affected by income increases. Instead, development-related activities like

education and health are more affected by rising income levels, population-induced demand and financial resources.

7. This explains, for instance, the curious phenomenon of graduate unemployment in countries like India and Sri Lanka where unemployment is more prevalent at the two extreme ends of the labour market (see Jolly, *et al.*, 1977). In 1971, 71.8 per cent of all Indian graduates were in public sector employment, the preferred employer (Desai and Desai, 1988: 84). While the average wage in the government sector in developing countries appears to be less than that in the non-agricultural private sector, the average public sector pay could still be much higher than the average per capita income. More importantly, public sector employment involves security of tenure as well as other perks.

8. The Indian government of V.P. Singh tried to secure the support of the lower castes for his weak electoral coalition by announcing higher employment quotas for these castes in the government machinery in October 1990.

9. Puthucheary (1978) found many Malaysian government employees had chosen public administration jobs for non-wage considerations. Similarly, a SERU (Socio-Economic Research Unit) survey in 1983 found that despite lower wages in the public sector, most workers in the public sector still preferred public to private sector employment. Even those in the lower rungs of the bureaucracy tended to encourage their children to work for the government, possibly because public sector employment used to be the preserve of the Malay aristocracy. See below, and also Khasnor (1984).

10. Employment in public enterprises expanded even faster than overall public sector employment, from 94,600 in 1975 to 131,000 in 1980 and 305,000 in 1985 (cf. Table 5.4), before the privatization policy was implemented from the mid-1980s.

11. The use of public sector employment as a restructuring instrument contributes to changing employment and occupational patterns to reduce the identification of economic roles with ethnicity.

12. Employees of the banking industry are defined as employees of firms covered by the Banking and Financial Institutions Act, 1989, i.e. commercial banks, merchant banks and finance companies, discount houses, foreign exchange brokers, insurance companies, building societies, leasing companies (see Khong, 1991: Statistical Annex 9). Self-employed insurance agents affiliated with insurance companies, and small-scale pawnbroker shops are excluded.

13. The respective average annual growth rates since 1957 are calculated from Tables 4.1 and 4.2. Figures for financial services are understated because they do not include insurance agents, who are not considered part of the financial workforce in official statistics.

14. "Tontine" was a popular informal form of rotating consumer credit for people without any form of asset credit guarantee. A "tontine group" usually consists of several members previously known to one another. One person is elected leader and treasurer. Every month or week, each member contributes a fixed amount of savings into the group's pool of funds. The members then take turns borrowing (interest-free) from the pool as and when needed, or can redeem their savings when

desired. Those who cannot offer any formal collateral are often forced to use such informal arrangements.

15. The Malayan Administrative Service created in 1910 complement the elite Malayan Civil Service (MCS). However, promotion prospects to the more prestigious MCS were slim since the MCS was only opened to non-Europeans from 1904, but cultural bias continued — "the pre-war officer who did not appreciate English tea and could not intelligently discuss the finer points of cricket was not a likely candidate for the Malayan Civil Service" (Tilman, 1964: 127).

16. They derived more prestige from their association with the administrative machinery than any power they wielded. Their importance lay in their position as intermediaries between the Malay community and their colonial rulers.

17. A vicious cycle denied Malays access to higher positions. The limited nature of the role assigned to them influenced the attitude of the authorities provision of their education. "That the British were able to impose such limitations upon the Malays and to circumscribe the prospects of Malay officers for advancement was largely due to their confidence that their protectionist policy gave adequate compensation to the Malays for the lack of real substance and power in their administrative role" (Khasnor, 1984: 123). "On the part of the Malays, the material gains and the glamour of their official position in the eyes of the Malay society, as well as a false sense of a sharing of power with the British, made few among them inclined to question their inferior position in the Administrative Service" (Khasnor, 1984: 142).

18. Nearly all early Malay officers were drawn from the aristocracy. Although the rules governing selection were relaxed later, "good birth" remained an important qualification (see Khasnor, 1984; Yeo, 1980). As members of the traditional Malay elite, and being part of the Malay political structure, they participated actively in the politics of the country, vociferously defending Malay interests while performing their role as civil servants. With the creation of UMNO (United Malays National Organization) in 1946, led by civil servants at the time, the fusion of politics and administration rose with UMNO's attack on the Malayan Union's proposal of granting automatic citizenship to all Malayan-born non-Malays. The Malayan Union proposal was successfully defeated and replaced with a Constitution which granted citizenship to non-Malays born in the country after Independence Day.

19. Particularly in the Straits Settlements, where Malays were a minority and opportunities for English education in government or missionary schools were more easily available to other ethnic groups.

20. Their dissatisfaction escalated in the 1930s when the cumulative effects of the pro-Malay policy were exacerbated by the economic hardships caused by the Depression. The effects of the slump on the industrial and commercial sectors, where many non-Malays were found, meant that employment within the government sector became perceived as a far better guarantee of economic security than many other occupations.

21. Non-Malays, especially Indians, were already widely employed in the lowest occupational categories in the bureaucracy and in public works as they were first recruited by the British as English-speaking office workers and manual labour to

build and maintain the administration and infrastructure necessary for exploitation of the country's resources.

The Malayan Civil Service was opened to non-Malays as an incentive to cultivate Chinese loyalty to the colonial administration during the communist insurgency (1948–60) closely identified with ethnic Chinese sympathetic to communism. Ethnic barriers were mainly erected in the higher ranks of the bureaucracy due to fears that the Malayan Civil Service would eventually be dominated by non-Malays who had greater opportunities for better education because of their concentration in urban areas. The ethnic quotas were subsequently enshrined in Article 153: Section 2 of the Constitution, which safeguards the special position of the Malays and aborigines (*Orang Asli*). In fact, the Constitution does not actually specify the 4:1 quota, as is widely believed to be the case. This quota may be changed with the King's consent.

22. The majority of life insurance agents or direct sellers in 1989 were non-Malays; 82.5 per cent were Chinese, 11.6 per cent were Indians, and only 4.2 per cent were Malay (Khong, 1991: Table 5.4). Among full-time company employees in 1987, non-Malays were also significantly over-represented. Similar patterns are found in the non-corporatized stock-broking houses, mostly owned by Chinese.

23. However, this has changed with the transformation of demand as a result of structural changes in the economy such as increased public sector involvement in business as a means of restructuring ownership and employment in the modern services (see Mehmet, 1986).

24. Since the Malayanization of the public sector after Independence, entry into the Malayan Civil Service is no longer through the Malayan Administrative Service, but through open recruitment. To achieve the NEP's restructuring objectives through human capital investment, the government has sponsored many Malay students for higher studies in Malaysian and foreign universities.

25. Graduate unemployment was estimated at 35,000 in 1989, of whom 75 per cent were Malay (*Far Eastern Economic Review*, 22 June 1989). After the freeze in grade A recruitment from 1983, graduate unemployment soared to 15,000 by 1986. In response, the government implemented the Temporary Service Scheme, which employed about 4,000 graduates, who were paid a monthly salary of only RM400 (similar to the wages of category C workers). These temporary positions were renewed under pressure, with the promise of eventual absorption into permanent employment once the government's budgetary position improved.

26. Of course, the NEP guidelines and government directives affect other modern private services to ensure that at least 30 per cent of modern sector employment is allocated to Bumiputeras. However, many smaller non-Malay private firms mainly employed Bumiputeras only at lower levels.

27. Since 1976, the central bank has issued annual lending guidelines, which make it mandatory for financial institutions to set aside certain shares of their funds as loans to "special groups" such as small-scale enterprises, the Bumiputera community and prospective house owners.

28. Finance companies registered very fast growth in business and employment as rapid economic growth fuelled expansion in house and vehicle ownership,

leasing and hire purchases, and hence, greater demand for the services of finance companies.

29. Before the 1979 amendments to the Banking Act of 1973 and the Finance Companies Act of 1969, finance companies were not as stringently monitored as the commercial banks or merchant banks. Similarly, insurance services were not placed under the Central Bank's regulatory arm until 1988. With the new Banking and Financial Institutions Act, 1989, the central bank became the sole regulatory body (see Khong, 1991: Statistical Annexes 9 and 10).

30. Interviews with bank personnel managers suggest that financial institutions have been highly regarded as employers, perhaps because of the perception that the central bank's tight rein on these institutions and the existence of a strong union, ensured a modicum of economic security. Also, financial services were the first private source of large-scale white collar employment in Malaysia.

31. Before 1988, a "gentleman's agreement" existed amongst the financial institutions not to poach one another's staff. Since 1988, the central bank has formally imposed a penalty equivalent to a maximum of six months of the new staff's gross salary, on those financial institutions recruiting staff from another financial institution within six months of that worker's resignation. This fine is to be paid into the Central Bank's Staff Training Fund, which is used for staff training courses conducted by the central bank and the Malaysian Institute of Banks. Similarly, the Kuala Lumpur Stock Exchange discouraged job-hopping among salaried dealers through imposing a RM20,000 transfer fee.

32. Indians are more prominent as barristers, possibly because of their greater fluency in the English language. Chinese lawyers appear to be largely involved in conveyancing and other solicitor's work reflecting the longer history of greater Chinese involvement in private business. Malays are now over-represented in the public Judicial and Legal Service besides dominating private legal dealings with the government.

33. Malaysian jargon for non-Malay/Malay partnerships where the Malay is the dormant partner, contributing the privileged Bumiputera name in licence applications, tender bids, etc., but minimal capital with limited decision-making opportunities.

34. Gender-differentiated salary scales did not exist for the lower occupational grades or for clerical staff, but were practised at the upper occupational levels. The policy of gender differentiated salary scales for the higher occupational levels was abolished in 1969 with the implementation of General Orders (Service Circular Number 5). Before that, the Trusted Commission of 1947 had stated:

> Without propounding any theory regarding the relative rates of pay appropriated to men and women in any particular class of occupation, we have concluded satisfactorily in this department hitherto, and we do not propose a change except that the difference should be rather less than at present (as quoted in Norma, 1988: 28).

Subsequently, the Benham Report of 1950 set the pay scales of women employees at approximately four-fifth that of men officers, while also ensuring that these scales would end a few steps below the men's scales in the same service.

35. Even if a woman was appointed to an established post, she was not conferred pensionable status.
36. The demand for such services has risen with higher standards of living.
37. In December 1987, only 6.9 per cent of the 823 registered architects and 6.6 per cent of professional engineers were women. Although these shares have risen since, women are still greatly "under-represented" in these professions.
38. In Malaysia, men are not granted paternity leave, and they are less likely to help out with housework and family chores, i.e. unpaid care work.
39. In a patriarchal society, men's commitment to a career is unquestioned. However, career women have long faced social and cultural pressures to choose between family and job. The man is generally presumed to be the major breadwinner while the woman is usually in a less well-paid and less prestigious jobs due to historical gender prejudices. The main ideologies of about families presume women to be the ones responsible for family matters, and should therefore be willing to sacrifice her job, should the need arise.
40. Before Cabinet Committee Report of 1977, the terms and conditions of service differed between employees in the federal government, state government, statutory bodies and local authorities.
41. See Lee (1986) and Puthucheary (1978) for some criteria used in public sector recruitment, including fluency in the national language, ethnicity and class.
42. This perhaps explains why recruitment of group A and B workers is still under the centralized control of the Public Service Department, whereas recruitment of group C and D workers has been decentralized to individual government departments.
43. Interviews with representatives of unions for statutory bodies (Staff Side) and CUEPACS (Congress of the Unions of Employees in the Public and Civil Service). Some argued the public sector compensated for the private sector's discrimination against Malays by favouring Malays who may be less qualified than non-Malay applicants.
44. For instance, interviews with the personnel managers of merchant banks suggest that departmental heads have excellent paper qualifications (not necessarily maximum seniority) because this confers a psychological advantage in business dealings with competitors and in dealings with subordinates.
45. Barriers to entry increase substantially at the upper occupational levels. Free of institutional regulations, the recruitment of senior executive staff in modern corporations and partners in professional service firms tends to be more class-biased. For instance, top executives in the oligopolistic merchant banking industry are expected to have good business contacts to help secure loan syndications. Potential partners must have the right connections since the development of the practice often thrives on social contacts. Similarly, in the stock-broking industry, remisiers are recruited on the basis of the volume of business they will generate for the firm through their social and business contacts.
46. At times of urgent organizational need, experienced staff needed for trouble-shooting may be temporarily seconded from other firms.
47. During a recession, employers set longer probationary periods for non-unionized

occupations to avoid the higher costs associated with permanent employment, such as higher pay, termination notices, and bonus.

48. The accounting profession is monitored by the Malaysian Institute of Accountants (MIA) and the Malaysian Association of Certified Public Accountants, a private self-appointed association founded in 1958 to regulate accounting and auditing standards (the MIA was founded in 1967 to oversee the development of the profession according to the Accountant Act, 1967). The Malaysian Bar is the regulatory body in the law profession, while the Persatuan Arkitek Malaysia (Malaysian Architects Association) regulates the architectural profession.

49. Historically, secondary manual and general non-clerical labour do not need to have paper qualifications. However, rampant credentialism has resulted in paper qualifications being increasingly used as a rationing device.

50. In Malaysia, it is not uncommon for a job application form to contain questions on ethnic (race) origins, gender, age or religion, and a request for a photograph of the applicant. Applicants are also questioned as to whether he/she has any friends or relatives already working in the firm. Whether kinship helps in securing interviews and job access (implying the existence of an extended internal labour market) depends on whether the firm's board of directors and the chief executive officer see virtue in nepotism or actively discourage it. (Information from interviews with the Industrial Relations Manager of a local bank, a trade union representative, and a representative of the employers association for commercial banks.)

51. Exceptional grades are regarded as a liability because they are taken to indicate independence of mind and the increased likelihood of quitting for a better job or further education (from interviews with bank personnel managers).

52. Seventy per cent of all public and private sector interviewers considered personality important in their final selection (see Lee, 1986).

53. Existing employees, through peer pressure, may help to indirectly control a new recruit whom they helped recruit.

54. With the exception of petroleum companies, clerical, non-clerical and manual jobs in the banking industry are the best remunerated (unpublished survey, Malayan Commercial Banks' Association, 1985/86).

55. The collective agreement among the Malayan Commercial Banks Association, the National Union of Bank Employees (NUBE) and the Association of Bank Officers of Malaya (ABOM) standardized pay across the unionized segment of the industry for full-time permanent staff in non-executive positions. Only fringe benefits, such as subsidized housing and car loans, are discretionary.

56. Attitude encompasses many factors such as loyalty to the firm, devotion to the job and absenteeism.

57. Peripheral firms — such as smaller firms in terms of employment size, market share and volume of assets, e.g. non-bank finance companies, small insurance firms and small professional firms — tend to neglect training because of limited resources.

58. Owing to the bottom-heaviness of the occupational pyramid, opportunities for internal promotions within the firm are limited by the central bank's restriction on new branch openings.

59. A survey by the PA Consulting Group in Malaysia found that in tight labour markets, larger firms were losing staff to smaller firms, which provided comparable benefits but offered better prospects for upward mobility (30 November 1990).

60. The Institute of Banks and the Malaysian Institute of Insurance offer courses for clerks and junior officers. Diplomas from these institutes are prerequisites for all staff with general skills who aspire for vertical mobility.

61. Unlike Japan, where employees of large companies almost always have a life-long attachment to their first employer, Malaysian employers are loath to invest voluntarily in comprehensive industrial training because of the substantial costs involved.

62. Otherwise, a penalty equivalent to a percentage of the firm's investment in training costs is imposed on the errant employee. However, the penalty generally recoups only a proportion of the real costs, and may not be a sufficient deterrent. Bonding is most common for "skilled" and supply-constrained occupations in the air transport, telecommunications and banking industry.

63. According to interviews with some "head-hunters", the mobility of employees at the very top of the occupational ladder is less motivated by pecuniary benefits than by other factors, such as job satisfaction, prestige and power.

64. Before the central bank's restriction in 1966 on foreign banks' opening new branch offices, foreign banks were highly valued as potential employers. However, their prestige has declined somewhat since then, although the largest foreign banks have retained their desirability largely because of better fringe benefits for employees. Among locally-incorporated banks, the preference is for banks with large branch networks and greater potential for faster growth, and correspondingly, greater promotion prospects. Small local banks, small foreign-incorporated banks, small finance companies which are non-bank subsidiaries, and other non-unionized firms are at the bottom of the pecking order.

65. Based on interviews. Merchant banks can do this because they are not governed by the collective agreement negotiated between the commercial banks and the National Union of Bank Employees. Hence, merchant banks have an active role in wage policy, rather than the reactive role common in the rest of the industry.

66. The first commission was the Trusted Commission in 1947, which recommended that public sector employment should compare favourably with the private sector in terms of employment. This was followed by the Benham Report in 1950. The Suffian Report, which only covered some public services, was in effect from 1970 to 1976. The Aziz Report in 1973 only covered those in the teaching profession. Subsequently, the Harun Report in 1975 was designed for those in statutory bodies and local government services. The recruitment and compensation criteria were both inconsistent over time as well as across the government services. It was not until the Cabinet Committee Commission of 1977 chaired by Mahathir that the terms and conditions of service for all government services were finally integrated.

    The 1977 Report was reviewed and amended twice during the eighties, once in 1980, and again in 1988. Before each review, the five departmental joint councils for the public services (public sector unions) were consulted. In 1992, the government introduced its New Remuneration Scheme, another radical departure from the preceding framework.

67. This principle is seldom followed in reality. For instance, graduate teachers are paid almost twice as much as non-graduate teachers even if their job functions and responsibilities are similar. Also, it appears that responsibility is generally associated with educational qualifications and work experience, not the labour-intensity of a job. The most tedious but responsible manual jobs are still paid the least because of the low status of the workers involved.

68. In most developing countries, the single largest modern sector employer is the public sector. Heller and Tait (1984: 35) found that the share of public sector employment as a proportion of non-agricultural employment ranges from a high 87 per cent in Benin and 72 per cent in India to 19.6 per cent in the USA, averaging 44 per cent in developing countries and 24 per cent in the OECD economies.

69. It has never been clear what how a productivity increase in the public sector is measured. In interviews in January 1988, MAMPU (Malaysian Modernization and Management Planning Unit) and the NPC (National Productivity Centre) admitted they do not have clear productivity measurements for the public sector, except for indirect indicators such as the length of queues for public services and the number of public complaints.

70. The Malaysian Professional Centre suggested that the main reason for professionals left the civil service was for better remuneration in the private sector (*The New Straits Times*, 10 June 1982) although this is only true in good times. In bad times, the public sector offers far more security; lower wages can be compensated for by not having to be liable for wrong decision-making.

71. The relatively higher wages in the public sector must be viewed in the context of the limited promotion prospects in these segments, which are extremely bottom-heavy. Also, opportunities for overtime work are more limited in the public sector. Hence, secondary-primary and secondary workers in unionized firms are better off in the long run.

72. Historical evidence suggests that wage increases in the public sector encourage demands for wage increases in the private sector. For instance, when the government introduced the Special Relief Allowance in October 1973 to minimize the effects of the inflationary 1970s on the lower-paid workers, there was strong pressure from organized private sector labour to obtain similar concessions from private employers. In 1980, when the Cabinet Committee announced new salary scales for civil servants, such that some lower and even middle-level occupations in the public sector became comparable or more highly-paid than in the private sector, the move sparked off a fresh round of wage increases in the private sector (see Sivananthiran, 1986: 12).

73. In this respect, the Cabinet Committee Report differed from the earlier pay review commissions, which established that fair comparison with the private sector should be the guiding principle in determining salaries and conditions of service in the public sector.

74. Although merchant banks are not unionized, they are considered to be highly desirable employers because of their excellent wages and non-pecuniary benefits.

In a tight labour market, their non-unionized position is a boon to workers because the remuneration package is limited only by what the firm is willing to offer.

75. Historically, bonuses were not part of the standard wage packet, but discretionary perks used to attract and retain the best workers. Over time, it has become a standard feature of all NUBE-MCBA collective agreements. Although they were not pro-rated into monthly wages in overtime or gratuity calculations until the 1980 amendments to the Employment Act of 1955, employer claims about Malaysia's wage rigidity and lack of labour competitiveness during the mid-1980s' recession, soon reversed this gain. Amendments to the country's major labour legislations in 1989 (including the Employment Act of 1955) redefined wages to exclude bonuses, thus reducing the base on which overtime and employers' contributions to the Employees' Provident Fund are calculated (*Malaysian Business*, 16 November 1989).

76. During economic booms, the MCBA wanted to control wages and limit inter-bank competition for clerical staff across the industry by having one standard wage, leaving only non-pecuniary benefits — such as car loans, housing loans and merit increments — discretionary. However, this strategy left the weaker firms little room for manoeuvre in times of economic hardship.

77. Between 1986 and 1989, the central bank declared a moratorium on wage increases greater than five per cent, while bonuses were restricted to one month's basic salary except where such payments were contractual. Only firms which could prove that their profits exceeded the previous year's profits by at least ten per cent, were exempted from this ruling. While this affected the terms negotiated in the 1988 collective agreement, the greatest effect of the central bank moratorium was on non-bargainable positions at both ends of the occupational hierarchy, i.e. management workers in unionized firms and all workers in non-unionized secondary firms.

78. The exception is self-employed stockbrokers who require substantial financial capital before they can obtain a licence from the Kuala Lumpur Stock Exchange.

79. A licence is attached to a firm so that the firms can control the movement of remisiers and salaried dealers.

80. "Internal labour markets ... play a special role in meeting the needs of companies poised for expansion. Today, however, with increasing uncertainties and the dual tendencies towards increasing competition as well as increasing concentration, companies are poised for contraction, and employers are less concerned with developing promotional ladders to keep their most prized employees and more interested in finding cheap and efficient ways of reducing the number of workers at the first sign of a downturn in sales" (Eileen Appelbaum, as quoted in Harrison and Bluestone, 1988: 45).

Edgren (1990: 637) reports incidents of some regular workers being sacked and subsequent recruitments by the same employer of casual workers at much lower rates during the 1985–86 recession. This type of practice was more prevalent in unionized firms than in non-unionized firms because wages of unionized workers could not be cut easily. Internal labour markets, particularly for secondary-primary or secondary labour, therefore do not serve employers' interests as well as in an age of increasing economic uncertainty.

81. Moreover, "lifelong" employment is a misnomer as compulsory retirement is at age 55. Referring to Japan, Muto (1983: 112) says, "the system of life-long employment collapsed in the capitalist crisis of the 1970s where hundreds of thousands of workers, assumed to be protected under this system, were kicked out, the older ones first." Being in the primary core is no guarantee (even if its position is better off than in the external secondary segment) against the threat of lay-offs. Older workers are nearing the end of their productivity peaks; the on-the-job training, recruitment and other replacement costs would have been recovered during their long employment within the firm (see Chandra, 1983).

82. For instance, Malaysian Airlines was structured in a similar way after privatization. De-structuring of employment generally happens to the lowly-skilled workforce so that they can be replaced by contract or casual workers.

83. But this disregards the class aspects — "good connections", or "social capital" in contemporary parlance — still matter. There is room in the upper elite classes of different ethnic groups cooperating in meeting NEP targets, e.g. through joint ventures or partnerships or ethnic-functional specialization.

Glossary

ABOM	Association of Bank Officers of Malaysia
CUEPACS	Congress of the Unions of Employees in the Public and Civil Services
FMS	Federated Malay States
HSC	Higher School Certificate
ICAA	Inter-Company Agreement on Agencies
KLSE	Kuala Lumpur Stock Exchange
KTM	Keretapi Tanah Melayu (Malayan Railways)
LCE	Lower Certificate of Education
LIAM	Life Insurance Association of Malaysia
MAMPU	Modernization and Management Planning Unit
MARA	Majlis Amanah Rakyat
MAS	Malay Administrative Service
MAS	Malaysian Airline System
MCBA	Malayan Commercial Banks' Association
MCE	Malaysian Certificate of Education
MCS	Malayan Civil Service
MII	Malaysian Insurance Institute
NEP	New Economic Policy
NPC	National Productivity Centre
NUBE	National Union of Bank Employees
NUCW	National Union of Commercial Workers
NUHBRW	National Union of Hotel, Bar and Restaurant Workers
NUPW	National Union of Plantation Workers
OECD	Organization for Economic Cooperation and Development
PIAM	Persatuan Insurans Am Malaysia (General Insurance Association of Malaysia)
PSV	public service vehicle
SOMIA	States of Malaya Insurance Association
SS	Straits Settlements

SSCS	Straits Settlements Civil Service
TDC	Tourist Development Corporation
TWU	Transport Workers' Union
UMNO	United Malays National Organisation
UMS	Unfederated Malay States
UNIDO	United Nations Industrial Development Organization

Bibliography

Aanestad, J.M. (1987). "Measurement problems of the service sector". *Business and Economics* 22 (2) (April): 32–7.

Abraham, Collin E.R. (1997). *Divide and Rule: The Roots of Race Relations in Malaysia.* Kuala Lumpur: INSAN.

Adams, F.G., and B. Hickman, eds. (1982). *Global Econometrics.* Cambridge, MA: MIT Press.

Ampalavanar, R. (1981). *The Indian Minority and Political Change in Malaya, 1945–1957.* Kuala Lumpur: Oxford University Press.

Amsden, Alice, ed. (1980). *The Economics of Women and Work.* Harmondsworth, UK: Penguin.

Anand, Sudhir (1983). *Inequality and Poverty in Malaysia.* Oxford: Oxford University Press.

Azizah Kassim (1989). "The squatter women and the informal economy: A case study". In Rokiah Talib, Hing A.Y. and Nik Safiah Karim, eds., *Women and Work in Malaysia.* Special issue of *Jernal Manusia dan Masyarakat,* 1987. Anthropology and Sociology Department, University of Malaya, Kuala Lumpur.

Bacon, R., and W. Eltis (1979). *Britain's Economic Problem: Too Few Producers.* 2nd edition. London: Macmillan.

Baer, W. and L. Samuelson (1981). "Toward a service-oriented growth strategy". *World Development* 9 (6).

Bank Negara Malaysia (1989). *Money and Banking in Malaysia.* 2nd edition. Kuala Lumpur: Bank Negara Malaysia.

_____ (1999). *Money and Banking in Malaysia.* 4th edition. Kuala Lumpur: Bank Negara Malaysia.

_____. *Annual Report.* Various years. Kuala Lumpur: Bank Negara Malaysia.

_____. *Monthly Statistical Bulletin.* Various issues. Kuala Lumpur: Bank Negara Malaysia.

_____. *Quarterly Economic Bulletin.* Various issues. Kuala Lumpur: Bank Negara Malaysia.

Baumol, W.J. (1967). "The macroeconomics of unbalanced growth: The anatomy of urban crisis". *American Economic Review* 57 (June): 415–26.

Becker, Gary S. (1957). *The Economics of Discrimination*. London: The University of Chicago Press.

Beechey, V. (1982). "The sexual division of labour and the labour process: A critical assessment of Braverman". In S. Wood, ed., *The Degradation of Work? Skill, Deskilling and the Labour Process*. London: Hutchinson.

Berger, Suzanne, and Michael Piore (1980). *Dualism and Discontinuity in Industrial Societies*. Cambridge: Cambridge University Press.

Berry, Albert (1978). "A positive expansion of urban services in Latin America". *Journal of Development Studies* 14: 210–31.

Berry, Albert, and R. Sabot (1978). "Labor market performance in developing countries: A survey". *World Development* 6 (11/12) (November–December): 1199–249.

Bhalla, A.S. (1970). "The role of services in employment expansion". *International Labour Review* 101: 519–39.

Bilton, Tony, Kevin Bonnet, and Philip Jones (1987). *An Introduction to Sociology*. London: Nelson.

Birks, S., and I. Hamzah (1988). "An evaluation of the employment potential of modern sector services". The Malaysian Human Resources Development Plan Project, Module 3, Study 9C, December, Economic Planning Unit, Kuala Lumpur.

Blackaby, F., ed. (1979). *De-industrialization*. London: Heinemann.

Blades, D., Johnston, D.D., and Witold Marczewski (1974). *Service Activities in Developing Countries*. Paris: Organisation of Economic Cooperation and Development.

Bluestone, Barry (1970). "The tripartite economy: Labor markets and the working poor". *Poverty and Human Resources* 5 (July–August): 15–36.

Bluestone, Barry, and Benedict Harrison (1982). *The Deindustrialization of America*. New York: Basic Books.

Breman, Jan (1976). "A dualistic labour system? A critique of the 'informal sector' Concept". *Economic and Political Weekly*, 27 November, 4 December, 11 December: 1870–1944.

Bromley, R.C. (1978). "Introduction — The urban informal sector: Why is it worth discussing?" *World Development* 6 (9/10): 1033–39.

Bromley, R.C. and Gerry Rodgers, eds. (1979). *Casual Work and Poverty in Third World Cities*. Chichester, UK: John Wiley.

Brown, William, and Peter Nolan (1988). "Wages and labour productivity: The contribution of industrial relations research to the understanding of pay determination". *British Journal of Industrial Relations* 26 (3) (November): 339–61.

Cain, G. (1976). "The challenge of segmented labor market theories to orthodox theory: A survey". *Journal of Economic Literature* 14 (December): 1215–57.

Cham, B.N. (1977). "Colonialism and communalism in Malaysia". *Journal of Contemporary Asia* 7 (2): 178–99.

Chandra Muzaffar (1983). "Overkill: In-house unions for Malaysian labour". In Jomo K.S., ed., *The Sun Also Sets: Lessons in 'Looking East'*. Kuala Lumpur: INSAN.

Chenery, Hollis, and Moshe Syrquin (1975). *Patterns of Development: 1950–1970*. New York: Oxford University Press.

Chua, J.M. (1989). "Human resource development: Key issues after 1990". Paper presented at the MCA (Malaysian Chinese Association) National Economic Seminar, Kuala Lumpur, October.

Clark, Colin (1957). *Conditions of Economic Progress*. 3rd edition (first edition 1940). New York: St. Martin's Press.

———— (1979). "Productivity in the service industries". In C.H.H. Rao and P.C. Joshi, eds., *Reflections on Economic Development and Social Change*. Oxford: Martin Robertson.

Cornia, Giovanni Andrea, Richard Jolly, and Frances Stewart (1987). *Adjustment with a Human Face: Protecting the Vulnerable and Promoting Growth*. Oxford: Clarendon Press.

Craig, C., Jill Rubery, R. Tarling, and Frank Wilkinson (1985). "Economic, social and political factors in the operation of the labour market". In B. Roberts, R. Finnegan and D. Gallie, eds., *New Approaches to Economic Life*. Manchester: Manchester University Press.

Credit Guarantee Corporation, Malaysia. *Annual Report, 1987*. Kuala Lumpur: Credit Guarantee Corporation.

Damis, A., ed. (1987). *The Malaysian Hotel Industry Survey, 1987*. Kuala Lumpur: Young and Associates.

Department of Statistics (2005). *Annual Survey of Manufacturing Industries, 2004*.

————. *Labour Force Survey*. Various years.

Desai, A., and E. Desai (1988). "India". In Gus Edgren, ed., *The Growing Sector: Studies of Public Employment in Asia*. New Delhi: International Labour Office.

Doeringer, P.B., and M.J. Piore (1971). *Internal Labor Markets and Manpower Analysis*. Lexington, MA: Heath Lexington Books.

Driver, C., and B. Naisbitt (1987). "Cyclical variations in service industries' employment in the UK". *Applied Economics* 19 (4) (April): 541–54.

Eckstein, A.J., and D.M. Heien (1985). "Causes and consequences of service sector growth: The US experience". *Growth and Change* 16 (2) (April): 12–7.

Edgren, Gus (1988). "The growth of public sector employment in Asia". In Gus Edgren, ed., *The Growing Sector: Studies of Public Employment in Asia*. New Delhi: International Labour Office.

———— (1990). "Employment adjustment and the unions: Case studies of enterprises in Asia". *International Labour Review* 129 (5): 629–48.

Edgren, Gus, ed. (1988). *The Growing Sector: Studies of Public Employment in Asia*. New Delhi: International Labour Office.

Edwards, Richard, Michael Reich, and D.M. Gordon, eds. (1976). *Labor Market Segmentation*. Lexington, MA: Heath Lexington Books.

Emerson, Rupert (1937). *A Study in Direct and Indirect Rule*. New York: Macmillan.

Emi, K. (1971). "The structure and its movements of the tertiary industry in Japan". *Hitotsubashi Journal of Economics* 12 (1) (June): 22–32.

Fabricant, S. (1972). "Productivity in the tertiary sector". *Acta Oeconomica* 8 (2–3): 207 –19.

Faridah S. and Madeline Berma (1989). "Economic development trends and women's participation in the service sector: A macro level analysis of inter-relationships, impact and implications on development planning, 1957–1980". Paper presented at the Colloquium on "Women and Development in Malaysia: Implications for Planning and Population Dynamics", University of Malaya, Kuala Lumpur, 10–12 January.

Fisher, A.G.B. (1935). *The Clash of Progress and Security*. London: Macmillan.

———— (1945). *Economic Progress and Social Security*. London: Macmillan.

Friedman, J. F. and Flora Sullivan (1974). "The absorption of labor in the urban economy". *Economic Development and Cultural Change* 22 (3) (April): 385–413.

Fuchs, V.R. (1968). *The Service Economy*. New York: National Bureau of Economic Research.

Gershuny, J.I., and I.D. Miles (1983). *The New Service Economy: The Transformation of Employment in Industrial Societies*. New York: Praeger.

Gintis, Herbert (1976). "The nature of labor exchange and the theory of capitalistic production". *Review of Radical Political Economics* 8 (Summer): 36–54.

Gordon, D.M., Richard Edwards, and Michael Reich (1982). *Segmented Work, Divided Workers: The Historical Transformation of Labor in the United States*. New York: Cambridge University Press.

Griffin, Keith and A.R. Khan (1978). "Poverty in the Third World: Ugly facts and fancy models". *World Development* 6 (3): 295–304.

Griffin, Keith and Jeffrey James (1981). *The Transition to Egalitarian Development*. New York: St. Martin's Press.

Gullick, J.M. (1964). *Malaya*. London: Ernest Benn.

Harrison, Benedict and Barry Bluestone (1988). *The Great U-Turn: Corporate Restructuring and the Polarizing of America*. New York: Basic Books.

Hart, K. (1973). "Informal income opportunities and urban employment in Ghana". In Richard Jolly and Emmanuel De Kadt, eds., *Third World Employment: Problems and Strategy*. Harmondsworth: Penguin.

Heller, P.S., and A.A. Tait (1982). "International Comparisons of Government Expenditure". IMF Occasional Paper 10, International Monetary Fund, Washington, DC.

_____ (1984). "Government employment and pay: Some international comparisons". IMF Occasional Paper 24 (original 1983, revised 1984), International Monetary Fund, Washington, DC.

Henderson, R.F. (1979). "Employment in the tertiary sector". *Australian Economic Review* 46 (2): 72–7.

Hill, T.P. (1977). "On goods and services". *Review of Income and Wealth* 23: 315–38.

Hirschman, Charles (1975). *Ethnic and Social Stratification in Malaysia*. Washington, DC: American Sociological Association.

Hoerr, O.D. (1973). "Education, income and equity in Malaysia". *Economic Development and Cultural Change* 21 (2) (January).

Hua, Wu Yin (1983). *Class and Communalism in Malaysia*. London: Zed Books.

ILO. *World Employment Programme Papers*. Geneva: International Labour Office.

_____. *World Labour Report*. Volumes 1–4, various years. Geneva: International Labour Office.

Inman, R.P., ed. (1985). *Managing the Service Economy: Prospects and Problems*. Cambridge: Cambridge University Press.

Ipoh Municipal Council, Malaysia (undated). *Report of the Ipoh Structure Plan*. Ipoh: Municipal Council.

Ismail Salleh (1986). "Public sector employment in Malaysia". Paper presented at the "Public Sector Employment" workshop, Universiti Kebangsaan Malaysia, Bangi, Malaysia, 22 September.

James, J. (1978). "Growth, technology and the environment in less developed countries: A survey". *World Development* 6 (4): 937–65.

Joll, Caroline, Chris McKenna, Robert McNabb, and John Shorey (1983). *Developments in Labour Market Analysis*. London: George Allen and Unwin.

Jolly, Richard, and Emanuel De Kadt, eds. (1973). *Third World Employment: Problems and Strategy*. Harmondsworth: Penguin.

Jolly, Richard, Emanuel de Kadt, Hans Singer, and Fiona Wilson, eds. (1977). *Third World Employment: Problems and Strategy*. Harmondsworth: Penguin.

Jomo K.S. (1984). "Education and inequality in Malaysia". *Ilmu Masyarakat* 7 (July–September): 68–80.

———— (1986). *A Question of Class: Capital, the State and Uneven Development in Malaya*. Singapore: Oxford University Press.

———— (1990). *Growth and Structural Change in the Malaysian Economy*. London: Macmillan.

———— (2003). "Malaysia's September 1998 controls: Background, contents, impacts, comparison, implications, lessons". G-24 commissioned paper, UNCTAD, Geneva <www.g24.org/ksjomgva.pdf>.

————, ed. (1983). *The Sun Also Sets: Lessons in 'Looking East'*. Kuala Lumpur: INSAN.

————, ed. (1985). *The Sun Also Sets: Lessons in 'Looking East'*. 2nd edition. Kuala Lumpur: INSAN.

————, ed. (1995). *Privatizing Malaysia: Rents, Rhetoric, Realities*. Boulder, CO: Westview Press.

————, ed. (2001). *Malaysian Eclipse: Economic Crisis and Recovery*. London: Zed Books.

Jomo K.S. and Ishak Shari (1986). *Development Policies and Income Inequality in Peninsular Malaysia*. Institute of Advanced Studies, University of Malaya, Kuala Lumpur.

Jomo K.S. and Patricia Todd (1994). *Trade Unions and the State in Peninsular Malaysia*. Kuala Lumpur: Oxford University Press.

Jomo K.S., H. L. Khong, and K. A. Shamsulbahriah, eds. (1987). *Crisis and Response in the Malaysian Economy*. Kuala Lumpur: Malaysian Economic Association.

Jones, Sidney (2000). *Making Money off Migrants: The Indonesian Exodus to Malaysia*. Wollongong, NSW: CAPSTRANS, University of Wollongong.

Junaenah Solehan (1987). "Strategies to regulate the informal sector". Paper presented at the Seminar on "Human Resource Development", Kota Kinabalu, Malaysia, 17–19 August.

Kaldor, Nicholas (1966). *Causes of the Slow Rate of Growth in the UK*. Inaugural Lecture, 2 November. Cambridge: Cambridge University Press.

Katouzian, M.A. (1970). "The development of the service sector: A new approach". *Oxford Economic Papers* 22: 363–82.

Kaur, Amarjit (1985). "An historical study of transport in Malaya". In Syed Husin Ali, ed., *Masalah Pembangunan Sosio-Ekonomi Malaysia*. Kuala Lumpur: Malaysian Social Science Association.

Kendrick, J.W. (1987). "Service sector productivity". *Business Economics* 22 (2) (April): 18–24.

Kerr, Clark (1977). *Labor Markets and Wage Determination: The Balkanization of Labor Markets and Other Essays*. Berkeley: University of California Press.

Khasnor Johan (1984). *The Emergence of the Modern Malay Administrative Elite*. Singapore: Oxford University Press.

Khong, H.L. (1985). "Labour and employment trends in Peninsular Malaysia". Bachelor of Economics graduation exercise, Faculty of Economics and Administration, University of Malaya, Kuala Lumpur.

_____ (1986). "Export-oriented industrialization, employment and real wages in Malaysia". *Kajian Ekonomi Malaysia* 23 (2) (December): 1–30.

_____ (1991). "Service Employment in the Malaysian Economy: Structure and Change". PhD thesis, Cambridge University, Cambridge, England.

Khong Kim Hoong (1984). *Merdeka! British Rule and The Struggle for Independence in Malaya, 1945–1957*. Kuala Lumpur: INSAN.

Kravis, I.B., Alan Heston, and Robert Summers (1982). "The share of services in economic growth". In F.G. Adams and B. Hickman, eds., *Global Econometrics*. Cambridge, MA: MIT Press.

Kuznets, Simon (1966). *Modern Economic Growth: Rate, Structure and Spread*. New Haven: Yale University Press.

Lam, T.F. (1977). "Urban poverty — The case of hawkers and vendors". In B.A.R. Mokhzani and Khoo S.M., eds., *Poverty in Malaysia*. Kuala Lumpur: University of Malaya Press.

Lawson, Tony (1981). "Paternalism and labour market segmentation theory". In Frank Wilkinson, ed., *The Dynamics of Labour Market Segmentation*. London: Academic Press.

Lee, K.H. (1986). "Affective, cognitive and vocational skills — the employers' perspective". *Economics of Education Review* 5 (4): 395–401.

Lengelle, M. (1980). "Development of the service sector in OECD countries — economic implications". In I. Leveson and J.W. Wheeler, eds., *Western Economies in Transition: Structural Change and Adjustment Policies in Industrial Countries*. London: Croom Helm.

Leveson, I., and J.W. Wheeler, eds. (1980). *Western Economies in Transition: Structural Change and Adjustment Policies in Industrial Countries*. London: Croom Helm.

Lewis, W.A. (1954). "Economic development with unlimited supplies of labour". *The Manchester School* 22 (2) (May): 139–91.

_____ (1955). *Theory of Economic Growth*. London: Allen and Unwin.

Li, D.J. (1982). *British Malaya — An Economic Analysis*. 2nd edition. Petaling Jaya, Malaysia: Institute for Social Analysis (INSAN).

Life Insurance Association Malaysia (1989). Unpublished statistics. Kuala Lumpur: LIAM.

_____ (1994). unpublished statistics. Kuala Lumpur: LIAM.

Lim, L.Y.C., and L.A.P. Gosling, eds. (1983). *The Chinese in Southeast Asia: Identity, Culture and Politics*. Vol. 2. Singapore: Maruzen Asia.

Lim, M.H. (1980). *Ownership and Control of the One Hundred Largest Corporations in Malaysia*. Malaysia: Oxford University Press.

Lim, T.G. (1984). "British colonial administration and the ethnic division of labour in Malaya". *Kajian Malaysia* 2 (2) (December): 29–66.

Liow, B.W.K. (1987). "The New Economic Policy and the training of Bumiputra Bank Officers". *Ilmu Masyarakat* 12 (July–September): 62–76.

Lo Sum Yee (1972). *The Development Performance of West Malaysia, 1955–1967, with special reference to the industrial sector*. Kuala Lumpur: Heinemann.

Loh, P.F.S. (1975). *Seeds of Separatism: Educational Policy in Malaya, 1874–1940*. Kuala Lumpur: Oxford University Press.

Loveman, G., and Charles Tilly (1988). "Good jobs or bad jobs? Evaluating the American job creation experience". *International Labour Review* 127 (5): 593–611.

Loveridge, R., and A.L. Mok (1979). *Theories of Labour Market Segmentation: A Critique*. The Hague: Martinus Nijhoff.

Maddison, Angus (1980). "Economic growth and structural change in the advanced countries". In I. Leveson and J.W. Wheeler, eds., *Western Economies in Transition: Structural Change and Adjustment Policies in Industrial Countries*. London: Croom Helm.

Majlis Bandaran Melaka, Malaysia (undated). *Laporan Pemeriksaan Rancangan Struktur Majlis Perbandaran Melaka, 1987–2010*. Melaka: Majlis Bandaran Melaka.

Malaysia (1971). *The Second Malaysia Plan, 1971–1975*. Kuala Lumpur: Economic Planning Unit, Prime Minister's Department.

_____ (1973). *The Mid-Term Review of the Second Malaysia Plan, 1971–1975*. Kuala Lumpur: Economic Planning Unit, Prime Minister's Department.

_____ (1976). *The Third Malaysia Plan, 1976–1980*. Kuala Lumpur: Economic Planning Unit, Prime Minister's Department.

_____ (1977). *Cabinet Committee report on the remuneration and terms and conditions of service in the public sector*. Kuala Lumpur: Prime Minister's Department.

_____ (1979). *The Mid-Term Review of the Third Malaysia Plan, 1976–1980.* Kuala Lumpur: Economic Planning Unit, Prime Minister's Department.

_____ (1981). *The Fourth Malaysia Plan, 1981–1985.* Kuala Lumpur: Economic Planning Unit, Prime Minister's Department.

_____ (1983). *Pendapatan Corak Perbelanjaan dan Taraf Sosioekonomi Pekerja-Pekerja Sektor Awam.* Socioeconomic Research Unit, Prime Minister's Department, Kuala Lumpur.

_____ (1984). *The Mid-Term Review of the Fourth Malaysia Plan, 1981–1985.* Economic Planning Unit, Prime Minister's Department, Kuala Lumpur.

_____ (1986). *The Fifth Malaysia Plan, 1986–1990.* Economic Planning Unit, Prime Minister's Department, Kuala Lumpur.

_____ (1989). *The Mid-Term Review of the Fifth Malaysia Plan, 1986–1990.* Economic Planning Unit, Prime Minister's Department, Kuala Lumpur.

_____ (1991a). *The Second Outline Perspective Plan, 1991–2000.* Economic Planning Unit, Prime Minister's Department, Kuala Lumpur.

_____ (1991b). *The Sixth Malaysia Plan, 1991–1995.* Economic Planning Unit, Prime Minister's Department, Kuala Lumpur.

_____ (1993). *The Mid-Term Review of the Sixth Malaysia Plan, 1991–1995.* Economic Planning Unit, Prime Minister's Department, Kuala Lumpur.

_____ (1996). *The Seventh Malaysia Plan, 1996–2000.* Economic Planning Unit, Prime Minister's Department, Kuala Lumpur.

_____ (1999a). *The Mid-Term Review of the Seventh Malaysia Plan, 1996–2000.* Economic Planning Unit, Prime Minister's Department, Kuala Lumpur.

_____ (1999b). *White Paper: Status of the Malaysian Economy.* Economic Planning Unit, Prime Minister's Department, Kuala Lumpur.

_____ (2001a). *The Eighth Malaysia Plan, 2001–2005.* Economic Planning Unit, Prime Minister's Department, Kuala Lumpur.

_____ (2001b). *The Third Outline Perspective Plan, 2001–2010.* Economic Planning Unit, Prime Minister's Department, Kuala Lumpur.

_____ (2003). *The Mid-Term Review of the Eighth Malaysia Plan, 2001–2005.* Economic Planning Unit, Prime Minister's Department, Kuala Lumpur.

_____ (2006). *The Ninth Malaysia Plan, 2006–2010.* Economic Planning Unit, Prime Minister's Department, Kuala Lumpur.

Malaysia, Ministry of Human Resources. *Labour Force Survey Report, 2003.* Ministry of Human Resources, Kuala Lumpur.

_____. *Labour and Manpower Report.* Various years. Ministry of Human Resources, Kuala Lumpur.

_____. *Labour Market Report*. Various issues. Ministry of Human Resources, Kuala Lumpur.

Malaysia, Ministry of Labour. *Survey of the Banking and Finance Industry, 1986* (Laporan Tinjauan Gaji dan Pekerjaan Industri Bank/Kewangan). Ministry of Labour, Kuala Lumpur.

Malaysian National Reinsurance. *The Malaysian Insurance Directory, 1988/89*. Malaysian National Reinsurance Berhad, Kuala Lumpur.

Manwaring, T. (1984). "The extended internal labour market". *Cambridge Journal of Economics* 8: 161–87.

Mark, J.A. (1982). "Measuring productivity in service industries". *Monthly Labor Review* 5 (6) (June): 3–8.

Marquand, J. (1979). "The service sector and regional policy in the UK". Centre of Economic Studies Research Series 29, July, Centre of Economic Studies, London.

Marquez, C., and Jaime Ros (1988). "Labour market segmentation and economic development in Mexico". Paper presented at the International Conference on "Economic Development and Labour Market Segmentation", University of Notre Dame, 17–20 April.

Mazumdar, Deepak (1981). *The Urban Labor Market and Income Distribution: A Study of Malaysia*. New York: Oxford University Press for The World Bank, Washington, DC.

_____ (1983). "Segmented labor markets in LDCs". *American Economic Review* 73 (2) (May): 254–59.

Meerman, Jacob (1979). *Public Expenditure in Malaysia: Who Benefits and Why*. New York: Oxford University Press for The World Bank, New York.

Mehmet, Ozay (1972). "Manpower planning and labor markets in developing countries: A case study of West Malaysia". *Journal of Development Studies* 8 (4) (January): 277–89.

Mehmet, Ozay (1988). *Development in Malaysia: Poverty, Wealth and Trusteeship*. Petaling Jaya, Malaysia: Institute for Social Analysis (INSAN).

Mokhzani, B.A.R. and Khoo S.M., eds. (1977). *Poverty in Malaysia*. Kuala Lumpur: University of Malaya Press.

Momigliano, F., and D. Siniscalco (1982). "The growth of service employment: A reappraisal". *Banca Nazionale del Lavoro* (September): 269–306.

Moore, G.H. (1987). "The service industries and the business cycle". *Business Economics* 22 (2) (April): 12–17.

Moser, C.O.N. (1978). "Informal sector or petty commodity production: Dualism or dependence in urban development". *World Development* 6 (9–10): 1041–64.

Murthi Semudram (1988). "The services sector of the Malaysian economy:

Macroeconomic issues". In M.L. Sieh, ed., *Services in Development: An Agenda for Research in ASEAN.* Ottawa: International Development Research Centre.

Muto Ichiyo (1983). "Japanese labour in the 'company world'". In Jomo K.S., ed., *The Sun Also Sets: Lessons in 'Looking East'.* Kuala Lumpur: INSAN.

Nelson, Richard (1980). "Technical advance and productivity growth: Retrospect, prospects and policy issues". In I. Leveson and J.W. Wheeler, eds., *Western Economies in Transition: Structural Change and Adjustment Policies in Industrial Countries.* London: Croom Helm.

Nelson, Richard, and Sidney Winter (1986). "From an evolutionary theory of economic change". In L. Putterman, ed., *The Economic Nature of the Firm: A Reader.* Cambridge: Cambridge University Press.

Nor Aini H.I. (1989). "The development process and its impact on women in the small market place: A case study of women small-scale traders in Kelantan". Paper presented at the Colloquium on "Women and Development in Malaysia: Implications for Planning and Population Dynamics", University of Malaya, Kuala Lumpur, 10–12 January.

Norma Mansor (1988). "The development process and women's participation in the government sector: A macro level analysis of trends and implications, 1958–1987". Paper presented at the Colloquium on "Women and Development in Malaysia: Implications for Planning and Population Dynamics", University of Malaya, Kuala Lumpur, 10–12 January.

Oi, W.Y. (1962). "Labor as a quasi-fixed factor". *Journal of Political Economy* 70 (6) (December): 538–55.

Peattie, L. (1987). "An idea in good currency and how it grew: The informal sector". *World Development* 15 (7): 851–60.

Petit, P. (1986). *Slow Growth and the Service Economy.* London: Frances Printer.

Piore, Michael (1975). "Notes for a theory of labor market stratification". In Richard Edwards, Michael Reich and D.M. Gordon, eds., *Labor Market Segmentation.* Lexington, MA: Heath Lexington Books.

Pryor, R., ed. (1979). *Migration and Development in Southeast Asia: A Demographic Perspective.* Kuala Lumpur: Oxford University Press.

PSD, Malaysia. "Central Staff Lists". Various years. Unpublished. Public Services Department, Prime Minister's Department, Kuala Lumpur.

Puthucheary, J.J. (1960). *Ownership and Control in the Malayan Economy. Singapore*: Eastern Universities Press.

Puthucheary, M.C. (1978). *The Politics of Public Administration in Malaysia.* Singapore: Oxford University Press.

Putterman, L., ed. (1986). *The Economic Nature of the Firm: A Reader*. Cambridge: Cambridge University Press.

Rao, C.H.H. and P.C. Joshi, eds. (1979). *Reflections on Economic Development and Social Change*. Oxford: Martin Robertson.

Razali Agus (1987). "The integration of informal sector on planning of low income settlers: The Malaysian experience". Paper presented at the UNCRD Congress, United Nations Center for Regional Development, Nagoya, Japan, 21–27 July.

Rema Devi, P. (1986). "Job and labour contracting in Peninsular Malaysia". M.Phil. thesis, University of Malaya, Kuala Lumpur.

_____ (1987). "Features of labour utilization: The contract system". Paper presented at the seminar on "Current Issues in Labour Migration in Malaysia", Kuala Lumpur, 24–28 August.

_____ (1996). *Contract Labour in Peninsular Malaysia*. Kuala Lumpur: Institut Kajian Dasar.

Riddle, D. (1986). *Service-led Growth: The Role of the Service Sector in World Development*. New York: Praeger.

Roberts, B., R. Finnegan and D. Gallie, eds. (1985). *New Approaches to Economic Life: Economic Restructuring, Unemployment and the Division of Labour*. Manchester: Manchester University Press.

Rodgers, Gerry, ed. (1989). *Urban Poverty and the Labour Market: Access to Jobs and Incomes in Asian and Latin American Cities*. World Employment Programme, International Labour Office, Geneva.

Rogayah Mohamed (1995). "Public Sector". In Jomo K. S., ed., *Privatizing Malaysia*. Boulder: Westview Press.

Rokiah Talib and Fauzi Yaacob (1986). "Laporan akhir — penjaja dan penjajaan di Bandaraya Kuala Lumpur: Keadaan semasa, masalah dan cadangan". Processed, Anthropology and Sociology Department, University of Malaya, Kuala Lumpur.

Rokiah Talib, A.Y. Hing, and Nik Safiah Karim, eds. (1989). *Women and Work in Malaysia*. Special issue of *Jernal Manusia dan Masyarakat*, 1987. Anthropology and Sociology Department, University of Malaya, Kuala Lumpur.

Rosenberg, S. (1989). "From segmentation to flexibility". *Labour and Society* 14 (4) (October): 363–406.

Rowthorn, R.E., and J.R. Wells (1987). *De-industrialization and Foreign Trade*. Cambridge: Cambridge University Press.

Rubery, Jill (1980). "Structured labour markets, worker organization and low pay". In Alice Amsden, ed. *The Economics of Women and Work*. Harmondsworth, UK: Penguin.

_____ (1981). "Secondary jobs and secondary workers". In Frank Wilkinson, ed. *The Dynamics of Labour Market Segmentation*. London: Academic Press.

Rudnick, Anja (1996). *Foreign Labour in Malaysian Manufacturing: Bangladeshi Workers in the Textile Industry*. Kuala Lumpur: INSAN.

Runyon, H. (1985). "The services industries: Employment, productivity and inflation". *Business Economics* (January): 55–63.

Ryan, Paul (1987). "Primary and secondary labour markets". In John Eatwell and Murray Milgate, eds. *The New Palgrave Dictionary of Economics*. Hampshire: Palgrave Macmillan.

Sabolo, Y. (1975). *The Service Industries*. Geneva: International Labour Office.

Seow, G.F.H. (1980). "The service sector in Singapore's economy: Performance and structure". Occasional Paper 2, Economic Research Centre, University of Singapore, Singapore.

SERES (1985). "Small retail business: An analysis of issues and trends in the urban areas of Peninsular Malaysia". Final Report submitted to the Kuala Lumpur Selangor Chinese Chamber of Commerce and Industry Subcommittee on Small Retail Business. Kuala Lumpur: SERES.

SERU (Socioeconomic Research Unit) (1979). "Kesulitan-kesulitan yang dihadapi oleh Peniaga-peniaga Melayu di dalam Perusahaan dan Perniagaan dari Sudut Sosio-ekonomi: Kes Kampung Baku". Processed, Prime Minister's Department, Kuala Lumpur.

_____ (1983). *Pendapatan, Corak Perbelanjaan dan Taraf Sosioekonomi Pekerja-pekerja Sektor Awam*. Kuala Lumpur: Prime Minister's Department.

Shamsulbahriah K.A. (1988). "Stratification and occupational segmentation in the Peninsular Malaysian labour force: A case for gender-oriented development planning". Paper presented at the Colloquium on "Women and Development in Malaysia: Implications for Planning and Population Dynamics", University of Malaya, Kuala Lumpur, 10–12 January.

Shelp, R.K. (1981). *Beyond Industrialization: Ascendancy of the Global Service Economy*. New York: Praeger.

Shireen Hashim (1998). *Income Inequality and Poverty in Malaysia*. Lanham, Maryland: Rowman and Littlefield.

Sieh Mei Ling, ed. (1988). *Services in Development: An Agenda for Research in ASEAN*. Ottawa: International Development Research Centre.

Singelmann, J. (1978). *From Agriculture to Services: The Transformation of Industrial Employment*. Beverly Hills: Sage Publications.

Siow, M. (1983). "The problems of ethnic cohesion among the Chinese in Peninsular Malaysia: Intra-ethnic divisions and inter-ethnic accommodation". In L.Y.C. Lim and L.A.P. Gosling, eds. *The Chinese in Southeast Asia: Identity, Culture and Politics*. Singapore: Maruzen.

Siti Rohani Yahya (1988). "The development process and women's labour force participation: A macro level analysis of patterns and trends, 1957–1987". Paper presented at the Colloquium on "Women and Development in Malaysia: Implications for Planning and Population Dynamics", University of Malaya, Kuala Lumpur, 10–12 January.

Sivananthiran, A. (1986). "Public Sector Employment in Malaysia". Paper presented at the Workshop on "Public Sector Employment", Universiti Kebangsaan Malaysia, Bangi, Malaysia, 22 September.

Smith, A.D. (1972). *The Measurement and Interpretation of Service Output Changes*. London: National Economic Development Office.

Snodgrass, Donald (1980). *Inequality and Economic Development in Malaysia*. Kuala Lumpur: Oxford University Press.

Soon Lee Ying (1988). "Labour market monitoring in Malaysia". Appendix 6, Report of the Tripartite National Seminar on Labour Market Information, Kuala Lumpur, 11–13 April.

Squire, Lyn (1979). "Labor force, employment and labor markets in the course of economic development". World Bank Staff Working Paper No. 336, June, World Bank, Washington, DC.

Squire, Lyn (1981). *Employment Policy in Developing Countries*. London: Oxford University Press.

Stanback, Jr., T.M. (1979). *Understanding the Service Economy: Employment, Productivity and Location*. Baltimore: Johns Hopkins University Press.

Standing, Guy (1983a). "Migration in Peninsular Malaysia". Technical Report, Geneva: International Labour Office.

_____ (1983b). "A labour status approach to labour statistics". Working paper no. 139 (WEP 2-221), August, World Employment Programme, International Labour Office, Geneva.

_____ (1989). "The growth of external labour flexibility in a nascent NIC: Malaysian labour flexibility survey (MLFS)". Working paper no. 35 (WEP 2-43), November, World Employment Programme, International Labour Office, Geneva.

Statistics Department, Malaysia (undated). *Population Census, 1957*. Department of Statistics, Kuala Lumpur.

_____ (undated). *Population Census, 1970*. Department of Statistics, Kuala Lumpur.

_____ (undated). *Population Census, 1980*. Department of Statistics, Kuala Lumpur.

_____ (undated). *Census of Professional and Institutional Establishments, 1985*. Department of Statistics, Kuala Lumpur.

_____ (undated). *Census of Selected Service Industries, 1985.* Department of Statistics, Kuala Lumpur.

_____ (undated). *Population Census, 1991.* Department of Statistics, Kuala Lumpur.

_____ (undated). *Population Census, 2000.* Department of Statistics, Kuala Lumpur.

_____ (undated). *Sample Survey of Wholesale and Retail Trades in Peninsular Malaysia, 1974.* Department of Statistics, Kuala Lumpur.

_____ (undated). *Sample Survey of Wholesale and Retail Trades in Peninsular Malaysia, 1980.* Department of Statistics, Kuala Lumpur.

_____ (2004). *Yearbook of Statistics, 2004.* Department of Statistics, Kuala Lumpur.

_____. *Labour Force Survey.* Various years. Department of Statistics, Kuala Lumpur.

_____. *National Accounts Statistics.* Various years. Department of Statistics, Kuala Lumpur.

Stenson, Michael (1980). *Class, Race and Colonialism in West Malaysia.* Brisbane, Queensland: University of Queensland Press.

Stigler, George (1956). *Trends in Employment in Service Industries.* Princeton: Princeton University Press.

Sundram, S.T., and A. Sivananthiran (1987). "Dynamics of the Malaysian labour market: Trends and prospects". *Ilmu Masyarakat* 12, July–September: 37–45.

Supian Ali (1988). "Malaysia". In Gus Edgren, ed. *The Growing Sector: Studies of Public Employment in Asia.* New Delhi: International Labour Office.

Tai Yuen (2000). *Labour Unrest in Malaya, 1934–1941: The Rise of the Workers' Movement.* Institute of Postgraduate Studies and Research, University of Malaya, Kuala Lumpur.

Taira, K. (1988). "Dualistic economic development, labour market segmentation and structural adjustment". International Conference on "Economic Development and Labour Market Segmentation", University of Notre Dame, 17–20 April.

Tan Poo Chang and Siti Rohani Yahya (1987). "The role of socio-economic and demographic variables in determining labour force participation and employment in Peninsular Malaysia". Occasional Paper no. 13, February, Population Studies Unit, Faculty of Economics and Administration, University of Malaya, Kuala Lumpur.

Tan T.W. (1982). *Income Distribution and Determination in West Malaysia.* Kuala Lumpur: Oxford University Press.

Tilman, R.O. (1964). *Bureaucratic Transition in Malaya.* Durham, NC: Duke University Press.

Tokman, Victor (1988). "Economic development and labour market segmentation in the Latin American periphery". International Conference on "Economic Development and Labour Market Segmentation", University of Notre Dame, 17–20 April.

Treasury, Malaysia. *Annual Report of the Director-General of Insurance*. Various years. Ministry of Finance, Kuala Lumpur.

_____. *Economic Report*. Various years. Ministry of Finance, Kuala Lumpur.

Udall, A.T. (1976). "The effects of rapid increases in labour supply on service employment in developing countries". *Economic Development and Cultural Change* 24: 765–86.

UNIDO (United Nations Industrial Development Organisation) (1985). "Industrialisation and employment generation in the service sector of developing countries". *Industry and Development* 15.

Urquhart, M. (1981). "The service industry: is it recession-proof?" *Monthly Labor Review* 104 (10) (October): 12–19.

_____ (1984). "The employment shift to services: where did it come from?" *Monthly Labor Review* 107 (4) (April): 15–22.

Villa, P. (1986). *The Structuring of Labour Markets: A Comparative Analysis of the Steel and Construction Industries in Italy*. Oxford: Clarendon Press.

Waldinger, R. (1985). "Immigrant enterprise and the structure of the labour market". In B. Roberts, R. Finnegan, and D. Gallie, eds. *New Approaches to Economic Life: Economic Restructuring, Unemployment and the Social Division of Labour*. Manchester: Manchester University Press.

Wang Gungwu, ed. (1964). *Malaysia – A Survey*. London: Pall Mall Press.

Wee Chong Hui (2006). *Fiscal Policy and Inequality in Malaysia*. Kuala Lumpur: University of Malaya Press.

Wee Chong Hui and Jomo K.S. (2005). "Macroeconomic Policy, Growth, Redistribution and Poverty Reduction: The Case of Malaysia". In Giovanni Andrea Cornia, ed.. *Pro-Poor Macroeconomics: Potential and Limitations*. Oxford: Clarendon Press, for United Nations Research Institute for Social Development, Geneva, chapter 9.

Wilkinson, Frank (1985). "Deregulation, structured labour markets and unemployment". Processed, Department of Applied Economics, University of Cambridge, November.

_____ (1989). "Wage inequalities, segmented labour markets and economic progress". Processed, Department of Applied Economics, University of Cambridge, Cambridge.

_____, ed. (1981). *The Dynamics of Labour Market Segmentation*. London: Academic Press.

Williamson, O.E., M. Wachter, and J.E. Harris (1975). "Understanding the employment relation". *Bell Journal of Economics* 6: 250–78.

Winstedt, Richard (1966). *Malaya and Its History*. London: Hutchinson.

Wong Lin Ken (1965). *The Malayan Tin Industry to 1914*. Tucson: University of Arizona Press.

Wong Poh Kam (1979). "The dynamics of labor absorption in post-colonial Peninsular Malaysia". PhD thesis, Massachussetts Institute of Technology, Cambridge, MA.

_____ (1983). "Economic development and labour market changes in Peninsular Malaysia". ASEAN-Australia Joint Research Project, December, Kuala Lumpur.

Wong, Steven, and Mustapha Mohd Nor (1988). "Employment prospects for Malaysia: A survey of terrain". ISIS Research Note, Institute of Strategic International Studies (ISIS Malaysia), Kuala Lumpur.

Wood, S., ed. (1982). *The Degradation of Work? Skill, Deskilling and the Labour Process*. London: Hutchinson.

World Bank (1988). *World Development Report, 1988*. New York: Oxford University Press for the World Bank, Washington D.C.

Yeo Kim Wah (1980). "The grooming of an elite: Malay administrators in the Federated Malay States, 1903–1941". *Journal of Southeast Asian Studies* 11: 286–319.

Periodicals (Magazines and Newspapers)

Far Eastern Economic Review
Malaysian Business
New Straits Times
Business Times (Kuala Lumpur)
National Echo
Malay Mail

Index